Origins of the Israeli Polity

Translated from the Hebrew by Charles Hoffman

Origins of the Israeli Polity

Palestine under the Mandate

Dan Horowitz Moshe Lissak

University of Chicago Press

Chicago and London

DAN HOROWITZ teaches political science and sociology at the Hebrew University of Jerusalem, and is coauthor of *The Israeli Army* (1975). MOSHE LISSAK teaches sociology, also at the Hebrew University. He is the author of *Social Mobility in Israel* (1969) and coauthor of *Moshava, Kibbutz and Moshav* (1969).

The University of Chicago Press, Chicago 60637
The University of Chicago Press, Ltd., London

© 1978 by The University of Chicago
All rights reserved. Published 1978
Printed in the United States of America

82 81 80 79 78   5 4 3 2 1

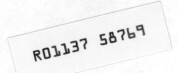

Library of Congress Cataloging in Publication Data

Horowitz, Dan.
    Origins of the Israeli polity.

    Revised translation of the work published in 1977 by Am Oved, Tel Aviv under title: Mi-yishuv li-medinah.
    Bibliography: p.
    Includes index.
    1. Jews in Palestine—Politics and government.
2. Palestine—Politics and government. I. Lissak, Moshe, 1928–   joint author. II. Title.
DS126.H6713   1978   320.9'5694'04   78–3175
ISBN 0–226–35366–4

Contents

v

Tables

Figures

Preface

Despite the recent wave of interest in the study of the Yishuv (the preindependence Jewish community in Palestine), no comprehensive political or social histories of the Yishuv have as yet been written. The authors of this book are social scientists whose major interest was not a detailed description of historical developments but an analysis of the social and political structure and of the processes influencing it. Nevertheless historical events have a role in this study, mainly to illustrate and explain phenomena which are meaningful from the perspective of the social sciences. We hope that this book will serve two purposes. The first is to present a reliable description of the Yishuv as a political community. It is necessary to emphasize this apparently obvious aim, since over the years, whether consciously or unconsciously, many myths have been created about the Yishuv. The second aim is to improve understanding of present phenomena in the State of Israel which are rooted in the period of the Yishuv. It is our belief that many characteristics of the social and political structure of Israel may be explained by reference to the persisting influence of processes and structures that originated in the Yishuv.

Since this book belongs in the categories of political sociology and political science, it naturally treats its subject matter in terms of the theoretical interests of these fields. Complete understanding of several sections of the book is therefore contingent upon some prior acquaintance with the social sciences.

The book as presented here is a revised, shortened version of the Hebrew edition published in 1977 by Am Oved, Tel Aviv. The omissions in the English edition consist mostly of references to events and personalities which we believe are of minor interest to the non-Israeli reader. In addition, a number of references to Hebrew sources were omitted from the notes.

This book is the fruit of many years of research; portions of it have appeared previously in professional journals. It is based on three types of sources: (1) original research including the analysis of statistical data and studies of the composition of political elites and the characteristics of organizations in the period of the Yishuv; (2) scholarly studies of specific historical aspects of the Yishuv, based on primary sources such as memoirs, speeches, newspapers, and journals; (3) the personal experience of the authors, who grew to maturity during the turbulent period of the end of the Mandate and the birth of the State.

In the course of writing this book, we have subjected our assumptions, hypotheses, and conclusions to the critical examination of colleagues and students. We are particularly indebted to the following for their advice and comments: S. N. Eisenstadt, Shlomo Avineri, Israel Kolat, Dov Weintraub, Emmanuel Gutmann, Shlomo Aronson, Ovadia Shapira, Moshe Samet, Baruch Knei-Paz, and Meir Barelly. We are greatly in debt to our translator from Hebrew, Charles Hoffman, and to Mrs. Ilene Gregg, who edited the English version. We would also like to thank our research assistants who participated during various stages of the work: Meir Cialic, Yehezkel Meroz, Aviad Bar-Haim, Aviva Middelman (Aviv), Shoshana Shtiftel, Gabriel Arieli, Ora Mizrahi (Shoked), Beverly Mizrahi, and Israel Katz.

Financial aid has been given by the Faculty of Social Sciences and the Leonard Davies Institute of International Relations of the Hebrew University. We are profoundly grateful to all for their support, advice, and assistance. Needless to say, full responsibility for any weak points and inaccuracies that have crept into the work falls on the authors alone.

1

Introduction: The Historical and Sociological Perspectives

The Yishuv: Historical Background

Under the British Mandate, Palestine was a state without a national identity which contained two national movements seeking statehood. From a juridical point of view the nationality of this territorial entity was "Palestine." But, as the Palestine Royal Commission (better known as the Peel Commission) concluded in 1937: "It is time, surely, that Palestinian 'citizenship' . . . should be recognized as what it is, as nothing but a legal formula devoid of moral meaning." This statement was based on the realization that each national community—the Arab majority and the Jewish minority—possessed a separate national identity. Moreover, there was never a time when the primary loyalty of either group was focused on the formal framework of the Mandatory government. As early as the beginning of the Mandate, the first indications of separate embryonic political systems appeared. These later developed into nearly autonomous political systems oriented symbolically and institutionally to wider frameworks: the Zionist movement in one case and the Arab national movement in the other. As a result, Mandatory Palestine could not be considered a nucleus of a nation-state for two reasons: the population was divided into two separate ethnonational groups, and each group saw itself as part of a larger national entity whose borders extended beyond Mandatory Palestine. Against this background, the concept of "the Jewish community in Palestine" (the Yishuv) emerged. Perceived as an autonomous political system in embryo, the Yishuv was often defined as a "state in the making" or a "state within a state." The institutional framework was that of a quasi state which in many spheres of political and social activity operated in a statelike manner.

We use the term "quasi state" to characterize the Yishuv as a political system because three traits distinguish it from a full-fledged state.

First, the Yishuv was a minority in a dual social-political system. Moreover, not only was Mandatory Palestine a binational political unit, but large sections of the country had a mixed population; there were almost no continuous areas of Jewish settlement without an Arab population.

Second, in terms of the functions it performed, the system was of a partial nature. In particular, it lacked judicial functions, with no legal code or courts of its own. Other areas, such as postal and telegraph services, customs, and the maintenance of the transportation infrastructure, were a monopoly of the Mandatory government. In the sphere of security the Yishuv had several paramilitary organizations, mainly the Hagana, but these organizations did not usually engage in enforcing law and order.

Finally, the Yishuv was dependent on the Diaspora. Without the latter's resources of manpower, funds, and political support the Yishuv would not have been able to amass economic power or to maintain its political institutions.

The transformation of the Yishuv from a quasi state into a state in 1948 involved demographic changes that made possible the creation of a society with an overwhelming Jewish majority and the acquisition of sovereign status entailing the three functions of a sovereign state: legislative, executive, and judicial. On the other hand, the special relationship between the Yishuv and the Diaspora persisted—along with the need for the Diaspora's resources. Nevertheless, the political implications of this connection were reduced by the separation of the functions of immigration and settlement—in which the Diaspora continued to take an active part through the institutions of the Zionist movement —from other spheres of policy making that passed into the exclusive jurisdiction of the Israeli government.

Despite these changes, considerable continuity between the political
system of the Yishuv and that of Israel can be discerned in the composition of the leadership, the political party structure, and the political
culture—that is, the rules of the game and relations between political
parties, ideological movements, and interest groups.

The evolution of a semiautonomous Jewish community in Palestine
was a gradual process which began with the wave of immigration to
Palestine in 1882. This wave occurred in the wake of pogroms against
the Jews in Russia and was part of the tide of Jewish immigration from
Eastern Europe to the west.

At this early stage, Zionism was still an ideological and cultural
movement rather than a political one. Its ideology, developed by Leon
Pinsker, Moshe L. Lilienblum, and other thinkers, called for settlement
of Jews in Palestine to achieve a territorial concentration of Jews. The
desire for a Jewish state became part of Zionist thought after the appearance of Theodor Herzl and the convention of the First Zionist Congress
in 1897.

In the last two decades of the nineteenth century, some of the Jews
who came in the First Immigration established settlements in Judaea
and the Galilee; others turned to Jerusalem and Jaffa, which became
the centers of the New Yishuv. The socioeconomic pattern which
evolved as a result of the dependence of the early settlers on hired
Arab labor was challenged by the immigrants of the Second Immigration, which began in 1904 and continued until 1914. Inspired by
socialist ideas, they advocated the replacement of Arab workers by
Jewish "self labor." As immigration to Palestine continued on a limited
scale, the Zionist movement in the Diaspora developed its institutional
framework in the form of the World Zionist Organization (WZO),
established by Herzl in the First Zionist Congress in 1897. After Herzl's
diplomatic endeavors to enlist international support for a Jewish com-
monwealth in Palestine failed, the Zionist movement concentrated its
efforts on immigration and settlement in Palestine.

The First World War ended the first phase in the development of
the New Yishuv. The Ottoman Empire collapsed, the British occupied
Palestine, and for the first time the Zionist movement had the support,
albeit qualified, of the ruling power in Palestine. In the Balfour Declaration of 1917, the British government stated its commitment to permit
the establishment of a Jewish national home in Palestine. This commit-

ment was confirmed by the League of Nations, which granted Britain
the Mandate of Palestine. The British authorities recognized the WZO
as the official agency to implement the establishment of a Jewish national
home. This status enabled the Executive of the WZO in Jerusalem to
become the authoritative representative of the Jewish community in
Palestine. An institution whose functions were complementary to the
WZO Executive in Jerusalem was the National Council of Knesset
Israel, the central community organization of the Jewish population in
Palestine which obtained official recognition in the mid-twenties.

The favorable conditions for the advancement of the Zionist cause
created by the Balfour Declaration and the post–First World War
climate supporting self-determination encouraged renewed Jewish immigration to Palestine. The Third Immigration, which began in 1919,
brought thirty-seven thousand immigrants to Palestine between 1919
and 1923. As in the Second Immigration, most of the newcomers were
young pioneers who became the backbone of the Jewish Labor movement in Palestine.

The renewal of large-scale immigration provoked violent Arab reactions. The "Arab disturbances" of 1920 and 1921 were the first of a
series of political riots which accompanied each stage of expansion of
Zionist endeavor in Palestine. In 1922 the British made their first con-
cession to Arab resistance to Zionism by creating the amirate of Transjordan in the territory east of the Jordan River, an area originally
included in Mandatory Palestine.

The Third Immigration was followed by an even larger wave of
immigration, the Fourth Immigration, 1924–30, which brought more
than sixty thousand Jews to Palestine, thirty-five thousand in the year
1925 alone. Unlike the previous immigrations, most of these people
came from Poland rather than from Russia. They brought some capital
that was invested mainly in the building industry and triggered a boom.
But there was not enough of the imported capital to create an infrastructure capable of allowing the economic absorption of these immigrants. Thus the prosperity was soon replaced by a severe recession
which halted the expansion of the Jewish economy in Palestine. Immigration fell to its lowest point in the entire period of the Mandate. At
the end of the twenties, a nascent economic recovery was accompanied
by a new outburst of Arab riots.[1] The riots led to a reevaluation of
British policy in Palestine. But a white paper (the "White Paper of
Lord Passfield," 1930) stating the British intention to impose limitations

on Jewish immigration and land purchases[2] was not implemented as a result of vehement Jewish protests led by Chaim Weizmann.

Another development in 1930 involved the internal politics of the Jewish community in Palestine, when the two largest labor parties merged. The unified party, Mapai, led by David Ben-Gurion, became the central political force in the Yishuv. At this stage of the Yishuv's development, the Zionist Executive and the National Council assumed control over the underground self-defense organization of the Jewish community, the Hagana.

In January 1933, Hitler came to power in Germany. This external event gave new impetus to Jewish immigration to Palestine, which in 1935 reached a peak of sixty-two thousand in one year. During the entire wave of immigration from 1932 to 1939, no less than one hundred ninety thousand immigrants arrived in Palestine from central and eastern Europe. As a result, the Jewish population increased from one hundred ninety thousand in 1932 to four hundred forty-five thousand in 1939. While German immigrants made up only 20 to 25 percent of the total, they were the dominant group among these immigrants, and this wave is sometimes called the German Immigration. More than any previous wave, this one—the Fifth Immigration, was accompanied by extensive importation of investment capital, which laid the foundation for the economic take-off of the Jewish community in Palestine.[3]

The peak year of immigration, 1935, was followed by the most intense Arab reaction:—the Arab revolt of 1936–39. This revolt left a strong impression on the attitudes and policies of the three parties involved in the determination of Palestine's fate—the Arabs, the Jews, and the British. The Arabs failed to achieve their military objectives, their guerrilla force was suppressed by the British army, and their political leadership obliged to leave the country. Yet they succeeded in demonstrating their ability to disrupt law and order, which induced the British government to reconsider its policy in Palestine.

The impact of the Arab revolt on the Jewish community was to call forth new approaches to the political struggle with the Arabs, particularly in the area of self-defense. The Hagana ceased to be a decentralized organization for the defense of life and property in a local context and became a centrally directed armed force. Its command supervised not only Hagana units armed with illegal weapons, but also, indirectly, the Jewish constabulary force which operated within the framework of the Palestine police. The central control of the Jewish self-defense forces

was, however, incomplete. A splinter group, the armed Irgun Zvai
Leumi or IZL (National Military Organization), operated under the
auspices of the nationalist right-wing Revisionist party, which had
seceded from the WZO in 1935 in protest against the moderate policies
of the WZO president, Dr. Weizmann, and the Labor movement.

The British reaction to the Arab revolt was a reappraisal of the
policy in Palestine. This led to the proposal, by a royal commission,
to partition Palestine, a proposal which was rejected by the Arabs and
became a controversial issue in the Zionist movement.[4] In response
to Arab opposition, the British government abandoned the idea of
partition and convened an Arab-Jewish "Round Table" in London to
discuss the Palestine problem.[5] As no agreement was reached, in 1939
the British government, in an effort to appease the Arabs, issued a white
paper which recommended far-reaching restrictions on Jewish immigration and purchases of land, as well as the grant of Palestinian independence after an interim period in which the Arabs would remain the
majority.[6]

The Second World War and Hitler's European successes brought on
a self-imposed suppression of most forms of resistance to this British
policy—with the exception of illegal immigration, which continued on
a reduced scale. The leadership of the Yishuv urged active participation
in the war effort, and over twenty-five thousand men and women
volunteered to serve in the British armed forces out of a population of
five hundred thousand. In 1941–42, the danger of German invasion in
the Middle East resulted in the resumption of cooperation by the
Jewish leadership with the Mandatory authorities, especially in promoting war effort. In 1942, under Ben-Gurion's leadership, the Zionist
movement officially adopted the demand for a Jewish state and tried to
enlist the support of American Jewry and American public opinion.
Aspirations for independence were enhanced when the first news of the
Holocaust in Europe reached the Yishuv. The official leadership of the
Jewish community continued to hope for a change in the British policy
when the war was over, but the splinter illegal military organization,
the IZL, declared a revolt against British rule in Palestine. This act of
defiance against both the British and the official Jewish leadership
prompted the Hagana to resort to sanctions against IZL. However,
when the war ended and the new Labour government in England continued the implementation of the 1939 White Paper, the official leadership of the Yishuv resumed the struggle against British policy.

The cumulative effect of American pressure, Jewish resistance in Palestine, and the Jewish refugee problem in Europe ultimately led the British government to submit the Palestine question to the United Nations. An international commission of inquiry nominated by the United Nations General Assembly recommended the partition of Palestine into a Jewish state and an Arab state. This recommendation was adopted in the resolution of 29 November 1947, supported by more than two-thirds of the member nations, including the two superpowers, the United States and the Soviet Union. The British refused to implement the resolution and withdrew from Palestine, which became an arena of bitter fighting between Arabs and Jews. On 14 May 1948, a Jewish state was established in the territories controlled by the Jewish armed forces. On the same day, the regular armies of neighboring Arab states invaded Palestine in an unsuccessful attempt to eradicate the newly established state.

The Frame of Reference

The scholar who seeks to study the internal political development of the Yishuv from the perspective of the social sciences must confront the problem of the relation between history and social science. The raw material, or data, is the same for both the social scientist and the historian, which raises the problem of applying the methods of the social sciences, which strive for comprehensive generalizations based on features common to different societies and historical periods, to the study of unique historical phenomena. There is also the problem of emphasis. The social scientist stresses the functions performed by components of political and social structures at a given time, while the historian concentrates on development and change through time.[7] These differences of perspective require the social scientist who wishes to deal with historical materials to learn to live with the tension between the two disciplines. As a result, his work lacks uniformity; there will always be some problems which cannot be treated according to the standards of either discipline. Nevertheless, this study attempts to bridge both gaps, that between the specific and the general, and that between emphasis on structure and function and emphasis on process and change.

The split between the specific subject of historical research and the theoretical approach guiding the social scientist in the selection of facts is narrower in a case study that it is in a comparative study of several cases. In the latter, a model or theoretical framework is examined by comparison of a number of cases.[8] In the study of a single case, however, it is possible to apply a number of partial theories which are relevant to the subject in question; the *case* and not the theory determines the point of departure. It appears that comprehensive theories are not most valuable for students of particular cases, but rather what Robert Merton has called "theories of the middle range" which relate to various facets of the phenomenon under study.[9] Even so, it is clear that the authors' theoretical approach, or in Kuhn's terms their scientific "paradigm," has influenced the selection of middle-range theories to be applied.[10] The partial theories referred to in this study were not assembled eclectically, based solely on particular characteristics of the Yishuv. They reflect the authors' general approach to the basic theoretical problems examined in the comparative study of political systems. We believe that the application of relevant middle-range theories has facilitated our efforts to examine unique phenomena in relation to theoretically meaningful notions and concepts.

Actually, there is no inherent contradiction between the study of a unique case and the application of theoretical concepts. Social scientists who have dealt with the methodological problems of comparative political analysis have identified several ideal types of case studies: the theoretical case study, the interpretative case study, the hypothesis-generating case study, the theory-confirming case study or theory-infirming case study, and the deviant case study.[11] The importance of deviant cases derives from the assumption that the exceptional case, properly explained, is likely to aid not only the formation of theoretically fruitful hypotheses but also the understanding of the potential and the limitations of existing theories. Moreover, since it is assumed that "any particular study of a single case may fit more than one of the categories" of case studies,[12] it is clear that there is a reciprocal influence between the study of the exceptional case and the process of theory building, verification, and refutation.

We attempted to bridge the second gap—that between the structural-functional approach and the analysis of change—by focusing our analysis on the system as it was in its most "developed" (or "ripe") form, in the late 1930s and in the 1940s. We selected variables to focus on while analyzing previous developments, looking for developmental trends which in retrospect may be seen to have determined the

nature of the political system of the Yishuv in the "peak" of its development.

From the foregoing it is clear that the subject of our inquiry—the
characteristics of the political system of the Yishuv—has determined
our point of departure. From the historian's perspective the concept of
the Yishuv does not present any special methodological difficulties. But
from the viewpoint of a sociologist or political scientist who seeks to
grasp the Yishuv as a political system, the problem arises of providing
a precise definition of the boundaries of a political system that is not
a nation-state. It is, of course, no longer considered innovative or un-
usual to take exception to the once generally accepted approach which
defined the boundaries of political systems in terms of a nation-state.
Such phenomena as colonial rule in multinational or multitribal territories, national minorities with ties to "foreign" states, multinational
states, processes of regional integration comprising several states, and
international movements such as the Catholic Church and the communist
movement which foster allegiance to a political center beyond the
boundaries of the nation-state, all have raised serious doubts that the
nation-state is the meaningful framework for analyzing political processes in each and every case.[13] Under these conditions, state borders
and citizenship cease to be the exclusive determinants of the boundaries
of political systems. Territorial boundaries and citizenship, however,
have the advantage of distinguishing clearly between those who belong
to the system and those who do not. In contrast, political systems based
on partial allegiance or voluntary membership permit distinctions between different degrees of attachment to a system, as well as simultaneous attachments to different political systems. The problem of vague
boundaries is particularly acute in the case of the Yishuv, which was
both a national minority group dispersed among the majority and a
part of a people whose majority lived outside the political and territorial
unit of Palestine.

Despite the difficulties in defining the boundaries of the system and
the criteria of membership, there are good reasons for studying the
Yishuv as distinct political system. First, the Yishuv possessed a distinct
political party structure that had no connection with the politics of the
Arab community. Second, there was a considerably broad consensus
within the Yishuv on the "rules of game" governing relations between
political and ideological groups. Third, the authority of a common

political center was accepted, albeit in a limited and conditional manner, by most of the political movements and parties in the Yishuv which adhered to Zionist ideology.

The concept of "center" as a focus of charismatic and institutional authority was introduced into the social sciences by Edward Shils in his analysis of political development.[14] Shils's model is based on a distinction between center and periphery. A "center" possesses both institutional and symbolic meaning. It serves as a source of inspiration and as focus of authority and commitment for that population which accepts its legitimacy. The "periphery," on the other hand, comprises those sectors of society which are voluntarily or involuntarily subject to the center's authority, but which are not active partners in shaping the features of society and its regime. This conceptual framework enables us to delineate the boundaries of a system without resorting to the formal criteria of territory and citizenship; affiliation to a community is defined in terms of attachment to a center as a focus of authority.

Adoption of the center-periphery conceptual framework does not require acceptance of Shils' model in its entirety. It is possible to use it as a point of departure for analysis without accepting some of its underlying assumptions.[15] For example, to the extent that Shils's model implies a dichotomous distinction between center and periphery, it is not applicable to the Yishuv, not only because of the existence of sub-centers (a concept which Shils employs), but also because of the coalitionary structure of the center, which had several traits in common with the "consociational model" in nation-states (of which more below). Consequently, and in contrast to Shils's model, in the case of the Yishuv the center was not the predominant source of authority and was not the dominant source of entrepreneurship and symbolic creativity. It was the subcenters that engaged in the creation, interpretation, and transmission of symbols. The center's role was primarily that of co-ordination and regulation of the relationships between the subcenters, though it also cultivated certain values that served as the common normative basis of the subcenters. This perception of a center is compatible with the historical development of the Yishuv, since the national institutions of the Yishuv arose on the foundations of an agreement between parties and movements whose activity antedated the formation of the common representative framework.

These modifications of Shils's model may make it seem that the concepts of "center" and "periphery" have been emptied of content.

As the reader will soon discern, we feel that this is not the case. There are several reasons for applying the "center" concept. First, the role of the national center as the embodiment of an ideological consensus was expressed in a common system of symbols. Identification with these symbols facilitated the political mobilization of the Jewish community of Palestine for the attainment of collective goals. Second, the authority of the center was institutionalized and the resultant framework was supported by legitimacy accorded from within the Yishuv and by external recognition by the Mandatory government and the League of Nations. Third, the institutions of the national center controlled the allocation of resources essential for the activities of the subcenters, which made the subcenters dependent to an extent on the national center.

The concept of "periphery" is also useful for analyzing the politics of the Yishuv, despite the fact that only a few groups were peripheral in the full sense of the term as used by Shils. If we take the concept periphery in the relative sense of distance from the center, we can determine the extent to which different groups were peripheral. Differences among groups were expressed by the extent to which they participated in the coalition formed by the national leadership and by the extent of their willingness to submit to the authority of the national center. In addition, the concept of periphery can be employed to analyze the relationships between the various subcenters and their clients.

The notion of differential attachment to the center gives rise to a certain ambiguity as to the boundaries of the system: to what extent does the peripheral nature of individuals or groups place them beyond the boundaries of the system? For example, a distinction was made between the "Yishuv" as comprising the entire Jewish population of Palestine and the "organized Yishuv," referring to those groups and sectors that were represented in the national institutions and that accepted their authority.

The concepts of "center" and "periphery" can also be applied to the relations between a political community such as the Yishuv and other frameworks in its environment, the relevance of which stems from the Yishuv's lack of sovereignty. The interrelations between these systems or subsystems, each with an authority center of its own (for example, the two national groups in Palestine, the Mandate, and the Zionist movement in the Diaspora), create partial overlappings between what can be called the "fields of authority" exerted by the centers of each of these systems. The concept of "authority field" refers to the differential institutional attachment to an authority center of various groups on its periphery, or alternatively to the differential allegiance of various groups in a society to more than one authority center. Thus it is possible to speak of overlapping authority fields, a common feature of all nonsovereign political systems and of a considerable number of sovereign systems which deviate from the ideal type of the "nation-state" system.

Our modifications of the center-periphery model emphasize, then, two limitations affecting national centers in societies such as the Yishuv: (a) the partial nature of the authority of a center stemming from the existence of external authority centers; and (b) a relative decentralization of authority resulting from the considerable autonomy possessed by the subcenters.

This second limitation on the center's authority is analogous to certain tendencies found in consociational democracies in fragmented sovereign societies. The regime of consociational democracy is characterized by cooperation between elites representing competing subcultures formed by ethnic, religious, linguistic, or (according to some versions) ideological cleavages. This cooperation exists despite political and social segmentation, expressed in a considerable degree of subcultural autonomy. The coalitionary governmental system thus comprises a common center that regulates conflicts by bargaining, rather than majority decision, and/or proportional sharing of positions of power and proportional allocation of rewards, all of which considerably restrict competition among the rival sectors.[16]

The central cleavage in the Yishuv was ideological, rather than ethnic or religious, despite the common ideological basis shared by all sectors, Zionism. Nonetheless, the resemblances between the political rules of the game in the Yishuv and the rules of the game characteristic of consociational democracy are immediately apparent:

1. The existence of subcultures cultivating symbols emphasizing the differences among them
2. The evolution of sectoral institutional frameworks for satisfying normative and instrumental needs as an expression of subculture autonomy
3. A common quasi-governmental system, based on cooperation among the different sectors, which tends to avoid making decisions in controversial areas

4. A tendency toward proportional allocation of resources among the various sectors
5. Cooperation among competing elites despite the unfavorable reciprocal images held by the groups represented by these elites.

With regard to the last point, cooperation between elites was not based on neglect of the interests of the rank and file of the various sectors. Since the primary cleavages in the Yishuv were ideological, and since each ideology had a different order of priorities, bargaining could be based on the willingness of each sector to yield on certain interests, rewards, and values that it regarded as peripheral in return for concessions on interests, rewards, and values that it regarded as central but that were seen as peripheral by other partners. Such non–zero-sum perception of politics facilitated consociational practices.

Organization of This Book

In the following chapters various aspects of the development of the Yishuv and its structure are presented. Each of these aspects can be presented as questions that serve as the focus of the following chapters.

The first question is dealt with in chapter 2: what were the conditions which permitted the development of a unique dual system composed of two national communities within a common territorial and political framework? This dual system did not resemble societies with an ethnic division between groups at similar levels of modernization, nor did it resemble societies in which a more developed ethnic group became the ruling stratum in a politically and economically uniform structure. In Mandatory Palestine two separate and parallel economic and stratification systems of different levels of modernization emerged which maintained only limited mutual relations. Our contention is that this phenomenon arose due to the influence of ideological and political pressures exerted within each of the two national communities.

Our second question, discussed in chapter 3, concerns the institutionalization of the Yishuv's political center, which enjoyed a large degree of authority even though it lacked the sanctions available to a sovereign power. The factors that contributed to the emergence of such a political center included the recognition granted to the central "national institutions" by the Mandatory government. The center itself was a coalition of innovative subcenters associated with ideological movements, political parties, and economic interest groups. The importation of resources, which were allocated largely under the supervision of the national center, and the existence of an ideological consensus over basic Zionist aims provided a basis for the legitimacy of the national center and the loyalty of the Yishuv toward it.

Chapter 4 examines how the subcenters in the Yishuv contributed to the crystallization of a national center. The political system was based on the capacity of subcenters to mobilize resources, particularly manpower, for the building of institutions which they themselves initiated. The entrepreneurial capacities of the subcenters thus created an institutional foundation for the Yishuv's political center, with the subcenters acting as agencies of the center.

The fourth question, dealt with in chapter 5, concerns the composition and characteristics of the political elites of the Yishuv. The Labor movement elite was more homogeneous than that of other sectors, had a higher level of political professionalization, and could rely on a loyal "constituency" in the form of a highly organized cadre of activists and the rank and file. These characteristics enabled the Labor elite to accumulate political power that was translated into decisive influence on the national center.

Chapter 6 focuses on a fifth issue: the central role played by ideology in the formation of the political system. Different ideological orientations implied different degrees of commitment to collective action. The most significant contribution was made by activist, collectivist, and future-oriented ideologies which required high levels of commitment. The movements which were the carriers of this type of ideology, in particular the Labor movement, were able to assume a prominent role in institution building and the shaping of the national center.

The sixth question, discussed in chapter 7, concerns the nature of the authority of the Jewish national center and its capacity to allocate resources. The legitimate authority of the national institutions enabled them to allocate resources according to political criteria and even to deny resources to groups which did not recognize their authority. Such control over allocation induced groups and sectors within the Yishuv to accept the authority of the national institutions in order to secure access to these resources.

The question dealt with in chapter 8 departs from the chronological framework of the period of the Yishuv to examine the impact of the political system of the Yishuv on the process of transition to statehood and on the political structure of Israeli society. The existence of an institutionalized national center and of subcenters oriented toward it made it possible to fill the vacuum created by the end of British rule in the country. Consequently, a political structure was created which preserved some of the characteristics of the Yishuv, especially the tendencies of the political parties to expand their activities at the expense of the government and to an extent the principle of allocating resources through the channels of political parties. These characteristics helped to prevent crises in the transition from community to state and facilitated the political absorption of mass immigration during the early years of the state, but they hampered the effectiveness of the government in the spheres of economic and social policy.

All the questions posed here can actually be reduced to one: what conditions made integrative processes stronger than disintegrative processes? The answer presented in chapter 9 lies in the conflict-regulating and tension-reducing mechanisms which functioned in the Yishuv. These mechanisms were based on a division of political authority between the national leadership and the various subcenters' elites; on the allocation of resources in a way that benefited most groups and sectors; and on the development of a political culture stressing compromise and bargaining, at least within the coalitionary framework of the "organized Yishuv." These mechanisms helped to create a dual balance in the political system: on the one hand, a balance between the functions performed by the center and the resources at its disposal (legitimacy, a common symbolic framework, and material resources); and on the other, a balance between the varied demands made on the center by different groups and the perception of the role of the center held by the elites that created it. This delicate balance made it possible for a people without a state to create the foundations of a nation-state in the space of a generation while dealing simultaneously with problems stemming from immigration, economic growth, and involvement in external political conflicts.

2

The Dual Society of Mandatory Palestine

The Yishuv in Mandatory Palestine cannot be considered a full-fledged polity since it formed a part of a larger entity. It was a minority group in a dual political system, binational in population, and ruled by a foreign power in accordance with the Mandate granted by the League of Nations.

Political scientists and sociologists who have studied the emergence of independent political systems in developing countries have developed models for analyzing these societies, but most of them are inadequate for describing the unique characteristics of the dual system in Mandatory Palestine.

There are models which describe societies characterized by tribal, ethnic, religious, or national heterogeneity where the groups composing them are at a similar level of modernization.[1] These models are unsuitable for describing the dual society of Mandatory Palestine because of the significant difference in level of modernization between the Arab majority and the Jewish minority.

There are also models describing heterogeneous societies which emerged as a result of Western colonization in Asia, Africa, and Latin America.[2] For the most part these models too fail to grasp the social and political pattern that developed in Palestine as a result of Jewish settlement. Such models generally describe societies

with a unified economic structure encompassing parts of the developed
and the underdeveloped components. This usually implies extensive
exchange between the two components of the economy, even though
part of the productive sector of the underdeveloped component (usually
termed a "subsistence economy") is relatively autonomous. Although
similar patterns were present at the beginning of Zionist settlement, the
dominant trend later departed from this pattern so greatly that two
distinct economic systems were formed with only limited market relations between them. This distinction between most examples of
Western colonization and the binational society of Palestine spilled
over to the sphere of stratification. Whereas in colonial societies the
developed strata composed of immigrants became a privileged upper
class in an explicitly or implicitly racist stratification system, in Mandatory Palestine there emerged two separate stratification systems of the
two communities. These two systems were based on completely different
principles of ranking which made them mutually irrelevant.

The most appropriate model for describing the heterogeneous character of the dual society of Mandatory Palestine appears to be one
which reflects the bipolar attributes of a society with two separate
centers exerting symbolic and institutional controls over the relations
between their respective peripheries. Yet the centers were not autonomous, since they were dependent on other, complementary centers.
The first complementary center corresponded to other colonial situations
—the center of the foreign ruler. But in addition there were also the
complementary centers outside Mandatory Palestine which had a direct
affinity to only one or the other of the component groups—the Zionist
movement in the Diaspora and the Arab nationalist movement.

A model based on a multiplicity of centers does not necessarily
assume a symmetrical relation between the centers. Where different
economic, stratificational, and cultural systems exist, different levels of
development of their political centers may also be presumed. These
centers may differ as to level of institutionalization, power, effectiveness
of political control, and capacity for mobilizing human and material
resources.

The characteristics of a model for the description of the divided
society of Mandatory Palestine kind can be summed up as follows:

1. It is constructed on the basis of two "internal" centers partially
   dependent on complementary "external" centers (the Diaspora

and the Arab national movement) and on a center with both an internal and an external territorial base (the British authorities).
2. The two internal centers differ in the degree of authority each exercises over the population in its sphere and in the nature of its relations with external centers.
3. The relations between the two national groups are influenced to a considerable extent by the differential capacity of these centers to exercise control over them.

Such a model seems to be most appropriate for describing the trends of political development in Palestine from the time of the British conquest (1917–18) until the partition of 1948. That development that was characterized by steadily increasing tendencies toward separation between the Jewish and Arab population, beginning with *cultural* separation and continuing with *ecological* separation in the form of all-Jewish neighborhoods, at first in rural areas, and later in urban areas as well. Eventually the process included increasing *economic* separation and the emergence of separate *political* institutions which, at least in the case of the Jewish community, were characterized by considerable authority even in the absence of sovereignty. This difference between the Arab and Jewish centers was of critical importance in 1948 when the British departed without transferring authority to a successor regime. The Jewish center was sufficiently effective to fill the political vacuum created in areas which in the course of the war were brought under Jewish military and political control. In contrast, despite the fact that it represented the majority of the population, the Arab leadership was forced to yield its independence to external forces, the Egyptians in the Gaza Strip and the Jordanians in the West Bank. Thus the complementary centers took over from the weak center of the Palestinian Arab community. The subjection of Palestinian Arabs to non-Palestinian Arab rule meant that the very idea of a Palestinian identity became problematic. As a result, the Arabs of the West Bank came to accept the authority of the political center in Amman on the instrumental level, and postponed the political realization of Palestinian identity until an indeterminate time in the future.

This chapter is divided into two parts: the first presents an overview of the cultural, economic, social, and political differences between the Jewish and Arab societies, while the second deals with the process of separation which paved the way for the formation of an effective Jewish political center striving for full autonomy.

Two Levels of Economic and
Political Development

The proportion of the Jewish population in Palestine increased steadily after the nineteenth century, but when the Mandate ended, the Arabs still composed two-thirds of the population. The 1922 census recorded a Jewish population of 83,790 out of a population of 752,048, or 11 percent of the total. Nine years later in 1931, a census showed the Jewish population to be 174,606 out of 1,033,314, or 17 percent of the total; in 1939 the Jewish population was estimated at 445,457 out of 1,501,698, or 30 percent;[3] and in 1947 on the eve of independence, the Jewish population was estimated at 650,000 out of 1,900,00, or 33 percent. (For population figures for the years 1922–45, see Appendix 1.)

Neither of the two communities was formally represented in the Mandatory government, which was administered directly by British officials according to directives from the Colonial Office in London. Proposals were made in the 1920s and 1930s to create a legislative council in which representatives of both communities would participate with "official" members representing the government, but these were never put into effect because of the tangled web of suspicion and hostility that linked Jew and Arab in Palestine. Finding mutually acceptable criteria of representation was the major stumbling block.[4] Proportional·representation would have given the Arabs a decisive majority among the representatives of the local population. The Jews argued that this would contradict the manifest purpose of establishing a "Jewish national home in Palestine."[5] The Arabs claimed, however, that if the Jews were overrepresented this would not reflect the actual composition of the local population.

As a result, the Mandatory government continued to the end to administer without any participation of the local population, contravening British policy in other colonial and Mandate territories, which sought to replace direct with indirect rule. The Peel Commission of 1937 pointed out that this type of rule was inappropriate for the Jewish community in Palestine. "The form of government . . . which circumstances have imposed on the whole of Palestine is not a suitable or natural form for the Jewish section of its population."[6] This conclusion was predicated on the commission's recognition that the "National Home is a highly educated, highly democratic, very politically-minded, and unusually young community." Therefore, the commission con-

cluded, the Jewish community "can never be at ease under an alien
bureaucracy."[7]

Differences between the two communities were apparent in all areas
of life. The Jewish sector was mainly urban while the vast majority
of the Arab sector was rural. At the time of the 1931 census 83.2
percent of the Jewish population lived in urban settlements and 16.8
percent in rural settlements. Conversely, only 24.8 percent of the
Muslim population lived in urban settlements while 75.2 percent lived
in rural areas.[8] The tendency of the Jewish population to concentrate
in urban areas increased over the years, and by 1945 84.6 percent of
the Jews resided in urban areas, including 64.3 percent in full-fledged
cities.[9]

In the economic sphere, two levels of wages existed for the same
occupations and even two levels of prices for the same agricultural
produce. The daily wages of an Arab baker were 219 mills in 1939
and 500 mills in 1944, and carpenters earned 200 mills a day in 1939
and 658 mills in 1944. Their Jewish counterparts earned 511 mills in
1939 and 1105 mills in 1944, for the baker, and 370 mills in 1939
and 1010 mills in 1944, for the carpenter. An unskilled Arab laborer
in the building industry earned 160 mills a day in 1939 and 500 mills
a day in 1945, while the daily wage of an unskilled Jewish laborer was
300 mills a day in 1939 and 1350 in 1945.[10] The prevailing daily wages
in mills for general agricultural laborers in the winter seasons were:[11]

	1938–39	1945–46
Jews	100–120	400–800
Arabs	175–200	700–1000

Of course wages are only one component of economic activity.
Estimates of national income per capita clearly show different levels
of development for the Jewish and Arab economies. Table 1 represents
the data on income distribution (at current prices) between Arabs and
Jews in gross and per capita terms.

No less significant were the differences between the two communities
in the sphere of education and culture. A vivid description of the
cultural differences between the Jewish and Arab populations appears
in the Peel Commission report which reaches the conclusion that: "With
every year that passes, the contrast between this intensely democratic
and highly organized modern community and the old-fashioned Arab

world around it grows sharper, and in nothing, perhaps, more markedly
than on its cultural side."[12]

It is only natural that these extensive differences would also be
expressed in the political sphere. The Jewish community established
elected representative institutions, while no elected institutions existed
in the Arab community. Political activity in the Arab community was
never fully institutionalized, and to the extent that a political center did
exist, it lacked formal authority recognized by the Mandatory govern-

Table 1
National Income Distribution: Jews and Arabs
1936–47

Year	National Income			National Income per Capita		
	Palestine	Jews	Arabs	Palestine	Jews	Arabs
1936	34.8	19.0	15.8	25.5	47.5	16.3
1939	30.2	17.2	13.0	20.2	27.8	12.5
1942	84.0	48.0	36.0	51.4	94.0	32.0
1943	92.3	52.1	40.2	55.0	99.3	34.8
1944	125.5	70.6	54.9	72.0	128.6	46.0
1945	143.4	80.1	63.3	79.1	138.3	51.3
1946	170.0	96.0	74.0	90.0	157.4	57.8
1947	200.0	110.0	90.0	101.0	169.3	67.7

SOURCE: *Encyclopaedia Hebraica,* 6:730.
Figures are millions of Palestinian pounds (LP).

ment. The Supreme Muslim Council was exceptional in that it possessed
considerable political influence, even though its formal functions were
nonpolitical. Among other things, the council controlled the vast prop-
erties of the Muslim religious endowments (Muslim awqaf)[13] and
supervised the network of Muslim religious courts (*sharia* courts).
But the Supreme Muslim Council could not be considered representative,
in national political terms, of the entire Arab population, in part, because 10 percent of this population was Christian.

There were repeated attempts to establish a representative authority
for the entire Arab population. In 1920 an Arab congress convened
in Haifa and elected a body from among its participants called the Arab

Executive Committee. Even though this congress referred to itself as the "legal representative of all classes and groups of the Arab people in Palestine,"[14] in fact it was an assembly of notables most of whom were associated with one of the two influential rival families, the Husseinis and the Nashashibis.

After 1920 a number of Arab congresses convened to protest Jewish settlement in Palestine, but neither these nor the Arab Executive Committee elected by them received government recognition. In 1923 a British proposal to create an "Arab agency" parallel to the Zionist Executive in Jerusalem was rejected. The later congresses were not basically different from the one of 1920, because they too reflected the elitist and particularistic nature of Arab politics, which was not based on permanent institutionalized mass participation. Political activity remained the province of a narrow elite, though sporadic attempts were made to mobilize the Arab masses for action against the Jewish community and at times against the Mandatory government.[15] A higher level of political mobilization was attained only in 1936–39 after the Arab parties established a new body, the Arab Higher Committee, which for all practical purposes succeeded the Arab Executive Committee. This body led the guerrilla movement of 1936–39 referred to in Jewish sources as the "disturbances" and in Arab sources as the "Arab revolt."

In the course of the revolt the Arab leadership resorted to terror and other forms of pressure in asserting its authority, and it may be assumed that without a considerable degree of consensus in the Arab community it would not have been possible to conduct a general strike and guerrilla operations over an extended period. Even so, without an organizational infrastructure, a cadre of political professionals, rules of the game for the resolution of internal conflicts, and other institutionalized patterns of action, Arab political organization returned to its previous state of weakness at the end of the revolt. This weakening was also caused by the expulsion of several leaders of the Arab Higher Committee to the Seychelles and the flight of the mufti of Jerusalem, at first to Syria and Iraq and later to Nazi Germany. But even when the committee renewed its activities in the 1940s with some of its formerly exiled leaders, it did not regain the stature it had achieved during the revolt.

Among the factors which explain the low level of institutionalization of the Arab political center, the most prominent are related to the characteristics of the traditional Arab elite. Its position was based not so much on political activity per se as on its social and economic preeminence. The power of the traditional leadership rested on family status and ownership of land. Only on rare occasions did this elite have recourse to strictly political processes in order to secure political leadership. In addition, the basis of the leadership's power was local, which hampered the emergence of a countrywide national leadership.

The character of the elite influenced its relations with the broader Arab society. The leaders had little authority over the followers and were not accountable to them. As in other societies characterized by the "politics of notables," most of the political activity among the Arabs in Mandatory Palestine was not directly connected to the mobilization of support based on articulation and representation of demands. Only for short periods in the years 1936–39 did the leadership function as an elite capable of wielding influence and mobilizing public support. But even in this period the level of mutual dependence between leaders and followers was low.

The Jewish political elite, by contrast, reached a higher level of political professionalization and developed recruitment patterns based to a large extent on achievement. The political organization of the Jewish minority was institutionalized in frameworks operating more or less continuously according to "rules of the game" accepted by the great majority of the Yishuv. The central political institutions, referred to as the "national institutions," operated through a permanent organizational framework according to an established division of labor and by means of formal administrative procedures. The first and most powerful of the two "national institutions" was the Jewish Agency, which enjoyed a legal status recognized by the Mandatory government and the League of Nations. Until the Jewish Agency was established in 1929, immigration and settlement activities were conducted by the Jerusalem office of the Executive of the World Zionist Organization (WZO), which assumed the functions of the Zionist Commission formed immediately after the British conquest.[16]

Because the interest of world Jewry in the Jewish national home was not limited to the WZO—a fact noted in the Mandate charter itself—it was decided to establish a more comprehensive institution than the Zionist Executive to represent the non-Zionist interest as well in the development of the "national home."[17] The executive of this institution, the Jewish Agency, consisted of the members of the WZO Executive and a few representatives of the "non-Zionists."

The second national institution was Knesset Israel, or the Jewish
Assembly, which was recognized by the Mandatory government as the
institutional system of the Jewish community. The broadest representative institution of the Knesset Israel was the Elected Assembly (Assefat
Hanivharim), which was chosen through general elections based on
proportional representation. The electorate was composed of Jews who
did not explicitly deny membership in the organized Jewish community.
A smaller parliamentary body which convened more frequently, the
National Council (Vaad Leumi), was chosen by the Elected Assembly.
The executive body of Knesset Israel was known as the Executive of
the National Council and was responsible to the plenum of the National
Council.[18]

Differences between the Supreme Muslim Council and the institutions
of the Knesset Israel reflected the differences between the two communities. The former was primarily a religious institution operating according traditional patterns, but it did not abstain from political activity, and
made no distinction between political roles and religious roles. In contrast, the Executive of the National Council was composed of politicians,
not religious leaders, and functioned in strictly secular fields. Supreme
religious authority was vested in another institution, the chief rabbinate,
also a part of the institutional framework of Knesset Israel.[19]

A striking difference between the national institutions of the Jews
and those of the Arabs was apparent in the scope of political participation in decision-making processes. The best expression of widespread
participation among the Jews was the elections to the Elected Assembly,
where voting ran between 56 and 70 percent. This was a relatively
high rate of participation in elections within a nonsovereign framework,
especially considering that the elections were boycotted at times by
various groups due to conflicts over the electoral system.[20]

Differences between the Arab and Jewish political systems were also
manifested in the regulation of internal political conflicts. The conflicts
themselves were indeed different. The most important political conflicts
in Arab society were struggles between parties which were actually
groups of notables divided along family and *hamula* lines.

The Palestine Arab party (founded in 1935), the dominant element
in the Arab Higher Committee, was identified with the family of the
mufti of Jerusalem, Haj Amin al-Husseini. The Husseini family attained
its powerful position due to the decision of the first high commissioner

for Palestine, Sir Herbert Samuel, to appoint Haj Amin to the presidency of the Supreme Muslim Council.[21] Despite the role the Mandatory government played in securing this key position for the Husseini family, the family and the party associated with it tended to assume an extreme nationalist stance, opposing not only Zionism but the British as well.

The second most prominent family-based party was the National Defense party led by the Nashashibi family. The head of the Nashashibi family and leader of the party was a former mayor of Jerusalem, Ragheb Bey Nashashibi. Another important leader of this party, who was later assassinated (probably by agents of the Husseini family), was Fakhri Nashashibi. The Nashashibi party was supported by several Arab mayors, the most prominent being Suleiman Ruqan of Nablus. Besides these two large parties there were several others led by members of other prominent families.

In addition to the disputes among family-based factions, there were conflicts between Christians and Muslims and, during the later years of the Mandate, conflicts between the traditional leadership and the young intelligentsia, who in many cases were not members of prominent families. Yet there was almost no political expression of conflicts rooted in the class structure of Arab society. The Arab peasant population lacked any sort of political articulation; it truly fit Shils's notion of a "periphery" as a sector guided by an elitist center without influencing the shape of the center and its functioning. The sector of urban workers was very small, and there were hardly any Arab trade unions until World War II.[22]

The low level of political institutionalization among the Arabs was reflected in modes of conflict regulation. The Arab elite did not develop institutionalized "rules of the game" to provide a foundation of legitimacy to political processes. Consequently, Arab political groups sought the support of the Mandatory government or of Arab political centers outside of Palestine in strengthening their position vis-à-vis other groups within Palestinian Arab society.[23] As a result, the Mandatory government at times found itself acting as arbitrator of the internal conflicts of the Arab community—for example, over control of the Supreme Muslim Council.

In the late 1930s an external political force appeared whose influence on internal Palestinian Arab politics grew steadily from year to year, the rulers of the independent and semi-independent Arab states. One of the important figures in this sphere was the ruler of Transjordan, Amir Abdullah, who usually supported the moderates in their opposition to the Husseini faction.

Another outcome of the absence of authoritative leadership and mechanisms for the resolution of conflicts was an inclination to employ violence, including assassination of political rivals. This form of conflict reached its zenith in a series of political murders during the revolt of 1936–39. The Husseinis especially resorted to this weapon of political struggle. The most prominent victims of political assassination were the dynamic leader of the Nashashibi party, Fakhri Nashashibi, who was murdered in 1941 in Baghdad; Hassan Sidhi Dajani, another important leader of the Nashashibi party, who was killed in 1938; and Sami Taha, the leader of the Arab trade unions, assassinated in 1947.[24]

The Separation of the Jewish Community

Two populations so different from one another can exist in the same territorial framework in only one of two ways. The two populations can be aligned in the same hierarchy, with the more "developed" population (according to generally accepted indices of modernization) located in the upper stratum and the less developed in the lower stratum. Or, each population can maintain a hierarchy of its own, which implies that the populations are, to a considerable extent, segregated from each other. The first pattern often developed in areas of European migration and settlement and in colonial societies such as South Africa and Rhodesia. In Mandatory Palestine, however, a social structure of the second type developed, a circumstance without parallel in the annals of European settlement in the underdeveloped colonial territories.

The critical difference between the two patterns may be attributed to the difference between a movement propelled by economic or imperial drives and one motivated by an ideology which combined a call for the political and cultural renaissance of a people and an aspiration for its social and economic transformation. The drive for the "productivization" of the Jewish people or, in the words of D. B. Borochov, "inverting of the occupational pyramid," was an integral part of the ideology of the Zionist settlement in Palestine from its start.[25] The concept of "productivization" was rooted in the belief that what set the Jews apart in the lands of their dispersion was not only religious differences, or even political ones in those countries where Jews had not yet been emancipated, but exclusive socioeconomic features, such as a tendency to concentrate in occupations of trade, the free professions, and services, or to act as middlemen. The demand for "normalization," for the creation of a Jewish society "like all other nations," was a part of the Zionist ideology and implied a transformation of the occupational structure of the Jewish people through the creation of a stratum of manual workers in agriculture and industry.

Realization of this goal required the creation of an entire stratification system in which the Jewish population would be dispersed among all occupations. This striving for a change from tertiary to secondary and primary occupations—which, by the way, opposed the trends of urbanization and modernization in developed countries—involved glorification of manual labor in general and agricultural labor in particular.[26] However, realization of this ideology was not possible under conditions of an integrated Arab-Jewish society and economy in Palestine, since the Arab population was already predominantly rural.

The process of separation began with the advent of the Zionist settlement in the 1880s. The establishment of exclusively Jewish villages (known as *moshavot* or colonies) was the first expression of the trend toward ecological separation, explained in part by the inability of settlers of European background to become integrated into the traditional Arab village. Ecological separation in urban settlements is another matter. Urban separatism, which reached its peak in the early period with the founding of Tel Aviv, can only be explained by an explicit desire to live in a separate social framework and to strive for municipal autonomy. It comes as no surprise, then, that later waves of immigration sought to settle in Tel Aviv and not Jaffa—even though the original intention of the founders of Tel Aviv was to establish a small and exclusive neighborhood. Thus, the new suburb and not the original area of Jewish residence (Jaffa) became the center of Jewish urban life in Palestine. In Jerusalem and Haifa this process did not go as far and did not lead to the establishment of autonomous municipalities —but in Jerusalem most of the Jewish population lived in separate neighborhoods and in Haifa such neighborhoods were founded as the Jewish population grew.

The extent of ecological segregation can be seen through an examination of data on the distribution of the Arab and Jewish population in towns and villages in the 1930s. In 1931, 655,600 out of 794,600 Arabs (about 82 percent) lived in villages or towns that were exclusively

Arab. In the same year 88,500 out of 174,600 Jews (about 50 percent)
lived in Tel Aviv or in rural settlements with an exclusively Jewish
population. The other half of the Jewish population lived in mixed
towns, but usually in separate neighborhoods. Only five years later, in
1936, 246,000 out of 404,000 Jews (about 60 percent) resided in Tel
Aviv or in exclusively Jewish villages. The rate of growth of the Jewish
population in the all-Jewish settlements was thus greater than the rate
in the mixed towns.[27]

Ecological separation reflected the state of Jewish-Arab relations.
The issue of cultural separation involved another central problem:
creation of a common cultural basis for the Jewish community itself in
the Hebrew language. The cultural separation which preceded the
Zionist settlement was rooted almost entirely in religious differences.
Absent the subsequent revival of the Hebrew language, the impact of
religious differences would probably have decreased over the years due
to the secularization which began with the rise of the Jewish and Arab
national movements. The Jewish immigrants who arrived after 1880
included growing numbers of nonobservant Jews. Secularization pro-
ceeded among the Arabs more slowly, but soon led to a certain dissociation between religion and nationality, visible in the extensive
activity of the Christian elite in the Arab national movement.[28]

The language problem became the central issue in the crystallization
of an autonomous national Jewish culture in Palestine. At the beginning
of Zionist settlement, the languages spoken by the Jews varied according
to their background and country of origin, and included Yiddish,
Arabic, and Ladino (a Spanish dialect). This diversity hampered the
creation of a homogeneous national culture, since no sector of the
Yishuv was inclined to allow the language of another to become the
dominant language. The revival of the Hebrew language as a modern
spoken language proved an ideal solution for three reasons: first,
Hebrew was not the everyday spoken language of any single sector
of the Yishuv; second, it was the traditional language of prayer and
scholarship for the entire Jewish community; and third, it possessed
a symbolic meaning because of its connection to historical memories
of Jewish sovereignty in the Land of Israel during the periods of the
First and Second Temple.

This symbolic significance gave the struggle over the revival of
Hebrew a political meaning.[29] The opposition of ultraorthodox circles
(who saw Hebrew solely as a sacred language) was related to their
complete rejection of the ideas of national revival and modernization

entailed in Zionist ideology.[30] Another source of opposition to the
revival of Hebrew was an outlook which considered immigration and
settlement as an individual affair, rather than a basis for the creation
of an autonomous society. This attitude nurtured the persistence of attachments to external cultural centers, such as Germany or France.

These divergent perspectives created the conditions for the "language
war" fought over the language of instruction in the schools of the Ezra
(Hilfsverein der Deutschen Juden) and Israelite Universelle Alliance
associations. The victory of the partisans of Hebrew helped make possible the cultural homogeneity of the Jewish community which enabled
it to exist as a separate cultural unit aspiring to economic and political
separation as well.

In the economic sphere, the major difficulty was the fact that the
Arab economy was for the most part an agrarian economy which could
compete successfully with the Jewish agricultural sector because of the
low standard of living of the Arab peasant. Moreover, since the beginning of the twentieth century, a surplus of agricultural labor appeared
in the Arab economy, as in other developing countries.[31] The small
scale of capital accumulation and industrial development in the Arab
urban sector made the Jewish economy and the government sector
natural foci of attraction for this surplus labor. This process was not
limited to the Arabs of Palestine; the employment opportunities created
by imported Jewish capital and Jewish settlement attracted workers
from the neighboring countries, especially southern Syria (the Hauran
region). The result of these processes was that the surplus Arab workers
from the Arab economy competed with Jewish immigrants for the
limited supply of jobs created by imported Jewish capital.

To ensure the existence of a stratum of Jewish manual laborers
called for by the ideology of "productivization" of the Jewish people,
it was necessary to restrict at least in part the access of Arab workers
to the Jewish economy. Consequently, a contradiction emerged between
the market forces operating in the economy of Palestine and the demand
for "Jewish labor" voiced by the mainstream of the Zionist movement.[32]

Jewish employers, particularly the farmers of the *moshavot* (the
agricultural settlements of the private economic sector) and building
contractors, faced the choice of employing cheap Arab labor or relying
on union-organized and expensive Jewish labor.

Moreover, Arab agricultural produce was cheaper than the produce
of the Jewish sector, due to the low cost of labor in the Arab sector.[33]
And the supply of agricultural produce was not limited to what could

be produced in Palestine, but also included produce imported from neighboring countries.

A basic conflict of interest developed within the Yishuv between those who were willing to pay the economic price for creating a separate Jewish economy and those who were not. The former were chiefly interested in expanding employment opportunities for Jewish workers while the latter—such as the farmers organized in the Farmers' Association—refused to sacrifice economic benefits to political and ideological demands.[34] This conflict escalated at times from verbal disputes to violent confrontations. The opposition to "Jewish labor only" was supported by the Mandatory government, which strenuously opposed attempts to compel economic separation through political means.[35]

In the course of the debate, the farmers of the *moshavot* tried to cast doubt on the political wisdom of deepening the economic and social cleavages between Arab and Jew. Paradoxically, the Jewish right wing shared views on this subject with some extreme left-wing groups in the Yishuv who opposed economic separation on the grounds of socialist internationalism.[36]

However, the tendency toward separation in the occupational sphere was aided by counter political pressure from the Arab sector. The Arab boycott and general strike at the outset of the Arab revolt of 1936 reduced considerably the number of Arabs employed in Jewish citrus farms. The percentage of Arabs employed in the citrus groves of the *moshavot* of Petach Tikva, Nes Ziona, Hadera, Rishon Le-Zion, and Rehovoth decreased from 66.3 percent of all workers in April 1936 to 27 percent by February 1937. In the construction industry in Jerusalem, where the percentage of Arab workers in 1935 was 42.2 percent of the total, the percentage had decreased by July 1938 to only 3.4 percent.[37] Ironically, Arab political pressures contributed to the realization of the idea of an autonomous Jewish society and economy in Palestine.

The controversy over "Jewish labor only" ended during World War II. The crisis that afflicted the citrus industry in the wake of a severe drop in exports ended the need for the Arab worker in the Jewish economy.[38] On the other hand, Jewish contractors employing Arab workers in projects for the British army did not meet any opposition because of the labor shortage after 1941.

Economic separation was eventually achieved because the conflict between ideological demands and market forces was confined to the lowest level of the hierarchy. Skilled workers and especially white collar workers were not subject to competition from Arab workers, who generally lacked the education and skills required for these occupations. Another factor that facilitated occupational autarchy in the Jewish sector was the demand of the Jewish population for a higher level of public services than the Mandatory government provided—for example, in the areas of health, education, and welfare. The institutions that were established to provide these services created a demand for professionals and white collar workers and enabled the Jewish intelligentsia to avoid competition with colonial officials for jobs. Nor was the supply of jobs subject to competition from the Arab intelligentsia. From this emerges yet another paradoxical conclusion: failure to carry the principle of "inverting the occupational pyramid" to its extreme facilitated the creation of an autonomous hierarchy for the Yishuv.

The over-all effect of the segregation of the Jewish and Arab economies can be expressed in terms of mutual inputs and outputs. The data for 1936 show that the input deriving from the sale of industrial goods and services to the Jewish economy from the Arab economy was 1,108,000 LP out of 33,524,000 LP total inputs into the Jewish sector (from agriculture, manufacture, construction and services). Or, in other words, only about 3 percent of the monetary value of inputs to the Jewish sector stemmed from interrelations with the Arab sector. As for the input of the Jewish sector to the Arab sector from the purchase of goods and services, this totaled 3,657,000 LP out of 33,524,000 LP, about 10 percent.[39] Even in the labor market the scope of relations between the two networks did not significantly deviate from this pattern. The total percentage of Arab workers employed in the Jewish economy a few weeks prior to the outbreak of the Arab revolt was 14.6 percent, which reflected the peak of Arab employment in the Jewish sector.[40] Jewish employment in the Arab sector, on the other hand, was always very small and was limited to certain skilled occupations where no suitable Arab workers could be found.

From the data above it is clear that the relations between the two economies were small and asymmetrical. Jewish capital flowed into the Arab sector to a greater extent than Arab capital flowed into the Jewish sector. True, the tendency for developed sectors in developing economies to maintain a small scale of relations with the less-developed sectors, as compared to their relations with external economic systems, was not unique to Mandatory Palestine. But in the case of Palestine, it seems that the restricted relationships reflected not only rational economic behavior but also the intensity of political pressures segregating the two economies. We may therefore view the economic segregation as a "spillover" from the political sphere which, as previously discussed, was organized along primarily national lines.

The Two Political Communities

In the period of Ottoman rule there was no separate unit of government whose jurisdiction encompassed the entire territory later designated as Palestine. There was no "central" government to serve as a focal point for the local political activity of the inhabitants of this territory. In spite of this, both communities had managed some rudimentary organization into political groups by the end of the Ottoman period. The political organization among the Jews was almost completely dissociated from the Ottoman Empire. Its frames of reference were the Zionist movement on the one hand, and the early attempts at local rule in the *moshavot* and urban neighborhoods on the other. Arab political activity was oriented to two frames of reference: the seat of Ottoman rule in Constantinople and the early stages of the Arab national movement in Damascus and the Arabian peninsula. Thus, at least during the Ottoman period, it may be said that an Arab political center of "Palestinian" character, a focus of authority and source of inspiration for the Arabs of Palestine, never crystallized.

Political relations between the Arabs and the government were conducted on two levels: the local level (town or village) and a higher administrative level (the *vilayet* of Beirut, which included northern and central Palestine, and the independent *sanjak* of Jerusalem, which included Jerusalem and southern Palestine). The Arab national awakening was expressed in pan-Arab sentiments which transcended Ottoman administrative frameworks, as well as that historical unit without distinct borders known as Palestine—or, as the Jews refer to it, the Land of Israel.[41]

Jewish immigration in general and Zionist immigration in particular expressed a religious or ideological bond to Israel as a territorial unit —even if the borders of this unit could not be precisely defined. This bond with the land determined the directions of Zionist settlement which were concentrated in the territory that could be identified with the biblical Land of Israel.[42] Despite the presence of a historical connection between a people and its territory, a political center for the Jews was not formed because the Yishuv in the Ottoman period was still too small and fragmented to do so. The cleavages between the "Old Yishuv"[43] and the "New Yishuv,"[44] between "Ashkenasim" and "Sephardim," and between Ottoman subjects and foreign citizens who enjoyed the protection of foreign consuls (according to the Capitulation agreements)[45] hampered the formation of institutions representing the entire Jewish community in Palestine. There was an abortive attempt in 1903 by the Odessa Committee of the Lovers of Zion headed by Menahem Ussishkin[46] "to create a comprehensive organization to direct the affairs of the Yishuv."[47] But the institutions established by this assembly actually represented only the New Yishuv and disintegrated after several months.

While the attempt to establish a comprehensive representative framework for the Yishuv failed, an institutional framework for directing the activity of the WZO was successfully established. This framework —the Palestine Office, established in 1903 under the direction of Dr. Arthur Ruppin—had no political authority with regard to the Yishuv.[48] Its importance derived from the fact that it controlled the allocation of financial resources alloted to the Yishuv by the WZO.

This connection between the drive for political autonomy of the Yishuv and the reservoir of resources in the Diaspora was more apparent in shaping the political life of the Yishuv after the replacement of Ottoman rule by the British. The British conquest of Palestine and the League of Nations grant of the Mandate to Britain transformed Palestine from a historical and geographical notion into a distinct political and territorial entity. Now there was an authoritative political center in Jerusalem (albeit subordinate to the British government in London), headed by a high commissioner. This structure created indirect ties between the two national communities, since both were subject to the Mandatory law and both had recourse to the center as a provider of services and a governmental authority.

It was the very establishment of a governmental center, with key positions filled by British officials, which facilitated the political separation of Arabs and Jews. It relieved the need for Arab and Jewish political elites to cultivate direct relationships, since it was possible to conduct most of the political bargaining through the British authorities in Jerusalem and in London. This technical possibility of avoiding direct political contacts was exploited by both sides in ways which reflected their respective national aspirations. From the Arabs' point of view,

direct contact with the Jews implied recognition of the Jews as a
national entity with a legitimate claim to Palestine. According to prevailing Arab attitudes, Palestine was Arab. Jewish immigration and
settlement were perceived as an attempt to deny the exclusive Arab
claim to Palestine. The Balfour Declaration, which recognized the right
of the Jews to establish a "national home" in Palestine, and the example
of the grant of independence to several Arab countries,[49] strengthened
the Palestinian Arab inclination to reject Jewish political aspirations.
Opposition to Jewish immigration and settlement was a central motive
in the Arab efforts to organize countrywide political bodies, such as
the Arab Executive Committee and the Arab Higher Committee. From
this perspective, it may be said that the national consciousness of the
Palestinian Arabs originated in the reaction to Zionist ideology and its
implementation in Palestine.[50]

In contrast to the Arabs, the Jews did not avoid political contacts
with the other side for fear that these contacts would imply political
recognition.[51] But the Jewish community did contribute to the process
of separation by the systematic creation of nationwide political institutions which struggled for autonomy. These institutions tended to
restrict the scope of political activity to within the Yishuv itself. Moreover, the institutions of the Yishuv nurtured ties with the Diaspora in
general and the Zionist movement abroad in particular. Jewish political
organizations were also aided by the formal recognition accorded the
Jewish Agency in the charter of the Mandate and the institutions of the
Knesset Israel in the Religious Communities Ordinance. But the main
impetus was provided by the social and demographic changes which
occurred after World War I. The new waves of Zionist-inspired immigrants changed the internal structure of the Yishuv by numerically
increasing the size of the New Yishuv in relation to the Old Yishuv,
which was composed mainly of ultraorthodox elements. This change
paved the way for the creation of a secular and Zionist-inspired central
institution for the Jewish community.

Despite the general separation between the communities, there was
at least one area where Jews and Arabs did establish direct relations
in a common political framework: municipal government in the mixed
cities. But even there, in the elected bodies, local representatives were
chosen on a basis which implied a recognition of each community's
distinct interests.[52] The Mandatory government set a fixed number of
representatives from each community, usually according to their pro-

portion of the population. Thus election results and rates of participation in different parts of the population had no effect on the balance of political forces between Arabs and Jews.

A different type of political contact between Arabs and Jews developed as a result of attempts at "joint organization" of Arabs and Jewish workers in trade unions.[53] This became a subject of ideological dispute among the parties of the Labor movement, over the contradiction between the nationalist concept of building an autonomous Jewish society and the international concept which formed a part of the socialist ethos infusing the socialist-Zionist parties of Palestine. The more radical socialists in the Labor movement rejected, on the basis of Marxist ideology, cooperation between the bourgeoisie and the Labor movement in the construction of a Jewish society and economy in Palestine. They sought instead to organize with allies on a class basis which transcended national lines. Thus, socialist left-wing groups in the Yishuv called for a policy of joint trade union organization for Arabs and Jews, at least in those occupations where they worked side by side. In contrast, the majority in the Labor movement followed Ben-Gurion, who called for parallel national trade union organizations linked at the federation level.[54]

Practical attempts to effect a "joint organization" were few indeed, their scope hardly justifying the intensity of the ideological conflict on this issue. The most prominent attempts were the founding of the International Organization of Railroad Workers in 1923, whose membership reached five hundred after several years, and the establishment of the Alliance of Palestine Workers in 1932 by the Histadrut (the General Federation of Labor) as a framework for organizing Arab workers.[55] These initial attempts fell apart during the 1936–39 Arab revolt, and several of the Arabs active in these organizations were tried and punished by tribunals set up by Arab guerrilla bands. Only during World War II was cooperation renewed between Arab and Jewish workers in government and military projects. This cooperation reached its peak in the strike of government workers in 1940. The Alliance of Palestine Workers also renewed its activity and, according to its own figures, its membership reached twenty-five hundred in 1944. However, by this time there were already larger all-Arab trade unions which operated under Communist or nationalist inspiration.[56] Thus in the sphere of labor relations, as in other spheres of Arab-Jewish relations, the cleavage along national lines ultimately dominated others types of cleavages which divided the population of Mandatory Palestine. The attempts at "joint organization" initiated by Jews remained paternalistic attempts which encompassed only small numbers of Arab workers.

Attempts to bridge the Arab-Jewish antagonism through common political activities succeeded only to the extent that they were undertaken by small groups which dissociated themselves from the prevailing political and ideological trends in the Jewish and Arab communities. The most important example was the Communist party[57] which, because of its anti-Zionist platform, was partly able to overcome the obstacles to common Arab-Jewish political organization. Most of the members of the Communist party were Jewish, but for ideological reasons and because of pressure from the Comintern, it was decided early in 1930 that an Arab would occupy the post of secretary general. The violent Arab outbreaks of 1929 and 1936 placed the party in a dilemma. Most of the Jewish members tended to accept the idea that the special interests of the Jewish population could not be ignored and that this implied different approaches to the two components of the population.[58] Thus, in the final analysis even the Communist binational party organization collapsed under the pressure of the political conflict which determined the scope and nature of Arab-Jewish relations in Palestine.

3

The Growth and Consolidation of the Jewish Political Center

Center, Subcenter, and Periphery in the Jewish Community

The development of the political institutions of the Yishuv to the point where they could serve as the foundation for an independent state occurred simultaneously with the crystallization of its social structure. Unlike many developing countries, the political organization of the Yishuv was not the culmination of social and economic processes spanning generations; the development of the political system was linked to the growth of other institutional spheres in a set of interrelations that in turn produced the foundation of a new society striving for autonomy. The Yishuv, therefore, was to a considerable extent free of the tensions and pressures which generally accompany the transition from traditional and posttraditional societies to what are referred to as "modern" societies.[1] In other words, because the Yishuv was essentially a new society, there was considerable synchronization between the various spheres of development, and the serious gaps or lags between these spheres that have impaired the political stability of many new states did not develop.[2] Moreover, as a new society the Yishuv did not experience the collapse of an indigenous political system following colonial conquest. On the contrary, British Mandatory rule, at least in its early stages, actually assisted the process of institution building in the Yishuv through formal recognition of the national institutions and cooperation with them.

A further difference distinguishing the Yishuv from most political systems in formerly colonial societies lay in the cultural, social, and demographic characteristics of the population of the "periphery." In most developing countries the sector that assumes a leading role in the construction of the national center is numerically small and distinct in its ecological and institutional location. It is usually the educated elite in the major cities which acts as an "agent" of modernization. Most of the population of the Yishuv, however, possessed a European cultural background, though they were not necessarily from the most advanced countries of Europe. But since the act of immigrating to Palestine was based on ideological motives, the level of political sophistication among the Jews of Palestine was relatively high, and closer to the political culture of the intelligentsia and middle class in their countries of origin that to other sectors of the population, such as peasants and workers.

The modern character of the Yishuv was also expressed in the high concentration of the population in urban centers—even though a large portion of the New Yishuv adhered to ideologies that called for a "return to the land." Moreover, even the agricultural sector was not the traditional peasantry which tends to lag behind in terms of cultural and political development. Most of the settlers in the rural sector were ideologically motivated and saw themselves as the vanguard of the New Yishuv. They possessed the qualities of an elite and were among those who created the values and political culture of the Yishuv. More-over, most members of the agricultural sector came from middle-class backgrounds, possessed a secondary school education, and were much influenced by the various ideological movements of early twentieth-century Europe.

This resulted in the paradox that the political center was not neces-sarily the primary source of innovation and social initiative, which often originated in sectors such as the agricultural settlements which in other settings would be considered strictly peripheral. At times the innovations of the so-called "pioneering sector" were of such an enterprising nature that the center found it difficult to absorb them.

This situation compels us to reconsider the extent to which the center-periphery model is applicable to the case of the Yishuv. Two questions emerge: to what extent was the center indeed "central," and to what extent was the periphery "peripheral"? Or, in other words, to what extent was the national center a source of inspiration and innovation and to what extent was the periphery subject to the dominance of the center, passively accepting its influence rather than actively participating in its formation? Here we can distinguish between two dimensions of a center: the locus of institutional authority and the source of charisma. We conclude that the distribution of charisma in Shils's sense was wider than the distribution of institutionalized authority.[3]

The issue of the centrality of the center involves its ability to enforce its rules without the ultimate authority of sovereignty, whereas the question of the extent to which the periphery was peripheral is essentially one of the defining the status of the subcenters and their spheres of autonomy. The ambiguity of a center that was not completely central and a periphery that was not strictly peripheral was a consequence of the historical development of the Yishuv. From the outset the Yishuv did not have a dominant center with recognized authority, an absence particularly apparent under Ottoman rule. Even in the early years of the Mandate, the evolving center (then embodied in the World Zionist Organization and Knesset Israel) possessed only limited authority. What eventually led to a strengthening of this center was a shift of orientation on the part of the most energetic groups in the Yishuv from concentration on the formation of separate subcenters to participation in the effort to create a national center.

Even with the consolidation of the national center, the authority of the subcenters did not collapse, as they continued to function as agencies of the center in certain spheres while preserving their autonomy in others. Hence, these subcenters could not be considered peripheral in the full sense of the term since they were not "composed of those strata or sectors of society which accept orders or beliefs whilst playing no part in their formation or dissemination."[4] The subcenters were largely autarchic enclaves which attempted to shape the image of society or at least the way of life of those they inspired. They were thus the source of a considerable amount of charisma. Moreover, the subcenters possessed many modern elements, both in their form of organization and in their value systems.

Nevertheless, the term "periphery" is not totally without relevance to the development of the Yishuv. The concepts of center and periphery may be perceived as two extremes of a continuum and not as a dichotomy, so that it is possible to locate different groups and subcenters according to their distance from or proximity to the center. The affinity of the various subcenters to the national center not only varied in a given period, but changed from period to period. Hence, it is possible to speak of the centripetal movement of some subcenters and the centrifugal movements of others.

The most important centripetal movement that led to the strengthening of the authority of the center—and to an increase in its control over resource allocation—was related to the shift in the political orientation of the Labor movement, which abandoned its separatist tendencies of the 1920s to play an active and even dominant role in the shaping of the center in the 1930s. In the 1920s the Labor movement, and especially the umbrella organization of the labor parties, the *Histadrut*,[5] tended to maintain its own symbolic and institutional frameworks. It possessed only minimal influence on the World Zionist Organization Executive: one of the two main Labor parties had a representative on the Executive, while the other had a nonofficial representative as it was not a party to the coalition. These parties, Hapoel Hatzair and Ahdut Ha'avoda,[6] tended to conceive their role as representing the interests of the Labor movement to the WZO, rather than participating in decision-making. This introspective period of the Labor movement did, however, have the positive effect that the Histadrut's range of activity was broad. For example, until the early 1930s the Histadrut dominated a central field of activity that concerned the entire Yishuv: it assumed responsibility for organized Jewish defense against Arab attacks.

The situation changed after the unification in 1930 of the main labor party, Ahdut Haavoda, with the smaller party, Hapoel Hatzair. The merger formed the new party, Mapai, which soon concentrated its efforts on the competition for key positions in the national institutions. This shift of orientation was expressed in the slogan coined by Ben-Gurion, "from class to nation," and involved a recognition of the necessity for interclass cooperation in establishing the Jewish national home,[7] with the Labor movement as the dominant partner in the coalition center. When Mapai won control of the key positions,[8] it became the chief proponent of the demand to strengthen the center's authority and impose it on those sectors that had displayed a negative, ambivalent, or apathetic attitude toward it.

This centripetal movement on the part of Mapai took place almost simultaneously with a centrifugal movement in the right wing of the

Zionist movement which resulted in the secession of the Revisionist party, the strongest subcenter of the right wing, from the World Zionist Organization.[9] More moderate right-wing parties and factions also exhibited centrifugal tendencies. They did not secede from the "organized Yishuv," but did try to reduce their dependence on the national center. However, these subcenters of the moderate right had no pretensions of creating an alternative national center. Despite their reservations at the tendency of the center to expand the scope of its authority and activities, they continued to operate within the framework of the quasi-state organization of the Jewish community. The scope of authority of the national institutions became a major focus of struggle in the Yishuv and rendered the center's authority redefinable through a process of bargaining among the center, the subcenters, and the periphery.

Four factors which contributed to the integration of the political system of the Yishuv are especially significant:

1. The Arab-Jewish cleavage resulted in a struggle with the Arab national movement which necessitated political organization for security purposes and for effective representation vis-à-vis the Mandatory government.

2. The organizational infrastructures of the subcenters, some of which were institutionalized before the center, enabled them to provide manpower for key positions in the center and at times act as agencies of the center in the political mobilization of the population.

3. The dependence of all groups in the Yishuv on the external flow of material resources and manpower, controlled in part by the national institutions, helped check disintegrative processes. This dependency created an incentive for the subcenters to participate in the allocative mechanisms of the center.

4. Paradoxically, the fourth factor was connected with the absence of a sovereign political framework, as that enabled each group to threaten withdrawal from the political framework. Since secession could weaken the representative nature of the entire system, most groups preferred to compromise rather than to attempt exclusive control of the system. The possibility of secession led to the adoption of rules for the regulation of conflicts in the absence of the sanctions available to a sovereign state.

The National Institutions

The quasi-state functions of the national center were embodied in the "national institutions": Knesset Israel which represented only the Yishuv, and the World Zionist Organization (and, later, the Jewish Agency), the joint framework for the Yishuv and the Zionist movement in the Diaspora.

The institutions of the Knesset Israel received legal recognition by the Mandatory government, pursuant to the regulations of the Religious Communities Ordinance, in 1926.[10] The first Elected Assembly of the Yishuv had been chosen in April 1920. The Yishuv's population at that time was 67,000, and 22,000 out of 28,000 eligible voters voted.[11] Establishing a representative political framework required determining who should vote and how. There were three issues implicit in these questions: (1) the universality of suffrage, (2) the "one man one vote" issue, and (3) proportionality of representation. The last two were partially related.

The principle of universal suffrage was not accepted by all sectors of the Yishuv. The main objection came from the ultraorthodox, who were opposed to women's suffrage and eventually withdrew from Knesset Israel over this issue. However, the establishment of suffrage for every man and woman in the Yishuv did not yet assure the principle of "one man one vote."

In the elections to the first Elected Assembly there were separate all-male polling booths for the ultraorthodox. In the elections to the second Elected Assembly (December 1925) there were also separate booths, this time for the Yemenites who did not participate in the regularly scheduled elections and voted later (January 1926). Twenty of their representatives were later added to the Elected Assembly.[12] The most marked deviation from the principle of the equal vote (i.e., an equal number of votes per representative) appeared in the regulations for the elections held in 1932 to the third Elected Assembly which were, for the first time, formally approved by the government under the Religious Communities Ordinance. These regulations stipulated that the elections would be held according to separate ethnic *curiae*: Ashkenazic, Sephardic, and Yemenite. The various parties submitted separate lists of Sephardic, Yemenite, and Ashkenazic candidates for each of the three *curiae*, and the Sephardic and Yemenite representatives were elected by a smaller number of voters than those in the Ashkenazic category.[13]

The only assembly elected according to the formula of "one man one vote" was the fourth Elected Assembly, chosen in August 1944, four years before the state was established. These elections were preceded by a dispute over the proportional and countrywide characteristics of the electoral system. The Sephardim, the farmers of the *moshavot*, and the Revisionists sought to divide the country into a number of electoral districts instead of a single district.[14] When their demand was rejected, the Sephardim and the right boycotted the elections; but this was ineffective, as 67 percent of all eligible voters eventually participated in the election.[15] The eventual organization of an electoral system based on "one man one vote" was the result of the determined efforts of the parties of the left, who were also the main exponents of extending the authority of the institutions of Knesset Israel beyond the functions specified in Mandatory law.

Published in December 1928, the regulations governing Knesset Israel gave legal recognition to a three-tiered pyramidal structure: the Elected Assembly, elected every four years, which convened only for special occasions; the National Council plenum, which acted as the permanent parliamentary framework for directing current affairs; and the National Council Executive, charged with implementing the decisions of the Elected Assembly and the National Council plenum. Because they were based on the Religious Communities Ordinance, the regulations were infused with the concept that the communal organization of the Yishuv was primarily religious. However, both the scope of authority and the spheres of activity of Knesset Israel's institutions exceeded the boundaries drawn in the regulations. The National Council saw itself primarily as the representative of a political community, religious services being only one of many needs.

The differences in approach between the Mandatory government and Knesset Israel in regard to authority embraced several issues. The first point of dispute centered on the withdrawal of ultraorthodox circles from the community organization. The National Council opposed the government's recognition in any form of the ultraorthodox as a separate religious community. The government, on the other hand, viewed membership in Knesset Israel as basically voluntary, and allowed individuals to withdraw from its registry if they were not prepared to accept its authority[16]—a right soon exercised by extremist orthodox groups. Moreover, the government was prepared to recognize separatist groups as distinct and parallel religious communities. This status was chosen by Agudat Israel and other ultraorthodox circles in Jerusalem, who organized as the Edah Haredit (the Orthodox Community).[17]

The second controversy concerned expanding Knesset Israel to new institutional spheres, such as education. In general, the Jewish educational system was supervised by the Zionist Executive and independent of the Mandatory government in the areas of budget and curriculum. It was a central federation of systems encompassing three ideological trends: the "general" trend, supported mainly by the parties of the right and the center; the Labor trend, controlled by the Histadrut; and the religious Mizrahi trend.[18] Efforts to expand the authority and spheres of activity of the Knesset Israel into education (and other areas) were hampered by the meager resources which could be mobilized by the National Council. Before the promulgation of the regulations in the late twenties, the lack of formal authority was the major constraint: attempts to levy taxes without compulsory legal apparatus or an adequate administrative mechanism brought a poor response from the community. Even in the 1930s when the regulations allowed taxes to be collected by local authorities and community councils, the amount of resources at the disposal of the National Council remained small and did not permit the Council to expand its activities extensively. Only after the World Zionist Organization transferred responsibility for the Jewish educational system to the National Council in 1932 and provided funds to subsidize that system[19] was a partial solution found through the infusion of resources from the WZO. The limited capacity of the National Council to mobilize resources on its own explains why it played a secondary role in the creation of the national center, in contrast to the other component of the national institutions, the WZO Executive.

The Jewish Agency and the WZO were connected by Zionist members of the Agency Executive who were also members of the WZO Executive. The latter were responsible to the quasi-parliamentary forum called the Zionist Actions Committee (the General Council). There was no equivalent to which the non-Zionists members of the Jewish Agency Executive were responsible. The Zionist Actions Committee was chosen by the biennial Zionist congresses and elected democratically. The right to vote was acquired by the purchase of a *shekel* certificate, which also symbolized membership in the WZO. After 1921, residents of Palestine who purchased a *shekel* enjoyed a special status in comparison to WZO members abroad, as their votes in elections to the Zionist congresses were weighted double.[20] These elections were proportional, but were held separately in different countries. In each country the parties presented separate lists to the voters; at the Zionist congresses those elected united to form party factions that transcended territorial divisions. The relative size of each faction determined its representation on the Actions Committee.[21]

The Jewish Agency derived its legal authority from article 4 of the Mandate:

> An appropriate Jewish Agency shall be recognized as a public body for the purpose of advising and cooperating with the Administration of Palestine in such economic, social, and other matters as may affect the establishment of the Jewish National Home and the interests of the Jewish population in Palestine.[22]

The Jewish Agency concentrated on conducting external political negotiations, primarily with the British government in London and the British administration in Palestine, and on organizing immigration, agricultural settlements, and economic development for the Yishuv. These functions necessitated considerable financial aid from Diaspora Jewry. These resources were acquired through two "national funds," the Foundation Fund (Keren Hayesod)[23] and the Jewish National Fund (Keren Kayemet),[24] and provided the WZO Executive with financial instruments to achieve its goals.

The activities of the WZO, and later the Jewish Agency, were assisted by the formal recognition accorded them, but they did not rely on the recognition alone. They sought to obtain a measure of autonomy that was not always consistent with the letter of the Mandate. According to the Mandate, the activities of these bodies should have been "subject always to the control of the Administration to assist and take part in the development of the country." The striving for autonomy of the WZO and the Jewish Agency was facilitated by the Mandatory government's policy of avoiding excessive involvement in the building of the national home. The Mandatory government was prepared to share the WZO's view that WZO should direct the process of Jewish colonization, since it did not seek responsibility for a task that could only exacerbate the conflict between the British and the Arab majority in Palestine. Under these circumstances, the government agreed to determine only the over-all allotment of immigration certificates[25] and to leave the individual allocation of most of the various types of certificates to the Jewish Agency. In other areas related to the strengthening of the national home, such as agricultural settlement, the government was not involved at all, and only in the later years of the Mandate sought to hamper Jewish settlement by restricting immigration and land purchase.

Under these circumstances, relations between the government and the Jewish Agency were marked by constant haggling over the scope and rate of growth of the national home—the Agency and the National Council pressing to speed development, the government attempting to restrain it. The WZO's most conspicuous deviation from the range of activities defined in the Mandate was in the area of defense and security. The WZO did not abide by the principle that responsibility for the security of the Jewish population rested exclusively in the hands of the Mandatory government, which as sovereign demanded a monopoly on the legitimate use of force within Palestine. For that reason, some of the activity of the WZO in the area of defense was conducted in the nebulous region of semilegality. In the 1920s, the national institutions helped to finance the Hagana. In the 1930s, after the WZO assumed supervision of *Hagana* activities, it became the military instrument of the evolving national center of the Yishuv.[26]

The existence of a dual institutional system gave rise to the term "national institutions," but the existence of a descriptive term did not solve the problem of the division of functions between the WZO and the National Council, nor the more difficult problem of relations between the Yishuv and the Zionist movement in the Diaspora. The problem of division of authority was twofold: representation of the interests of the Yishuv before the Mandatory government, and participation of National Council representatives in the WZO Executive on matters affecting the Yishuv. In both areas the position of the WZO Executive (and the Jewish Agency) was clearly superior. Its authority rested on the legal recognition in article 4 of the Mandate, the political backing of the world Zionist movement, and the control of resources in the two national funds. The WZO Executive's authority was especially apparent in the early 1920s when Knesset Israel still lacked official recognition and sufficient resources to cover operations beyond the clerical expenses of its small central office.

After 1930, the friction between the National Council and the Agency abated as the composition of the Agency changed. The accession of

Mapai members to key positions in the Agency Executive in Jerusalem created a situation where the key positions in both institutions were held by members of the same party, which permitted greater coordination between the two institutions. This change in the Agency Executive, the transfer of responsibility for education to the representatives of the Yishuv, and enhanced cooperation between the two national institutions were related to another change which was to have a major impact on the formulation of the national center. In the early 1930s, the Zionist movement's center of gravity, including the leadership and the day-to-day administration of the Agency, shifted to Jerusalem. This change was expressed in the increased proportion of Executive members living in Jerusalem and in the appointment of a chairman of the Executive in Jerusalem, giving the Agency the image of a cabinet.

Four factors were influential in augmenting the authority of the Jerusalem Executive. The first was the growth and consolidation of the Yishuv itself. After the Yishuv's great crisis at the end of the Fourth Immigration—when emigration exceeded immigration—an economic and demographic recovery occurred.[27] The political crisis following the Arab disturbances of 1929 and the publication of the Passfield White Paper in October 1930 passed—and the drastic restraints on immigration many feared did not materialize. On the contrary, Hitler's rise to power in 1933 brought on the largest wave of immigration to date and a marked rise in the amount of private capital imports. This created unprecedented prosperity in 1930–35, the influence of which on the economic development of the Yishuv continued until World War II and indirectly thereafter as well.

The second factor in the shift of the center of gravity was related to the first. As the Yishuv grew, so did its problems. These required expansion of the functions of the national institutions. The absorption of the German immigration was different from that of previous groups in that the immigrants' private capital was transferred by the Jewish Agency through an agreement with the German government that provided for a conversion of this capital into goods. This was an example of the new centralistic approach to economic development inspired by the leaders of the Labor movement. In this way the Agency became more involved in the sphere of economic development.

The third factor in shifting the center of the Zionist Executive's activity to Palestine was the accession to key positions in the Agency Executive of Labor political elite members who, in contrast to members of the Executive in the 1920s, possessed an organized political base in the Yishuv. Leaders such as Harry Sacher,[28] Col. F. H. Kisch,[29] David Eder,[30] and Henrietta Szold[31] were elected to the Executive in the 1920s by virtue of their position and activities in the Diaspora, while Labor leaders such as David Ben-Gurion, Chaim Arlozoroff, Eliezer Kaplan, and Moshe Shertok (Sharett) rose to prominence in the Agency through political activities in the Yishuv. Their political base in the Yishuv augmented their bargaining power within the Zionist Executive and their status as political spokesmen vis-à-vis the Mandatory government.

The fourth factor was a result of a policy change by the Mandatory government. In order to free itself from the pressures of the pro-Zionist lobby in London, the Mandatory government transferred the main arena of political contacts with Jewish representatives from London to Jerusalem.[32] Practically, this meant that matters of political significance were now dealt with by the high commissioner instead of the Colonial Office. Consequently, the status of High Commissioner Sir Arthur Wauchope (1931–38)[33] was enhanced in relation to that of his predecessors, Field Marshall Lord Plumer (1925–28) and Sir John Chancellor (1928–31).[34] The status of Agency Executive members also rose in relation to their London colleagues.

Thus, the Yishuv in the thirties grew in size and strength; it overcame the extended economic crisis of the late 1920s; it withstood the violent Arab disturbances of 1929; and it successfully endured the period of political uncertainty created by the Passfield White Paper. These changes were signs of a process of political and social consolidation of the Jewish community that was reflected also in the life-style of individuals and groups. The migratory existence of the pioneering sector, romantic yet full of hardship, vanished almost completely from the social landscape. As the pioneers of yesteryear became family men and women with a permanent place of residence and regular or semi-regular employment, the demand for a higher level of services arose. Following its *laissez-faire* approach, the Mandatory government did not feel obliged to provide these services, of which education was the most important; instead they were provided (in part) by the national institutions. Even when these services were provided by other public institutions, such as the Histadrut or local authorities, they were occasionally assisted by allocations of resources from "national" sources through the Zionist funds controlled by the Jewish Agency. This control over financial resources, as well as the control over distribution of immigration certificates, gave the national institutions an allocative function, strengthening their influence not only by the amount of resources at their disposal, but also by the judicious manner in which those resources were allocated.

The 1936–39 Disturbances: New Dimensions of the National Institutions' Activities

By the mid-1930's the "state in the making" was no longer a vague concept, but an increasingly viable reality. Thus, when the Arab revolt broke out in 1936, the Yishuv had an institutional foundation upon which it could construct new organizational frameworks to meet the challenge. The Arab revolt was a reaction to the Fifth Immigration and the settlement and economic development that accompanied it. The importance of the revolt lies not only in its extent and force, but also in the way it influenced the Arab image held by the Jewish public and political leadership. For the first time, an image formed of an effective Arab national center and leadership, whose authority rested on the identification of its following, which was capable of mobilizing resources and manpower for its political aims and controlling the political behavior of the Arab masses. During the course of the revolt it became increasingly apparent that this image was considerably inflated. In actual fact, the power of the center rested in part on internal political terror, which became less effective as the Mandatory government intensified its response to it. But at least in the first stage of the revolt and the concomitant general strike, it seemed that the Arab center was effectively employing its resources.

Jewish leadership viewed the armed force of the Yishuv as defensive in nature, which meant the forces were to be used only if intercommunal violence was initiated by the Arabs. This perception of a limited role for armed force affected the extent of control the national center exercised over this force and the operational doctrines which guided it. In the sphere of control, the most conspicuous fact was the existence since 1930 of parallel defense organizations, one "leftist" and the other "rightist," the latter composed of parties participating in the ruling coalition of the Jewish Agency and the Revisionist party. Such a situation could endure only as long as "security" was perceived as the defense of Jewish life and property against Arab riots; it was not

appropriate to the use of armed force for political ends. Another expression of the reigning concept of security was the decentralized
structure of the Hagana, which was characterized by considerable
autonomy for local commands in the disposition of manpower and
weapons. The operational doctrines of the Hagana also reflected this
concept until 1936, in that they were mainly defensive and based on
static defense forces for Jewish settlements and Jewish neighborhoods
in mixed cities.

The countrywide nature of the Arab revolt, along with the efforts to
institutionalize its leadership and to subordinate the armed Arab bands
to the command of a former Syrian army officer, Fawzi el-Kaoukji,
created a new challenge for the leadership of the Yishuv. The response
to this challenge was a change in the perception of the role of military
force and the role of settlement in the political conflict over the future
of Palestine.

One of the results of this changed perception was a drive to reunite
the two defense organizations. The merger effected in 1937 was incomplete, because the Revisionist element of the right wing continued to
maintain its separate organization, the Irgun Zvai Leumi. But at least
the anomaly of a separatist military organization supported by Zionist
coalition parties had ended. Along with this political change were
changes in the organization, system of recruitment, and operational
doctrines of the Hagana. The culmination was a growing centralization
expressed in the creation of the field squads (*plugot sadeh*) that were
under the direct control of the central command, even though their
operations were conducted under the Hagana district commanders.

An even more important expression of these new attitudes was the
attempt made after the Peel Commission's partition proposal to devise
a master plan for the defense of the envisioned Jewish state. Even
though this plan was never effected because the British decided against
partition, it demonstrated the new dimensions in the political and military thinking of the Jewish leadership which implied also a new concept
of the national institutions' role. The appropriate scope of functions
for the national institutions and for the Hagana national command
became a central issue in the Yishuv's internal politics as the national
institutions and the Hagana expanded their functions. A command cadre
emerged in the Hagana with a professional outlook which viewed the
defense forces of the organized Yishuv as a regular army in the making.
Consequently, the technical department of the Hagana became the

nucleus of a general staff, even before it was decided in 1939 to establish such a body.[35]

The development of professional military cadres and the existence of full-time units mobilized under the direct or indirect and covert (as in the case of the Jewish Settlement Police) control of the Hagana illustrates another aspect of the contribution of the Arab revolt to the organization of the Yishuv: recruitment and direction of manpower. Levels of mobilization were increased, whether for occasional guard duty or for full-time duty in the constabulary units of the JSP or the Hagana's own field squads. For the first time since the beginning of the Mandate, there were thousands of men mobilized in full-time military activity at the same time subject to the authority (or at least direction) of the national institutions.[36] Moreover, manpower needs were not confined to the area of military service. During the revolt it was also necessary to construct fortifications and meet the logistic requirements of life in warfare conditions.

Along with the manpower mobilized by the "organized Yishuv" to face the security problems created by the Arab revolt, there was also a need to mobilize financial resources. The framework established for this purpose—a special fund called Kofer Hayishuv—was the first effective effort at voluntary self-taxation and raised the sum of 150,000 LP in its first year, which covered 70 percent of the Hagana's budget.[37] This voluntary taxation had a political significance as well. The political groups whose members were among the largest contributors visualized the organizational framework of Kofer Hayishuv as a means of increasing the influence of the non-Labor elements in the Yishuv on policymaking in the security sphere. Consequently the political composition of the national command of the Hagana, which was formed on a basis of parity, was more congenial to the right wing of the organized Yishuv than it was to the Executive of the national institutions. These circumstances created a situation where the Hagana cadres were a source of Labor movement influence; the fund-raising apparatus for the Hagana was a source of bourgeois influence; and the national command was poised between them to mediate in a continuous process of political bargaining.

The tendency to formulate a comprehensive strategy guided by national political considerations also emerged in the sphere of settlement. From the beginning of the "Tower and Stockade" settlement program in December 1936 until May 1939, fifty-two new settlements

were established, some of them in new areas of the country, such as
the Beit Shean Valley and Western Galilee. The partition proposal of
the Peel Commission was a stimulus in subjecting the process of settlement to political and strategic considerations.

The nature of the Jewish Agency's involvement with the Yishuv's
economy also changed around 1935. The transfer agreement with
Germany, in which Jewish capital was converted into goods and ex-
ported to Palestine, was the first manifestation of the new trend. The
Agency also influenced the extension of credit for industrial development by the Anglo-Palestine Bank. The economic department of the
Agency would recommend granting of loans to investors whose projects
appeared worthwhile. The innovation here was not only in the investment of imported capital in economic development, but also in the
direction of investments made by private investors, as well as those
made directly with "national capital." This led to a greater involvement
of the national center in the urban industrial sector of the Jewish
economy, hitherto almost completely in private hands.

In contrast to the changes in the conceptions of security and settlement, the increased involvement of the national institutions in the
economy was not a result of the Arab revolt. However, the revolt did
lead to changes that were of both economic and logistic significance.
For example, when the port of Jaffa was closed to Jewish traffic, a
parallel port was set up in Tel Aviv, while in Haifa—the only deep-
water port in Palestine—for the first time Jewish stevedores appeared,
thus ending the Arab monopoly.

The Organized Yishuv and the
Mandatory Government:
From Cooperation to Conflict

The expansion and intensification of security activities undertaken by
the national institutions required frequent contacts with the Mandatory
government. Toward the end of the Arab revolt relations between the
national institutions and the government in the sphere of security
expanded as the British army assumed primary responsibility for enforcing law and order. The most notable assistance rendered by the
Hagana to the British army in this period was the special night squads
commanded by Orde Wingate in which Hagana volunteers served under

British officers in guarding the Iraq Petroleum Company pipeline to Haifa.[38]

In 1937–38, it seemed to the leadership of the Yishuv and the Zionist movement that new political options had unfolded, the most significant related to the partition plan recommended by the Peel Commission. These options closed in part in 1939 as the British government, facing the threat of war in Europe, adopted a policy of appeasement toward the Arabs in order to protect the flanks of the empire in the event of war. The collaboration between the Mandatory government and the Zionist leadership, which helped to expand the functions and strengthen the authority of the national institutions, drew strength from a temporary convergence of interests in preserving law and order in Palestine during the years 1936–39. This collaboration reached its peak toward the end of the revolt when, the British government decided to employ firm measures to put down the revolt. Yet, on the political level, the danger of war with Germany and Italy soon led the British to adopt policies which created a deepening rift between the British government and the leadership of the Yishuv and the Zionist movement. The Woodhead Commission Report, the St. James Conference, the White Paper of 1939, and the Land Transfer Regulations of 1940 —each marked a stage in the deepening of this rift.

The conflict over continued Jewish colonization between British policy and the interests of the Yishuv and the Zionist movement became so intense that it affected even those areas where there had been co-operation or tacit consensus during the Revolt—particularly the sphere of security. During the revolt the British were aided by the capacity of the organized Yishuv to mobilize and deploy its resources against Arab terror. However, as soon as the revolt subsided, the inclination toward cooperation disappeared. The British efforts to stifle further Jewish colonization drove the national institutions to resort to illegal means, such as initiating mass demonstrations and organizing illegal immigration or, as it was called in Hebrew, Aliyah (immigration) B. British outlook changed too. The Hagana, once a partner in the struggle against Arab terror, was now perceived as a challenge to the ability of the British to implement their policy in Palestine. This shift had practical application in the arrest and imprisonment of forty-three participants in a Hagana officers' course and the confiscation of weapons stored in Jewish settlements. Another result of the rift between the Yishuv and the

Mandatory government was the reduction in the amount of resources made available to the national institutions. The leadership of the Yishuv was deprived of the extra authority as well as the material resources received from active collaboration with the British during the revolt.

The problem of reduced levels of potential resources was not caused only by the crisis in relations with the British. The contact between the Yishuv and Eastern European Jewry was severed as a result of the German conquest of most of Poland, and the Soviet occupation of eastern Poland and the Baltic States cut the Yishuv off from its largest reservoir of potential immigrants. At the onset of war the importation of capital too was drastically reduced because of the occupation of Eastern Europe and the cessation of capital transfers from German Jews. Another factor which created difficulties for the national institutions during the early months of the war was a rise in unemployment,[39] which lowered morale. The idea that the policy of the national institutions had reached a dead end became widespread in the Yishuv—with the result that willingness to respond to its leaders diminished.

The capacity to lead the Yishuv and the Zionist movement in times of crisis was one of the sources of authority of the national institutions, but this was undermined by confusion and uncertainty in the face of the 1939 White Paper and the outbreak of World War II. The leadership of the Zionist movement had difficulty resolving the contradiction between an effective struggle against the White Paper and active participation in the war effort against Nazi Germany. The slogan Ben-Gurion coined, "We shall fight the White Paper as if there were no war against Hitler and we shall fight Hitler as if there were no White Paper,"[40] was a rhetorical answer to the dilemma, but impracticable. In the early months of the war, during the so-called "phony war," the Yishuv did not embark on a full-scale participation in the war effort because of the White Paper—and failed to launch an effective struggle against the White Paper because of the war against Hitler. Only in the summer of 1940, after the fall of France and the entry of Italy into the war, did the leaders of the Yishuv decisively resolve their predicament.

The threat that Axis forces might occupy the Middle East and the spectacle of Britain standing alone in the struggle against Germany caused the Yishuv and the British to rediscover their mutual interests and give priority to military considerations. The Yishuv would postpone the struggle against the White Paper until the end of the war and would place its resources at the disposal of the Allies.

The internal challenge to the authority of the national institutions focused mainly on the control and supervision of the armed forces of the Yishuv. It was twofold: outside the framework of the organized Yishuv, the IZL was a focus of attraction to groups of activist youths who had become disenchanted with the policy of the national institutions. At the same time the right wing of the organized Yishuv objected to the authority given the national institutions over the Hagana and demanded that the disputed authority be transferred to institutions with a different political basis.[41] This erosion of the leadership's authority stopped, however, and actually reversed itself in summer 1940, with the decision to support Britain and the increase in wartime prosperity.

Jewish enlistment in the British army was carried out within a framework provided by the Yishuv for recruitment and attending the needs of soldiers and their families. The Executive of the Jewish Agency and the National Council issued unofficial mobilization orders to the Jewish population for the British army, exerting pressure on those who refused to enlist. The resort to pressure, including such sanctions as denial of work, reflected a change in the method of mobilizing manpower, since it was a clear departure from the voluntary participation that had guided mobilization in previous emergencies. Thus, the national institutions moved another step forward in the direction of a "state in the making." Renewed collaboration with the British enabled the reestablishment of a new framework for full-time service in the Hagana. Their mutual interests led the British to train and finance a striking force of the Hagana, the *Palmach*. The threat of a German invasion of Palestine in the wake of Rommel's victories in North Africa in 1942 led the British to cooperate in establishing this unit.[42] The British support for the Palmach ceased, however, after the danger subsided with the Battle of El Alamein. Since the force already existed and its existence was compatible with the military conceptions of the Hagana, a new way was found to finance and maintain it within the framework of the settlements of the *kibbutz* movement.[43]

The integration of the economy of Palestine into the Allied war effort effected another change. The economic recession of the first year of the war was replaced by a new wave of prosperity as the British army, cut off from its regular overseas channels of supply, placed large orders and arranged large-scale contracts for the construction of fortifications, airfields, and military bases. Capital imports were also renewed during the war years as fund-raising efforts were transferred to the

United States. The Arab sector benefited from the increasing demand
for labor and agricultural products, but the chief beneficiary of the
wartime prosperity was the Jewish sector, primarily in the industrial,
construction, and service branches. Participation in the war effort
strengthened the national institutions, especially the Jewish Agency,
from two aspects; (*a*) the Jewish Agency renewed its contacts with the
British army and government by serving as an intermediary mobilizing
economic resources for the war; and (*b*) the relative economic power
of the sectors within the Jewish economy shifted as a result of a crisis
in the citrus industry—the major export sector of the Palestine economy
—and the boom in construction and manufacturing.

Citrus was the economic backbone of those parts of the organized
Yishuv which sought to restrict the policy-making authority of the
parliamentary institutions of the Yishuv and to transfer at least part of
this authority to frameworks composed on a corporative basis—such as
the directorate of the Kofer Hayishuv and the national command of
the Hagana. The outbreak of the war, the conquest of Western Europe,
and the shortage and difficulties of maritime transport led to the loss of
export markets for Palestinian citrus, the consequent neglect of most
citrus orchards, and the diversion of citrus capital and manpower to
other sectors. Those branches in which Histadrut capital played a
prominent role were flourishing. In agriculture, the *kibbutzim* and
moshavim based on mixed farming—and connected politically to the
parties of the Labor movement—benefited from the increased demand
for local agricultural produce created by the reduction of imports. The
most impressive economic gains were made by the construction industry,
which built fortifications, roads, and airfields in all parts of the Middle
East. Large contracting firms enjoyed a relative advantage, especially
Solel Boneh, owned by the Histadrut. The Histadrut and the *kibbutz*
movement also owned part of the canning industry which benefited
from large orders from the British army.

Change in the relative profitability of different branches of the
economy led to a shift in the relative economic power of different
sectors. With increased capital accumulation by the Histadrut sector
its weight in the economy grew so much that it was able to purchase
industrial firms from private owners. The impact of the shift was
extended by the reduction in private capital imports on the one hand,
and the increase in the flow of national capital from the United States
on the other.[44] This change in the relative economic power of the public
and private sectors affected the balance of political forces in the Yishuv

and consequently the authority of the national institutions. The demand to establish policy-making frameworks structured on a corporate basis was rooted in the lack of congruence between the power balance of the parliamentary forces in the elected institutions and the balance of economic power between the private and public sectors. Those who demanded that political authority be vested in corporate frameworks sought to express the relative economic strength of private farmers (and owners of private enterprises in trade, finance, and industry) in political terms; in relative electoral strength their weight was much less than their share in capital ownership and national income. Thus, the wartime shift in the relative economic power and distribution of capital between the sectors created greater congruence between economic and political power for all parties concerned. The political position of those groups who sought a monopoly of policy-making power for the elected national institutions, chief among them the Labor movement, was considerably enhanced.

The widespread feeling of having reached a political impasse, which had weakened the authority of the national institutions in the early months of the war, gave way to the hope that postwar political conditions would open new opportunities for the Zionist movement. This optimistic feeling was fed by several developments during the war:

1. The growing power of the United States and Britain's dependence on American aid was expected to have a major impact on the destiny of the Middle East; hence Ben-Gurion's choice of the United States as the place to proclaim a new political plan, known as the Biltmore Program.[45]
2. Because he was considered sympathetic to the Zionist cause, Winston Churchill's appointment as prime minister of Britain gave rise to hope for a change in the policy of the British government and the Conservative party toward Zionism in the postwar period.
3. The participation of the British Labour party—which came out openly in support of Zionist demands—in the government and the possibility that its strength would increase in the postwar period reinforced the hope for a change in British policy.
4. The active participation of the Yishuv in the war effort, in contrast to the neutral or hostile attitude of most Arabs to the Allies, created expectations for a political *quid pro quo* for the Yishuv and the Zionist movement. These expectations were reinforced by the British decision in 1944 to establish a Jewish Brigade in the framework of the British army.

Yet, toward the end of the war, there appeared to be an erosion of public support for the recognized leadership of the Yishuv. The expectations for a change in British policy did not materialize. The Mandatory government affirmed the White Paper of 1939, which continued to serve as the guiding principle of British policy. Restrictions on immigration and land sales remained effective. In addition, the British renewed the searches for illegal arms in Jewish settlements and brought Hagana activists accused of illegal possession of arms to trial. New British efforts to woo the Arab states led to the formation of the Arab League, which helped consolidate of anti-Zionist Arab attitudes.[46]

Meanwhile, changes in the theatre of war altered priorities in respect to the two objectives Ben-Gurion indicated at the outset of the war: the fight against Hitler and the fight against the White Paper. As the Allied victory came to be viewed as certain, a new aggressive mood took over some areas of public opinion in the Yishuv, insisting that the fight against the White Paper should be renewed even before the end of the war against Hitler. Awareness of the Holocaust in Europe and realization that the Allied governments were not willing to do anything substantial to save the Jews fed the fires of this "activist" mood.

These new attitudes created fertile grounds for the renewed activities of the separatist underground movements, the IZL and LHI (Lochami Herut Israel). The LHI, or Stern Group, was the only group in the Yishuv that did not put aside the fight against the White Paper to fight Hitler, while the IZL, which in the early forties had cooperated with the British in the war effort, changed its position in 1944 and declared a revolt against the British.

By exploiting the nonconformist mood to strengthen their positions, the IZL and the LHI threatened not only British interests but also the authority of the national institutions. Unlike their reaction in the 1930s, the response of the national institutions to this challenge was forceful. Stringent sanctions were applied against the IZL, the most severe of them involving the episode called Sezon (or "Season"), in which members of the IZL were apprehended and turned over to the British.[47] The sanctions were a show of force on the part of the national institutions, but they also revealed their inherent weakness, lack of sovereignty, which led to the decision to surrender the dissidents to the British. It should be noted that the IZL and not the LHI bore the brunt of the sanctions, even though it was LHI that first engaged in acts of terror against the British, the most overt being the assassination of Lord Moyne, the British minister in Cairo and senior representative in the Middle East, on 5 November 1944. The Hagana's policy can be explained as a response to the threat sensed to the authority of the national institutions, originating mainly in the larger of the two splinter organizations, and the one with wider public support, the IZL.

The end of World War II and the perpetuation of the White Paper policy by the Labour government in Britain brought the national institutions to take a further step toward national autonomy by authorizing the deployment of the organized armed force of the Yishuv in the struggle against British policy. The transition to violent means was gradual and selective, moving from the armed defense of illegal activities, especially immigration, to direct attack on British objectives. But at all stages the use of armed force was controlled, selective, and subordinated to political considerations. Political considerations also influenced the relations between the leadership of the organized Yishuv and the splinter organizations. Coordination and cooperation in the framework of the Hebrew Resistance Movement[48] during the period of armed struggle against the British in 1945–46 was followed by severance of contacts when the leadership felt that political considerations made it necessary to refrain from military activities.[49]

The need to resort to cooperation as a means of control of the splinter organizations' activities reflected the enhanced bargaining power of the separatists in relation to the organized Yishuv. Thus, the transition from close contact with the British to active political and military opposition was accompanied by a transition from a situation where the national institutions formed the sole recognized leadership to one where they had to concede, at least temporarily, their exclusive position in the conduct of the political and military struggles of the Yishuv. Even so, the national institutions continued to possess quantitative superiority over the separatists and controlled the lion's share of resources imported from the Diaspora. The national institutions also represented an institutional network with the ability to serve as a political and administrative infrastructure for an independent Jewish community. These advantages became fully apparent with the outbreak of the War of Independence and the establishment of the State of Israel in 1948.

The National Institution Budgets

The growing power of the national center was reflected in the increasing quantity of resources it controlled. The expenditures of the national institutions from early 1930 until 1948 reveal not only the expansion of activities, but also changes in the order of priorities.

The data on over-all expenditures permit a distinction among three major periods in the activity of the national institutions. The first period, from the beginning of the Mandate until 1933, was characterized by marked fluctuations in expenditures from the Foundation Fund (Keren Hayesod). From a relatively high rate of expenditure that ran from 451,000 LP to 789,000 LP in the years 1922–23 to 1926–27, over-all expenditures dropped for the years thereafter (with the exception of 1929–30) reaching a low point of only 257,000 LP in 1933–34 (see Table 2). These fluctuations mainly reflect the income from the funds; as a result of a drop in this source of income, the Zionist movement suffered a severe financial crisis.[50]

The second period began in 1934–35 and was marked by the gradual growth of the budget of the Zionist Executive from about 410,000 LP in 1934–35 to over 800,000 LP in the last year before the war, 1938–39.

The rise in expenditures after 1934 indicates the expansion of the national institutions' activities from the time of the large immigration from Germany and the accession of the leaders of the Labor movement to the Zionist Executive. Another increase occurred as a result of the Arab revolt and the accompanying outlays for defense. The increase in expenditures in the 1930s was facilitated by the improved financial condition of the Jewish Agency which stemmed from the increased income of the two national funds after the end of the economic crisis that struck most countries in the early 1930s.

The budget year 1941–42 marks the start of the third period. Characterized by a steep rise in expenditures, this period shows total expenditures from the income of the Keren Hayesod increasing eightfold, from about 865,000 LP in 1942–43 to about 6,560,000 LP in 1945–46. Part of this increase can be attributed to a decrease in the value of money, since the cost-of-living index for Palestine jumped about 250 percent from the outbreak of the war to the end of 1945.[51] A detailed examination of the relation between expenditures and changes in the index reveals that actually there was a decrease in expenditure between 1939 and 1942, since the nominal level of expenditure did not change, while the index rose by nearly 100 percent. On the other hand, in the period of the greatest increase in expenditure (from 1942 on) the index rose from 212 to only 259, or only slightly more than 20 percent.

Real expenditures increased, therefore, approximately sixfold. The large increase in expenditures reflects primarily the new fund-raising opportunities that emerged as American Jewry awakened under the impact of the Holocaust and as a result of augmented Zionist activity in the United States following the initiation of the Biltmore Program. However, expenditures also rose in this period and new items related to the organization of illegal immigration and the struggle against British policy were reflected in the budget.

Changes in the relative weight of different items in the budget reflect changes in the significance of different activities of the national institutions. The percentages of funds spent on the preparation and organization of immigration generally reflect the various waves of immigration to Palestine. For example, the percentage of expenditures in this sphere rose during the period of the Fourth Immigration in the years 1924–25 and 1925–26, but fell considerably in the years thereafter (1926–29), with 1927–28 representing a low point, not only in immigration, but also in funds spent on it (about 3 percent). The percentage of expenditures rose slightly in 1929–31, and then considerably in 1932–36, the height of the Fifth Immigration. During the Arab revolt of 1936–39 this item decreased in importance compared with the increase in the percentage for settlement and security. The percentage for preparation and organization of immigration reached its peak in 1943–1946 (between 23 percent and 36 percent of the budget). This increase reflects the renewal of preparatory activities for immigrants in Europe and the process of immigration itself, which was for the most part in the "illegal" category (see Table 2).

The agricultural settlement budget was less given to sharp fluctuations than immigration; it is the most stable component in the expenditures of the Keren Hayesod. Except for 1921–22, the settlement component of the budget did not fall below 24 percent. In most years the percentage moved between 25 percent and 35 percent, and only in the two years of 1934–36 did it reach a peak of about 40 percent of total expenditures. Sharp fluctuations occurred in expenditures on relief payments, for housing, and public works projects to alleviate unemployment (shown in the column "Labor and Housing"). During certain years, between 1931 and 1934, they fell to about .05 percent, while they rose to about 25 percent in 1926–27, the year of the economic crisis. Outlays for education represented a sizeable item until the education system was transferred to the National Council; from 1932–33 there was a con-

Table 2
Expenditure and Investments of the Jewish
Agency from Keren Hayesod Receipts
(percentages)

Financial Year	Immigration and Training	Agricultural Settlement
1921–2	11.4	20.5
1922–3	12.6	28.3
1923–4	10.0	32.2
1924–5	14.6	34.9
1925–6	15.3	29.1
1926–7	6.3	30.5
1927–8	2.9	28.7
1928–9	4.6	24.3
1929–30	10.3	33.0
1930–1	7.2	26.6
1931–2	6.7	24.3
1932–3	21.5	34.3
1933–4	30.0	27.7
1934–5	27.5	40.3
1935–6	22.1	39.5
1936–7	13.6	33.7
1937–8	8.0	33.0
1938–9	9.7	34.6
1939–40	10.9	33.0
1940–1	11.0	26.8
1941–2	4.6	30.4
1942–3	17.6	30.4
1943–4	36.1	25.8
1944–5	23.2	26.0
1945–6	30.8	25.7

Labor and Housing	Urban Settlement and Industry	Education and Culture	Health and Social Services	Security	Administration	Total (in LP)	Index
6.2	6.7	25.7	17.0	8.6	3.8	648,120	100
3.7	10.8	24.8	9.4	4.7	5.6	451,646	70
6.1	10.9	22.9	7.4	6.1	4.2	464,839	72
5.9	6.5	21.9	6.6	5.5	2.2	549,854	85
13.3	4.4	20.6	7.8	5.1	4.3	584,304	91
24.7	6.0	16.7	5.5	5.0	5.2	789,656	123
10.0	13.7	24.2	1.5	4.9	9.0	428,465	66
1.5	9.6	39.3	2.6	6.7	9.3	331,353	51
1.8	7.4	30.0	3.4	7.0	7.0	495,576	77
0.5	10.2	38.0	1.5	7.2	8.7	374,676	58
0.5	6.5	39.2	2.2	6.1	14.3	276,493	43
0.6	9.3	14.6	0.7	6.0	12.8	268,059	41
0.6	16.2	8.7	0.9	5.8	10.0	257,374	40
5.2	4.2	6.2	0.5	5.1	10.8	409,360	63
11.0	3.8	6.2	0.02	9.8	7.3	459,904	71
13.2	5.2	6.6	0.6	20.7	6.3	499,494	77
28.8	10.0	5.4	0.9	13.3	5.7	622,367	96
18.7	6.7	7.2	0.2	18.0	4.8	811,514	125
16.9	8.3	7.6	0.5	17.0	5.7	799,117	123
15.4	12.3	7.4	0.5	19.9	6.6	762,660	118
10.7	8.5	8.4	0.5	31.7	5.1	864,546	133
6.0	5.5	5.5	0.5	31.1	3.4	586,358	245
8.2	3.9	4.2	0.5	19.1	2.1	3,353,105	517
11.4	6.6	5.6	0.4	24.5	2.2	4,009,618	614
16.6	5.3	4.5	0.01	15.6	2.0	6,562,878	1013

SOURCE: A. Gertz, ed., *Statistical Handbook of Jewish Palestine, 1947* (Jerusalem: Jewish Agency, Department of Statistics, 1947), pp. 370–71.

siderable decrease in the portion of outlays for education from 39
percent to about 14.5 percent. Spending for social services fell to almost
negligible proportions by early 1930; the decline reflects the division
of functions between the Zionist Executive and the National Council.
Of particular interest is the increase in the percentage for security in
1936–37, as compared to previous years: about 6 percent in 1933, 10
percent in 1935–36. Another increase in outlays for security occurred
during the war when the danger of a German invasion led to an increase
for the years 1941–42 and 1942–43 to a height of over 31 percent.
Afterwards the amount more or less returned to the levels of the late
1930s. In administrative expenses, from the mid-1930s a decrease
began which became even more marked in the 1940s. Apparently the
growth of the administrative apparatus of the Jewish Agency was slower
than the increase in expenditures for immigration, settlement, security,
and other services.

Stages in the Development of a
National Political Center

We have described in this chapter two aspects of the process of growth
and consolidation of the national center: the crystallization of institutional authority and the concentration of "charisma" in the broader
sense of this concept. The crystallization of institutional authority was
expressed through the expansion and intensification of the activities of
the national institutions. The concentration of charisma was reflected in
the more total identification of most of the social and political groups
in the Yishuv with the national center and the values and symbols it
represented. As a result, the subcenters did not aspire to an exclusive
position in innovating and interpreting values, and recognized the
national center as the major source of authority and inspiration. These
two developments complemented and reinforced one another, enabling
the national institutions to establish politically effective decision-making
processes.

Despite the general trend, the process of the national center gaining
strength and authority was not unequivocal or constant. There were
periods when the authority of the national institutions was weakened,
and there were groups in the Yishuv which diminished or even severed
their allegiance to the center. It is possible to speak of centripetal
processes which strengthened the authority of the center (whether insti-

tutionally or as a focus of charisma) as opposed to centrifugal processes
which weakened that authority. Analysis of the processes of center
formation described above indicates that centripetal rather than centrifugal processes were dominant. This conclusion becomes even more
apparent when we examine the capacity of the center to control
resources and to exploit them for the purpose of strengthening its
authority.

The resources the center extracted from the Yishuv and its environment (the Diaspora or the Mandatory government) were of three types:
(1) legitimation of authority; (2) material resources, such as capital
and manpower; and (3) symbols of collective solidarity. These resources
determined the efficacy of the national institutions. Legitimacy gave the
institutions a limited ability to compel individuals and groups in the
Yishuv to accept their decisions as binding; in a qualified way it is
possible to see legitimacy as a source of "coercive-based" power. The
control of material resources (most of which came from sources outside
the system) provided the national institutions with external and internal
bargaining power. It was possible to exchange these resources for others
and thus to influence social, economic, and political developments in
the Yishuv. The power derived from these resources can be described
as "utilitarian-based" power. The national solidarity and identification
with common symbols enhanced the internal cohesiveness of the Yishuv
and facilitated the mobilization of public support for the policy of the
national institutions in times of emergency. The power stemming from
these resources can be termed "normative-based" power.[52]

Looking at the crystallization of the national center and the impact
of centripetal and centrifugal trends on this process, we can divide the
period of the British Mandate into eight subperiods:

1. The period of authority derived from external sources (1918–
   20). There was no effective political center in this period. The
   Zionist Commission acted as a substitute center, but its authority
   was ad hoc and rested on the political and material strength of
   the Zionist movement in the Diaspora. Moreover, the existence
   of the British military government prevented representatives of
   the Jewish community from institutionalizing autonomous
   authority. Thus, it may be concluded that the embryonic national
   center was controlled largely from the outside and whatever
   authority it possessed was derived from external sources.

2. The institutionalization of the national center (1921–26). In
this period the institutional patterns of the national center
crystallized in the form of the Zionist Executive in Jerusalem
and the National Council of Knesset Israel. These institutions
enjoyed the recognition of the Mandatory government and the
support of most of the Yishuv, which had grown considerably
after the Third and Fourth Immigrations.
3. The period of decreasing resources (1926–29). The external
and internal influence of the center diminished in this period as a
result of a dearth of resources, which in turn created an im-
balance between demands made on the center and the center's
capacity to respond. The drop in immigration, the lack of financial
means, and unemployment precipitated a crisis in the colonization
process, which resulted in a slackened identification of groups
and individuals with the Yishuv and the national center, and
witnessed a large emigration from Palestine.
4. The reconstitution of the authority of the center (1930–36).
This period was marked by the expansion of the functions of the
national center and a new division of functions between the two
components of the national institutions. The National Council
of Knesset Israel recovered from a shortage of resources and
assumed responsibility for the supervision of education. A new
Elected Assembly was chosen for the first time according to the
official regulations promulgated by the Mandatory government.
Responsibility for the Hagana was transferred from the Histadrut
to the national institutions. At the same time, a split occurred
in the Hagana and a right-wing military organization emerged.
This period was also marked by an increase in the quantity of
the material and human resources at the disposal of the center.
Additional factors in strengthening the authority of the center
were the Labor movement's shift in orientation "from class to
nation" and the shift in the political center of gravity from London
to the Mandatory government in Jerusalem.
5. The period of concentration of authority and role expansion
(1936–39). The shift in the political center of gravity to Palestine
and the internal solidarity demonstrated in the face of the Arab
revolt reinforced the quasi-state characteristics of the national
center. Security problems turned the military sphere into a central
area of activity for the national institutions and provided impetus
for mobilizing manpower and financial resources. The Labor

movement, which by the end of the previous period had won
control of the key positions in the national center, became the
major political force in the struggle to intensify and expand the
authority and functions of the center.

6. The period of weakened authority (1939–40). The center suffered
   a loss of power and authority due to a crisis of confidence and
   the obstructed flow of resources from Europe. After the White
   Paper and the outbreak of the war, the leadership of the Yishuv
   plunged into uncertainty as it searched for a new political orientation. The economic situation deteriorated, creating difficulties
   for the center and strengthening the bargaining position of those
   groups who sought to restrict the authority of the center.

7. A period of growth and diversification of resources (1941–44).
   In this period the national center renewed its authority—primarily
   due to its control of an unprecedented flow of material resources.
   The import of capital from the United States and the mobilization
   of newly available capital from internal sources due to participation in the war effort enabled the center to expand its activities.
   In the security sphere a new military force was established, at
   first with British financial support, and later through an arrangement with the *kibbutz* movements. Other characteristics of this
   period were a partial shift from a British to an American
   orientation and the role played by the national institutions in
   recruitment to the British army. The most prominent feature,
   however, was a marked increase in the size of the budgets of the
   national institutions, a circumstance that could be converted into
   political power. In contrast to this trend, however, the necessity
   of reliance on the coercive power of the British during the Sezon
   revealed the limits of the authority of the national institutions.

8. The period of separation from the system of Mandatory rule
   (1945–48). The political, material, and organizational ties of
   the national institutions to the Mandatory government were reduced to a minimum, and open conflict emerged between the
   Yishuv and the British government. The conflict escalated to the
   point of physical, though controlled and limited, confrontation.
   On one hand, the national center became more autonomous in
   relation to its external environment, but on the other, it met
   increasing difficulty in enforcing its internal authority, especially
   over the splinter military organizations. However, the autonomous
   patterns of action facilitated the establishment of sovereign rule.

The development of the national institutions was not a constant process of strengthening since, along with the centripetal trends, there were centrifugal ones as well. However, if we observe the national institutions from the perspective of an increase or decrease in the types of resources upon which its authority was based—legitimacy, material resources, and collective solidarity—we see that the centripetal trends were generally stronger than the centrifugal trends. The center's control over material resources steadily increased after early 1930. Except for two brief periods in the late 1920s and at the outset of World War II, national solidarity steadily increased—although this process was interrupted by the strengthening of the splinter military organizations in the period immediately preceding the establishment of the state. The formal legitimacy conferred on the national institutions by the Mandatory authorities was augmented during the diplomatic struggle on the eve of independence when the Jewish Agency represented the Yishuv in the United Nations. The combination of formal recognition, bargaining power derived from control of exchangeable resources, and national solidarity endowed the national institutions of the Yishuv with power and authority.

4

Political Mobilization and Institution Building in the Yishuv

The Role of the Parties in the Formation of the National Center

The political system of the Yishuv was the creation of political organizations that developed first as autonomous subcenters, only later joining to form a national center. The institutionalization of this center occurred gradually and was the result of two interrelated processes: the integration of the Yishuv itself as a political and social system, and the inspiration and support provided by the Zionist movement in the Diaspora.

The fact that the parties were formed before the crystallization of the center was of major importance in determining their character as foci of attraction and inspiration for their members. If a center, in Shils's terms, is composed of institutions or roles that wield economic, political, military, or cultural authority, then a subcenter would be a focus of authority whose existence detracts from the authority of the center.[1] This notion may be applied as well to a situation where the center is not institutionalized, but where the existence of a common identity or consciousness of belonging makes it possible to view the various subcenters as alternatives existing within one system. The notion of subcenter, then, may also be applied to political parties and organized collectivities that were active in the period preceding the institutionalization of the center. In our context, the efforts of the parties to mobilize power and resources in the early stages of their development were not aimed at gaining control of a political system, but toward satisfying the instrumental and symbolic needs of those within their spheres of attraction. Thus, the parties were enclaves whose main activities were generally focused inward and whose contacts with other parties were centered on ideological debate and competition for new members.

The first organized parties in the Yishuv were those of workers. One was Poalei Zion, founded in 1905; after World War I it joined with other workers' groups to form the Zionist-Socialist Association of the Workers of Eretz Israel—Ahdut Ha'avodah. The other was Hapoel Hatzair, founded in the same year as its counterpart. Both parties were linked with wider confederations in the Diaspora, the World Union of Poalei Zion[2] (Socialist Zionists) and the Tseirei Zion movement respectively.[3] In 1920, in conjunction with other political groups among the workers, these parties formed the General Federation of Jewish Workers in Palestine, the Histadrut. The workers' parties created organizational frameworks earlier than other parties in the Yishuv because the workers formed the majority of the pioneering waves of immigrants —the Second and Third Immigrations—when there was no institutional framework to provide for the immigrants' needs. As these pioneers arrived in the country without any independent means of support, they were dependent for their livelihood on obtaining employment either as hired labor or as settlers on publicly owned land. Political organization and activity were essential to ensure employment opportunities in the private sector, especially given the competition with the Arab laborer, who was willing to work for lower wages. The other alternative, agricultural settlement, also required political and organizational action since the perennial scarcity of resources within the WZO led to political struggles over resource allocation. The parties also dealt with social services, such as health services and unemployment assistance, which became institutionalized in the parties' organizational structures. The workers that arrived in the early pioneering immigration waves, more than any other group in the Yishuv, experienced the chasm between the level of services people of European background demanded and the level of services that was actually obtainable with the meager resources at their disposal.

In addition to collective needs, the ideological orientation and interests of the workers distinguished them as an educated and politically conscious group and favored the rapid and early organizational development of workers' parties. Moreover, the socialist component in the ideologies prevalent among the workers of the pioneering sector reflected a collectivist inclination that facilitated the institutionalization of party frameworks. These factors were either nonexistent or of lesser importance among other sectors in the Yishuv, and therefore it was the workers' parties which created the dominant model of party organization during the period of the Mandate.

Characteristic of this model was a tendency for role expansion. This meant that the parties were not content with strictly political roles, but also sought to organize the lives of their members in various spheres, primarily through cultural, economic, and welfare services. The early economic and welfare organizations in the workers' sector were thus connected to political parties, though most of them were later transferred to the Histadrut when it was formed in 1920. Furthermore, political parties were instrumental in fulfilling certain quasi-governmental functions within the Yishuv. Ahdut Ha'avoda, for example, initiated the establishment of the Hagana, which was later supervised by Histadrut and eventually brought under the control of the national institutions.[4]

The parties' tendency to role expansion was related to the fact that they preceded the formation of the national center. Because the parties could not focus their activities on acquiring power in an institutionalized political system, in their early stages they concentrated most of their intellectual and organizational energies on internal activities designed to provide for their members' needs. This tendency to turn inward was expressed in the constructivist ideology of building a new society from the ground up and in the construction of institutions within the subcenters. Only when broader political frameworks such as the Histadrut, Knesset Israel, and the Zionist Executive in Jerusalem were created did the parties devote more of their efforts to competing with other parties for power.

With the establishment and consolidation of the national center, the political parties became integrated in the new political system as agencies of the center by providing services, allocating resources originating in the center, and mediating between the center and the individual. Since there was no way to give full expression to the notion of citizenship in the "state in the making," rules defining the relation of the "citizen" to the center were based on the mediation of the subcenters. One of the important rules was the principle of the "political party key," according to which the allocation of resources—such as immigration certificates, land for settlement, employment, and positions in public organizations—was based on the relative strength of the political parties and other subcenters. Thus the balance of parliamentary forces was translated into a numerical "key" according to which the resources of the national center were distributed. The subcenters also continued to perform several quasi-governmental functions, such as maintaining school systems, for which they received financial support from national sources while preserving a considerable degree of internal autonomy.

The Mosaic of Subcenters:
Political Parties, Interparty Organizations,
and Nonpartisan Institutions

Although the parties were not the only political bodies active in the organized Yishuv,[5] they were by far the most important subcenters. Even so, it would be somewhat simplistic to claim that the parties alone created the political center, since this would detract from the role of other subcenters. Of the latter, some were associated with parties, some were formed in concert by several parties, while others were non-partisan. Some subcenters formed by several parties, primarily the Histadrut, possessed considerable economic and political power, and their influence on the center was at times greater than that of the parties that composed them. The Histadrut was invested by its component parties with several quasi-governmental functions that were originally in the hands of the parties themselves—employment and health services, security, and education. Other subcenters with affiliated political parties were those whose members were part of a specific party. For example, the *kibbutz* and *moshav* movements were affiliated to political parties, but their memberships did not exhaust the entire membership of these parties.

There were also subcenters which transcended party boundaries. Some of these took a politically neutral stance, while others were politically active, some to the point of participating in elections and becoming quasi-party organizations. This distinction applies to the Industrialists Association (organized in 1923) and the Farmers Association.[6] The Farmers Association approached the pattern of a political party more nearly than any other subcenter not formally defined as such. Certain *landsmanschaften*, that is, associations based on a common

country of origin or "ethnic" background, also served as bases of
political organization, such as the Association of Sephardim,[7] the
Association of Yemenites (founded in 1923), and the Association of
Central European Immigrants, which in the 1940s gave rise to a political
party called Aliya Hadasha.[8]

The interparty and nonpartisan subcenters created points of contact
and interchange among the various parties associated with them. They
became areas of interparty competition, yet they offered opportunities
for the parties to cooperate and reconcile their differences. These subcenters may be depicted as marketplaces where resources were exchanged and the rate of exchange was set by the balance of political
forces.[9] The subcenters also formed a favorable setting for the arrangement of coalitions (similar to those formed on the level of the national
center) between parties.

Not all parties participated in subcenters to the same extent, nor
were they equally involved in contacts among the subcenters and the
parties. These differences were directly related to the scope of a party's
activities and its power in the system. Here as well, the parties of the
Labor movement had the advantage of a higher level of institutionalization and their tendencies toward role expansion implied a wider range
of activities.

The process of institution building in the party and the subcenter
was a gradual one. Over the years, those parties with a greater mobilization capacity succeeded in increasing their influence in the national
center. Other parties were faced with the choice of either entering into
coalitions with the dominant parties in the center or reducing or
severing their contacts with the center. The solutions to this dilemma
devised by the various parties resulted in centripetal or centrifugal
trends in the political system of the Yishuv.

The Political Party Map:
Splits and Mergers

The parties and political organizations that existed in the Yishuv
immediately prior to the establishment of the State of Israel differed
considerably from the array at the outset of the Mandate. When steps
were taken at the beginning of the Mandate to create a comprehensive
political organization for the Jews of Palestine, four major political
groupings existed. The most articulate and organized was the Labor

movement, which in the twenties included only Ahdut Ha'avoda and
Hapoel Hatzair. In the early 1920s they were joined by smaller political
groups formed by the pioneers of the Third Immigration, such as
Hashomer Hatzair and Poale Zion Smol. The bloc known as the
Ezrahim was composed in part of quasi-political organizations, such as
the Farmers Association and the Artisans Association, and in part of
various political organizations that represented General Zionist ideological sympathies. The third bloc, composed of the Sephardim and
other Oriental ethnic groups, attracted some 25 percent of the vote in
the 1920 elections to the Elected Assembly. The fourth bloc, the
religious one, combined two separate movements, the Mizrahi and
non-Zionist ultraorthodox groups. After the withdrawal of the ultraorthodox from the organized Yishuv, the Mizrahi joined the Ezrahim
bloc, while the Sephardim and other ethnic groups were unevenly
divided between the Ezrahim and the Labor bloc, most of them choosing
the Ezrahim.

From the mid-1920's, the organized Yishuv was composed of two
major blocs, the Labor movement and the Ezrahim. After the late
1920s a new political force emerged within the Ezrahim, to gradually
become the nucleus of a separate bloc—the Revisionists. In the mid-
1930s, when the Revisionists seceded from the WZO and established
a rival movement, they were no longer considered part of the organized
Yishuv, although they continued to participate in Knesset Israel.

One of the distinguishing features of the Yishuv's political system
was the constant change in the composition of the party map, reflecting
numerous splits, mergers, and the rapid emergence and disappearance
of new political groups. This trend applied to the Labor bloc and to the
Ezrahim bloc, though not to the same extent; there was more continuity
among the parties and political groupings of the Labor movement.

Changes among the parties of the Labor movement were mirrored
in the elections for the Histadrut, as it was the umbrella organization
for these parties. Three major periods may be distinguished. The first
period, the 1920s, was marked by numerous splits and the emergence
of new groups, some of which later disappeared and some of which
continued to exist until the 1940s; the largest and strongest parties of
this period were Ahdut Ha'avoda and Hapoel Hatzair, which originated
in the Second Immigration and whose leaders arrived with this wave of
immigration. In the early stages of the Third Immigration, new political
groups emerged which participated in the Histadrut elections but not

in the elections for the Elected Assembly. The most important of these groups in terms of its impact on the Labor movement in the 1920s was the Labor Brigade. This group underwent several transformations, until it was dissolved following a split between the right and left wings within the organization. This division resulted in the emigration of part of the Brigade's left wing to the Soviet Union, and in the right wing's absorption into Ahdut Ha'avoda.

Hashomer Hatzair was the second political group in the Labor movement that emerged during the Third Immigration; it remained independent and to the left of Mapai. Until the mid 1930s, it saw itself as basically a settlement movement and possessed no formal party framework, but nevertheless took part in elections to the Histadrut and to the third Elected Assembly. In the mid 1930s an urban-based offshoot of Hashomer Hatzair called the Socialist League was formed, and only ten years later did Hashomer Hatzair organize formally as a political party.

The third political group to emerge after World War I, Poalei Zion Smol, was not exclusively composed of pioneers of the Third Immigration. This party arose as a consequence of the split in the Poalei Zion World Union; the right wing of the Union formed ties with Ahdut Ha'avoda, the left wing with Poalei Zion Smol. The split was caused by Poalei Zion Smol's opposition to cooperating with the "bourgeois" parties in the WZO and its insistence on following a policy based on "class struggle."

The Palestine Communist party had a somewhat ambiguous status in the political system of the Yishuv and the Labor movement. This party went through numerous transformations, splits, and mergers, at times driven to an underground existence. As a result, it operated under different aliases. The party may be considered as part of the Labor movement since it competed in Histadrut elections. On the other hand, its exceptional status in the Labor movement resulted from its anti-Zionist stance, its binational composition, and its illegality under Mandatory law.

The second period, the 1930s, may be described as a period of stability for the Labor movement. This stability was due mainly to the creation of Mapai in 1930 following the union of Hapoel Hatzair and Ahdut Ha'avoda. The new combined party won the support of between 70 percent and 80 percent of the electorate in the elections to the Histadrut conventions in 1933 and 1942.

The third period, covering World War II and the postwar struggle for independence, was again a time of divisions and mergers that altered the party map of the Labor movement. The most important change occurred in Mapai in 1944, when the left wing broke away to form a new party. The political base of this group was composed primarily of Hakibbutz Hameuchad, one of the two *kibbutz* federations affiliated with Mapai. The new party was called Hatenu'a Leahdut Ha'avoda, its name symbolizing the claim of the new party's leaders that they were returning to the path of "pure" socialism represented by Ahdut Ha'avoda of the 1920s. Most of the leaders of the original Ahdut Ha'avoda, however, remained in Mapai—particularly David Ben-Gurion. The split was followed by a merger between Poalei Zion Smol and Hatenu'a Leahdut Ha'avoda in 1946. Early in 1948 Hatenu'a Leahdut Ha'avoda joined the new party formed by Hashomer Hatzair, creating the United Workers Party or Mapam, which became the major left-wing force in the Zionist Labor movement.

While the various Labor parties were relatively well defined, stable, and institutionalized, the political party map of the right and center was a different picture. In the Labor movement, the same parties or political groups created through alignments and mergers appeared consistently in elections for the Histadrut, the Elected Assembly, and the Zionist congresses. On the right and center, however, less institutionalized parties manifested a greater tendency to fragment, at times combining in ad hoc groupings for a particular election campaign. Other trends that characterized the parties of the Ezrahim were wide divergences in the number and composition of the lists submitted in the various elections to the Elected Assembly, and the participation of organizations representing specific economic interests, such as the Farmers Association and the Artisans Association, in such elections. The extent of fragmentation and division among parties of the right and center and the changes in the number of parties participating in the elections to the Elected Assembly are indicated in Table 3, which presents the number of slates that appeared in the various election campaigns.

The parties and political organizations of the right and center included General Zionists, "Yishuvist" parties without ties to sister parties in the Diaspora, Revisionists, the different elements of the Mizrahi movement, and ethnic parties and *landsmanschaften*.

The first group includes parties affiliated to the General Zionist trend within the Zionist movement. They included a relatively large number of leading figures who had been active in Zionist politics in the Diaspora. In the 1920s the General Zionist parties appeared under this name only in elections to the Zionist congresses. In the elections to the third Elected Assembly in 1931, the parties appeared under the General

Table 3
Unity and Disunity of Political Sectors in
Elections to the Elected Assembly

Sector	Number of Lists				
	1920	1925	1931	1944	Total
Labor parties	3	3	4	4	11
Center and right-wing groups	9	16	4	7	33
Reilgious parties	3	4	1	5	12
Ethnic groups	4	2	3	2	6

SOURCE: Adapted from M. Atias, *The Book of Documents of the National Council of Knesset Israel, 1918–48* (Jerusalem: R.H. Cohen, 1953).

Zionist label, but by this time and throughout the 1930s there were two separate General Zionist slates in the elections to the Zionist congresses.[10] These two lists reunited only in 1945, in order to create a united front for the elections to the Zionist Congress in 1946. The two factions of the General Zionist movement differed mainly in their relations with the parties of the Labor movement. Led by Chaim Weizmann, the left wing of the General Zionists (the "A" General Zionists) collaborated with the Labor movement in the Zionist Executive, while the right wing (the "B" General Zionists) regarded the Labor movement as a bitter political opponent. The reluctance of the "B" General Zionists to cooperate with the Labor movement was seen in their refusal to participate in the Zionist Executive coalition in 1933–35 (the only period in which they were not represented); in their boycotting the 1944 elections to the Elected Assembly with the Farmers Association, the Association of Sephardim, and the Revisionists; and in their participation in the governing body of the dissident Hagana B group during the years 1931 to 1937. The close political and ideological ties of the "A" General Zionists with the Labor movement were exemplified, among other things, in the formation in 1936 of a General Zionist faction within the Histadrut called Ha'oved Hatzioni (Zionist Worker), which had its own settlement and youth movements. The "B" General Zionists maintained a labor organization independent of the Histadrut.[11]

The major political base of the old guard of the Ezrahim was composed of the local authorities of Tel Aviv and Petach Tikva and the larger *moshavot*. The leaders of these groups tended to view the local authorities of the Yishuv as a basis of independent Jewish rule parallel to the central national institutions. The oldest and strongest of these groups was the Farmers Association, which represented the farmers of the veteran *moshavot*. Other prominent organizations in this sector were the Landlords Association and the Merchants Association, which combined with other groups of the Ezrahim to form ruling coalitions in the larger local authorities, primarily in Tel Aviv. In the early 1940s, an attempt was made to unite all Ezrahim groups in a body called the Citizens Union (Ha-Ihud Haezrahi), but this proved a be a short-lived venture (see discussion below).[12]

Among the parties of the right and center, the group farthest to the right was the Revisionist party, a bitter opponent of the Labor movement, which was active continuously in Palestine and the Diaspora from its inception in 1925 until the establishment of the state. They remained members of Knesset Israel throughout, although they boycotted the 1944 elections to the Elected Assembly. The Revisionists maintained their own labor and trade union organization, the National Labor Federation, and their own health services. A split in the party occurred with the secession from the Zionist Organization in 1935, when a minority faction called the Jewish State Party continued to participate. The Revisionist party and its youth movement Betar served as the political base and major recruiting ground for the IZL in the late 1930s and early 1940s; but relations between the IZL commanders and the Revisionist leaders became strained in the mid-1940s after their leader's death, as the two groups of Jabotinsky disciples struggled for primacy within the movement. Ultimately victory went to the commanders of the IZL.[13]

Another set of parties in the right and center group was the religious Zionist bloc, affiliated to the Mizrahi World Union.[14] From the early 1920s, this bloc was divided into the Mizrahi party and the Hapoel Hamizrahi. The latter was nominally a labor organization, although it participated in the elections and institutions of Knesset Israel as a political party.

Also for various reasons belonging with the right and center bloc were the organizations of the various Oriental Jewish communities that participated in the elections to the Elected Assembly and the local authorities. The leaders and members of these groups did not necessarily hold views identical to those of the parties of the right and center, as there were some members of these groups that were ideologically closer to the Labor movement. Yet the patterns of political action that characterized some of these groups, especially the Association of Sephardim, were closer to the veteran groups of the Ezrahim, such as the Farmers Association. These patterns may generally be described as the "politics of notables," since the political status of the leaders of these groups was based mostly on their social status in the Yishuv as it was before the changes caused by the Second and Third Immigrations.[15] For example, the Sephardic leaders collaborated with the Ezrahim on questions concerning the structure and electoral system of Knesset Israel and joined the Farmers Association, the "B" General Zionists, and the Revisionists in boycotting the elections to the Elected Assembly in 1944.

The Association of Sephardim represented a traditional elite whose status was undermined by the demographic changes produced by the waves of immigration from Europe. In contrast, a new political group arose in the late 1930s based on a common country of origin, but representing an entirely different trend. While the Sephardic elite was attempting to preserve its declining social status through political action, the newly arrived German Jewish elite formed the Aliya Hadasha party to secure a political and social status corresponding to their other attributes. The transformation of this group into an established political party took place in the early 1940s. The German immigrants possessed a distinctive cultural background, economic assets, and professional and educational qualifications far above average, but when they arrived in Palestine they found the key positions in the political system occupied by Jews from Eastern Europe who formed the majority of the elite of the organized Yishuv. The German immigrants responded by organizing a political party that adopted a liberal outlook close to the "A" General Zionists but even more moderate on political issues such as relations with Britain and the Arab question.

At least one Jewish party did not participate in either the elections to the Elected Assembly or the Zionist congresses. This party, Agudat Israel, comprised the relatively moderate wing of the non-Zionist ultra-orthodox groups and belonged to the Agudat Israel World Union. The more extreme elements among the ultraorthodox were not even organized in political party frameworks.

The Structural Characteristics of the Parties

The different positions and roles of the various parties in the evolving political system of the Yishuv may be explained as the outcome of a variety of structural and substantive characteristics. These characteristics affected the capacity of the parties to mobilize manpower (both active members and voters in elections) and material resources, to build autonomous institutions and interparty organizations, and to influence the policies of the subcenters other than political parties. This capacity in turn helped to determine a party's ability to influence the decisions of the national center in respect to resource allocation and the allocation of positions within the center itself.

The differential capacity of the parties to mobilize and employ resources may be explained by the following variables which relate to different structural aspects of the parties.[16]

1. *The range of party functions.* This refers to whether or to what extent a party tended to limit its activities to the political sphere, i.e., competing with other parties for representation in the national center, or whether it expanded its range of activity to include areas not considered political in the strict sense of the word, such as welfare, housing, education, and employment.

2. *The level of institutionalization.* This refers to whether or to what extent a party had permanent party forums or governing bodies and maintained its own organizational apparatus.

3. *Organizational continuity.* This variable refers to whether a party was a permanent organizational entity or an ad hoc group formed for the sole purpose of participating in elections.

4. *Social composition.* This refers to the relative homogeneity or heterogeneity of the social groups that comprised a party's members and supporters. In this context "social groups" may be classified according to class, country of origin, ethnic background, length of residence, place of residence (i.e., urban or rural), and so on.

5. *Affiliations to political frameworks outside Palestine.* This refers to whether a party maintained ties to sister parties in the Diaspora which formed a worldwide confederation or union.

6. *Frame of reference.* This variable refers to the orientation of a
party, whether inward toward a solid nucleus of members, or
outward toward the public at large. This more or less encompasses
the distinction between a "sectarian" and an "open" party.

The relevance of these structural characteristics for understanding the
political system of the Yishuv becomes apparent in the context of the
problem stated above: the relation of a party's structural characteristics
to its capacity for resource mobilization, institution building, and influencing the center. The relation between these variables can best be
understood if they are combined in a model in which the structural
characteristics serve as independent variables, the capacities for resource
mobilization and institution building serve as intervening variables,
while the capacity for influencing the policies of the center is regarded
as a dependent variable. We assume that most structural characteristics
of a party did not directly determine its capacity to influence the center,
but rather influenced this capacity indirectly by means of their impact
on resource mobilization and institution building. A further assumption
holds that there is a reciprocal relation between capacity for resource
mobilization and institution-building capacity: the latter augments the
capacity for resource mobilization, while resource mobilization creates
appropriate conditions for institution building.

The Range of Party Functions

The tendency to expand the range of party functions, to encompass
nonpolitical activities in the orbit of party organization, is one of the
distinguishing features of the pattern of party organization in the Yishuv.
In sociological terms this tendency may be considered an adaptive
response by immigrants lacking independent means of support who
sought to create a social framework to provide employment and welfare
services for themselves and others who would come after them. These
immigrants realized that only political organization could assure employment and health services, education and culture, and relief assistance
in periods of unemployment.

The model of party organization with the widest range of functions
was created by the two largest parties in the Labor movement, Ahdut
Ha'avoda and Hapoel Hatzair, and adopted later by parties outside the
Labor movement. Role expansion was greatest for these two parties
in their early years. Later their range of functions was reduced as

certain functions were transferred to the Histadrut. This did not end the parties' involvement in the provision of services and the allocation of resources, but rather placed these activities under the direct supervision of party functionaries who manned the organizational apparatus of the Histadrut or of other interparty subcenters.

Just as the establishment of the Histadrut entailed the transfer of functions from the parties to the new interparty subcenter, so in the 1930s and 1940s a parallel movement occurred as the policy of "from class to nation" inspired a transfer of functions from the Histadrut to the national institutions. This was reflected, for example, in the transfer of the political supervision of the Hagana to the national institutions in the early 1930s. Another example was the joint labor exchanges operated by the Histadrut and other labor organizations, which were brought firmly under the supervision of the Jewish Agency by the 1940s.[17] The division of functions between the Histadrut and the parties that composed it was determined for the most part by the majority party in the Histadrut, Mapai. The minority parties were forced to develop different patterns of action in relating political and nonpolitical spheres. Hashomer Hatzair, which over the years evolved from youth movement to *kibbutz* federation to quasi party, continued to involve the organizational apparatus of its *kibbutz* federation, Hakibbutz Ha'artzi, in its political activities even after it became a full-fledged party; the boundaries between party and *kibbutz* movement became blurred.

In contrast to the parties of the Labor movement, which established a powerful subcenter in the Histadrut, the parties and organizations of the right and center were not able to create any durable common frameworks that would facilite the extention of the parties' functions. The organizations among the Ezrahim that included members of several parties usually represented a particular economic branch, such as the Industrialists Association or the Merchants Association. A different type of economic-based organization was the Farmers Association, which developed into a quasi party and even participated in the elections to the Elected Assembly. The only attempt to create a politically oriented umbrella organization (if not necessarily a party per se) to unite all the groups among the Ezrahim was the Citizens Union in the early 1940s. The members of this body included the economic organizations of the non-Histadrut sector, representatives of the center and right parties active in local government, and political figures in organizations such as the "B" General Zionists. The Citizens Union failed in

its attempt to create a counterweight to the power of the Labor movement in the Histadrut, because the Citizens Union was not based on
individual membership, it was not designed for the provision of services
to a mass membership, nor did it establish a complex organizational
apparatus. Another problem was the lack of a clear division of functions
between the Citizens Union and the parties composing it, especially the
"B" General Zionists. This meant that in practice, if not in theory, it
competed with the parties of the right and center instead of comple-
menting or supplementing their activities.

The tendency to expand the role of political parties according to the
example set by the Labor movement, also characterized the Revisionists
and the religious parties. The Revisionists created an institutional network parallel to that of the Histadrut which was intended to provide
most of the services the Histadrut dispensed.[18] The policy of establishing
parallel frameworks for the provision of services was in effect the
political approach later adopted by the Revisionists when they formed
the New Zionist Organization. All of the competing frameworks created
by the Revisionists suffered from the same limitations: lack of resources
and the problem of struggling for political primacy with larger and more
powerful opponents.

The circumstances leading to the emergence of the multifunctional
party as the dominant type in the Yishuv's political system were evident
in the development of the Mizrahi movement in Palestine. The Mizrahi
leaders who immigrated to Palestine organized a local party according
to the narrow functional pattern characteristic of Mizrahi parties in the
Diaspora. This pattern of organization could not meet the needs of
religious immigrants for employment opportunities and social services.
Hence, religious workers faced the alternative of either joining the
Histadrut or establishing a parallel organization. After prolonged deliberations, an intermediate solution was found in which a religious labor
organization parallel to the Histadrut, Hapoel Hamizrahi, was established which received medical services from the Histadrut and cooperated with the Histadrut in the operation of labor exchanges.[19] In other
spheres, such as cultural activities, Hapoel Hamizrahi developed frameworks of its own. The adoption of this type of framework influenced
the political future of the religious labor organization, since Hapoel
Hamizrahi gradually emerged as a political body that participated in
elections for the Elected Assembly as a distinct slate from its parent
party Mizrahi. The labor offshoot of Mizrahi gradually surpassed it,

both in numbers and electoral support in the Yishuv, though in the Diaspora the situation was reversed. Nevertheless, both continued their affiliation to the same world movement.

Level of Institutionalization

A second structural variable for the analysis of the parties' activities is their level of institutionalization. In this context institutionalization refers to two aspects: the creation of a permanent organizational apparatus manned by salaried functionaries, and the enactment of formal rules and regulations for governing the operation of party bodies. Given the circumstances of the Yishuv, it would be incorrect to conclude that the enactment of regulations to define roles and decision-making procedures arose directly from the existence of a complex network of party administrative organs or governing bodies.

Mapai serves as a case in point. Though it pioneered in the creation of different levels of party forums and governing bodies and in the development of administrative apparatus during the Mandate, Mapai did not enact a formal constitution governing the organizational aspects of the party's operations, nor did it devise rules governing the division of labor between various party bodies or processes of decision making.[20] When problems in these areas arose, in most cases ad hoc solutions were devised. The tendency to avoid enacting formal, binding rules governing party activities was perfectly compatible with the prevailing political culture in the organized Yishuv. The political system was to a considerable extent based on consensus and informal, generally ad hoc arrangements, and was not anchored by any permanent set of rules. In Mapai's case, at any rate, a flexible organizational infrastructure made it possible for party leaders to mediate between the sometimes conflicting interests of the party's varied constituency—*kibbutz* members, *moshav* members, urban workers, white-collar workers, and laborers in the *moshavot*.

Notwithstanding the often intentional neglect of the formal aspects of institutionalization, Mapai's organizational apparatus developed on both local and countrywide levels, though this activity was centered in the three large cities of Jerusalem, Haifa, and Tel Aviv. For instance, in 1936, there were nine full-time salaried functionaries employed in Mapai party headquarters, four in the Tel Aviv branch, three in the Haifa branch, and two in the Jerusalem branch. The total number of salaried functionaries was eighteen, making a ratio of roughly one functionary per thousand party members.[21] These figures do not convey an accurate notion of how many members devoted a good portion of their time to party activity. Some of the employees of the Histadrut and its enterprises were members of formal party forums; for them there was little distinction between party work and work on behalf of the Histadrut. Moreover, during election campaigns the party's organizational structure would be reinforced with many temporary and volunteer workers mobilized from *kibbutzim, moshavim*, and the cities. The party's organizational apparatus made further progress toward greater institutionalization in reaction to the split of 1944 when Hatenu'a Leahdut Ha'avoda was formed. At this point the organizational side of party activity took on the familiar features of a political "machine." In the intensive competition after this split, Mapai launched an organizational campaign that was successful in returning hundreds of members to active status and in registering new members from among those who voted for Mapai but did not belong to any party. This campaign doubled the party membership from less than twenty thousand to almost forty thousand.[22] The characteristic organizational pattern of Mapai was based on the pattern evolved in Ahdut Ha'avoda, the larger of the two parties that formed Mapai in 1930.[23]

The parties of the right-center bloc and the religious parties did not share a common organizational pattern. Hapoel Hamizrahi reached a level of institutionalization that equaled and perhaps surpassed that of Mapai. The Revisionists as well had a permanent organizational structure, and their efforts were aided by the organizational frameworks of the Betar youth movement and the groups of workers in the *moshavot* affiliated with Betar. On the other hand, the level of institutionalization in the parties of the Ezrahim was considerably lower. The organizational budgets and structures in the parties of the Ezrahim were small in comparison to Mapai, despite the fact that the constituency of the Ezrahim was considerably wealthier. In addition, these parties were not connected to any powerful subcenter that could provide additional organizational services. As a result, the meager organizational structures of the parties had to suffice. This problem was recognized clearly by one of the General Zionist leaders who compared his party's pattern of activity to a "Zionist intellectual club."[24] Even Hamacabi Hatzair, the large youth movement of the Ezrahim, was not formally affiliated to any political party and thus could not be used directly to further party interests.[25]

Organizational Continuity

The third structural variable distinguishes between regular party organizations and lists formed solely for the purpose of participating in
elections. This type of political organization should not be confused
with the formation of "fronts" or "blocs" composed of several parties
or political organizations that appeared on a joint list at election time,
a common practice among the parties of the Labor movement in
elections to Zionist congresses and local authorities.

The appearance of ad hoc lists unaffiliated to a regular party was
almost unknown in the Labor movement. It was, however, quite characteristic of the parties of the center-right bloc. These lists were based
on locally oriented or countrywide groups of politicians, or on supposedly nonpolitical organizations such as the Landlords Association,
Artisans Association, and various women's groups.

Social Composition

An attempt to deal with the social composition of the parties must first
consider several problems raised by the unique characteristics of the
social structure and stratificational system of the Yishuv. These characteristics stemmed from the nature of the Yishuv as a new society
which did not undergo the social transformations entailed in the industrial revolution, a process which scholars such as Lipset and Rokkan
have found of crucial importance in the development of European
political parties.[26] The European origin and background of the founding
fathers of the political movements in the Yishuv did mean, however,
that they were influenced, if only in an intellectual and ideological
sense, by the major social changes of the nineteenth and twentieth
centuries.

Moreover, the political system and institutions of the Yishuv were
not influenced directly by that cultural and social legacy of Europe
bound up with the transformation from feudalism to absolutism and
later to bureaucratic capitalism. Absent this legacy, and because the
Yishuv was a society of immigrants, there were practically no groups
who based their claims for special treatment and privileges on grounds
of inherited status. Despite the variety of intellectual influences and
ideologies present in the Yishuv, the fact remains that except for the
farmers of the *moshavot* and the Jerusalem Sephardim, the social back-

grounds of the members and leaders of all other parties were quite similar. Not only were most of the founders of the "B" General Zionists and the Mizrahi of middle-class origins, but the leaders of the Labor movement were as well; the latter became workers and settlers on the land only after their arrival in Palestine. Any differences in social status within the Jewish communities in their native lands were largely effaced by the changes entailed in the process of immigration to Palestine. There was one criterion of social status, however, that *was* transferred with the immigrants and which was to become an important source of status differences in the Yishuv and the State of Israel: differences in country of origin.

Another ascriptive criterion of status characteristic of immigrant societies was the criterion of the length of residence. Thus the children of the immigrants of the First Immigration based their claims for preferential status on the fact that they were native-born. Among the later immigration waves as well, status as an "old-timer" was a source of prestige, though in these cases this criterion was applied on an individual and not a group basis. Attempts to organize groups on this particularistic basis were more characteristic of the second generation of the *moshavot*, who formed the Sons of Benjamin,[27] and veterans of the Old Yishuv who organized their own association. The first attempts of the Sephardim to organize on an ethnic basis were also related to their efforts to preserve their privileged status as an elite group under Ottoman rule.

Traditional social differences played a minor role in the social structure and status hierarchy of the Yishuv; more important were stratificational differences arising in the new economic and occupational structure created in the process of Zionist colonization. The most prominent strata to emerge were that of wage laborers in the cities and *moshavot*, and that of farmer settlers. With respect to the second group, it is of the utmost importance to distinguish between this group i.e., the farmers of the *moshavot*, whose farms were based on private property and hired labor, and the other group of agricultural settlers affiliated to the Labor movement, whose settlements were based on public ownership and self-labor. From a comparative perspective the existence of the latter group of farmers in the *kibbutzim* and *moshavim* created an unconventional relationship between social structure and political structure in the Yishuv. One expression of this was the existence of radical left-wing parties such as Hashomer Hatzair that were composed primarily of agricultural settlers. The creation of strata of manual laborers and agricultural workers in the process of Zionist colonization, in fact, represented the realization of the ideal of productivizing the Jewish people, an ideal of particular importance to the Labor movement. To ensure the realization of this ideal, the Labor movement organized training programs to prepare immigrants for manual occupations, particularly in agriculture, and mobilized resources to provide employment opportunities and social services for the newly created working class. Membership in the parties of the Labor movement was formally limited on ideological grounds to those who earned their living from the fruits of their own labor without exploiting the labor of others. Ideology was also responsible for changing the amount of prestige associated with various occupations. Manual labor, especially in agriculture, was accorded high prestige, whereas the prestige of the free professions and white collar occupations declined.[28]

In the early stages of their development, the parties of the Labor and the Ezrahim blocs were characterized by a rather homogeneous composition of members and supporters. In the Labor movement this homogeneity was institutionalized in an occupational and class sense. Among the Ezrahim there were also organizations, such as the Farmers Association, which sought members from specific groups. The membership of the General Zionist parties was more varied, even though it was composed mainly of middle-class elements, professionals, and white-collar workers.[29] The composition of most parties in the Yishuv became less homogeneous over the years. Mapai's shift of orientation "from class to nation" in the 1930s enabled it to end its state of partial exclusion from the wider society and expand its base of support to include middle-class groups. The willingness to appeal openly to these groups was particularly apparent after the split in Mapai when several Tel Aviv–based Mapai politicians organized a campaign to win the support of groups such as artisans and small merchants. On the other hands, in the Revisionist camp the activities of Betar and the IZL won the enthusiastic support of numerous Oriental Jews of Tel Aviv and Jerusalem, most of whom were unskilled laborers.

There is another aspect of the parties' social composition which relates specifically to the registered membership and not to the wider circles of supporters and voters. In the political system of the Yishuv, we recall, the parties served as intermediaries between the national center and the individual and as channels of resource allocation. In this context, the question arises as to the extent to which a party's membership was composed of organized groups, such as *kibbutzim* and *moshavim,* which maintained a group affiliation. The composition of Mapai's membership is particularly instructive in this respect. According to a survey conducted in 1933–34, 4,490 members of Mapai were urban residents, 3,590 were members of *kibbutzim* and *moshavim* and 2,247 resided in *moshavot* as hired workers. In 1944 the portion of party members from settlements was at least 57 percent; the portion residing in cities, all-Jewish neighborhoods, and industrial towns reached 35 percent; while 18 percent of party members resided in the *moshavot*.[30] The composition of Mapai's membership changed considerably after the 1944 split, with the entry of previously unaffiliated members. Some fifteen thousand to eighteen thousand members remained in *Mapai* after the split and to these were added some twenty thousand new members, the vast majority of whom had no connection with any of the organized frameworks affiliated to the party. In Hashomer Hatzair and Hatenu'a Leahdut Ha'avoda there was a much higher percentage of members belonging to an organized group affiliated with the party.

Affiliations to Political Frameworks outside Palestine

Most "Palestinian" Jewish parties had sister parties in the Diaspora. The Diaspora parties affiliated to the Labor movement were led by the Labor leadership in Palestine and their activities were directed by special emissaries sent abroad by the Labor parties in the Yishuv. In contrast, many of the leaders of the General Zionists lived abroad. The Revisionist movement was led by one man, Vladimir (Zeev) Jabotinsky, but after 1929, by order of the British authorities, he was prevented from returning to Palestine. Some of the other Revisionist leaders lived abroad, others in Palestine, but most of them began their political careers in the Diaspora.

Another aspect of the relation between the parties in the Yishuv and their counterparts in the Diaspora was the electoral dimension. In the 1930s and 1940s, the percentages of votes received by the Labor parties' candidates for Zionist congresses were consistently higher in

Table 4
Comparison of Zionist Election Results in
Palestine vs. Total Results by Political Sector
(percentages)

| | 1931 | |
Sector	Pales-tine	Pales-tine & Dias-pora
Labor	62.0	29.0
Mizrahi movement	9.1	14.0
Revisionists	16.8	21.0
General Zionists	7.8	36.0

Palestine than the comparable percentages for the Diaspora (see Table
4). Electoral support in Palestine for the Labor parties was between
60 percent and 70 percent, while their over-all support never reached
50 percent.

The General Zionists parties present a completely different case.
Notwithstanding the shifts in the extent of General Zionist support in
Palestine—explained in part by the fact that the Revisionists did not
participate in the elections of 1935, 1937, and 1939—the percentage
of their electoral support in Palestine was always less than half their
over-all support in elections to the Zionist congresses.

Mizrahi, Hapoel Hamizrahi, and the Revisionists had a more balanced
record of electoral support in Palestine and the Diaspora. The over-all
percentage of votes for the two religious parties was always somewhat
higher than the percentage of votes they attracted from the voters in
Palestine. The same was true for the Revisionists on the two occasions
in the thirties that they participated in elections for the congresses.

Frame of Reference

The sixth structural variable distinguishes between "closed" parties
oriented to more or less select and homogeneous groups and "open"

1933		1935		1937		1939		1946	
Pales-tine	Pales-tine & Dias-pora	Pales-tine	Pales-tine & Dias-pora	Pales-tine	Pales-tine & Dias-pora	Pales-tine	Pales-tine & Dias-pora	Pales-tine	Pales-tine & Dias-pora
68.0	44.0	66.8	48.8	69.5	46.3	70.6	46.8	60.5	39.9
8.0	12.0	13.9	16.0	15.4	16.5	10.4	14.2	12.4	15.0
12.2	14.0	—	—	—	—	—	—	13.7	10.6
6.6	28.0	16.0	32.2	14.9	35.3	17.6	36.4	12.2	33.2

SOURCE: Compiled from the protocols of the
Zionist Congresses, the Zionist Archives in
Jerusalem.

parties oriented to a broader, undifferentiated public. The first type is
the sectarian party that concentrates on serving the instrumental and
ideological needs and interests of its organized membership. The second
type attempts to influence the wider society and thus must mobilize
support from beyond its immediate circle of members and supporters.[31]
The sectarian party tends to relate to its constituency as a social enclave
populated by a select group. For this type of party, fulfilling the goals
and aspirations of its constituency and preserving the "purity" of their
values become primary political preoccupations.

On a continuum relating these two poles, the General Zionists would
occupy one extreme, Hashomer Hatzair the other. The General Zionists
appealed ideologically to the widest spectrum of groups, though in the
later stages of development their appeal tended to be aimed at more
specific strata. Hashomer Hatzair was the most sectarian and elitist
party among the Zionist political groups in the Yishuv. It was oriented
primarily inward toward what it considered the elect of the pioneering
groups—the members of Hakibbutz Ha'artzi kibbutzim and the Hashomer Hatzair youth movements. In the early 1920s sectarian and elitist
tendencies were also characteristic of other groups within the Labor
movement. The establishment of Mapai and the adoption of the "from
class to nation" approach indicated a shift away from sectarian ten-

dencies, for most of the Labor movement at any rate, and a movement toward greater openness.

The parties' location on each of the continua representing the different structural variables affected their differential capacities for resource mobilization and for institution building. The existence of sister parties in the Diaspora also had a more direct influence on the potential for mobilization and institution building. The organization and training of potential immigrants in the Diaspora conducted by the sister parties influenced a party's mobilization capacity, while the potential for institution building was augmented by the additional inputs of material and symbolic resources from the Diaspora. These capacities for resource mobilization and institution building to a large extent determined the party's capacity to influence decision making and determine policy in the national center.

The Nonparty Subcenters

The ramified network of subcenters other than political parties which existed in the Yishuv may be categorized and compared according to several variables. First we will look at the subcenters of the Labor movement and the Ezrahim and also at those of the ultraorthodox community; then the subcenters of each sector will be compared with the transsectoral subcenters. This comparative analysis will focus on the following variables:

1. *Type of membership*, in this case either individual or group membership in a subcenter. In the group membership, the subcenter assumes a federative structure and the individual is associated with the subcenter through membership in one of the groups or organizations that make up the subcenter.

2. *Relations to political parties*, in which context four types of subcenters may be distinguished: nonpartisan subcenters; multiparty subcenters where party affiliation is relevant; subcenters dominated or composed of a single party that may also contain those who are not members of any political party; and quasi-party subcenters, which are not political parties but do participate in elections.[32]

3. *Geographical scope*, that, is whether a subcenter is local or nationwide.

4. *Range of activities*, which can be categorized according to the criteria the structural-functional school of sociology has developed

for distinguishing between institutional spheres: political goal
attainment, instrumental-adaptive, solidarity-integrative, and
cultural pattern maintenance. This schema enables us to determine
numerically the range of functions of a subcenter. The political
goal attainment sphere refers to the mobilization, regulation, and
allocation of resources, particularly manpower, for the attainment
of collective goals. The instrumental sphere refers to activity
designed to further the adaptation of the individual or group to
its environment. Economic activity occupies the most prominent
place in this category, but activity designed to assure individual
or group security must also be included in the instrumental category. The solidarity-integrative sphere refers to the development
and maintenance of society's institutional patterns of action and
to the creation of the solidarity necessary to ensure the continuity
of these patterns. Solidarity may refer to national solidarity or
to group solidarity, such as within classes, status groups, political
movements, and so forth. The fourth sphere, that of cultural pattern maintenance, refers to activity connected with the formation
and transmission of values. This includes socialization carried out
through formal educational institutions and other forms of communication. Activities usually designated as "cultural" are of
course included in this sphere.

5. *Level of institutionalization*, which differentiates between subcenters that possess a permanent organizational apparatus and
   staff which operate according to formal rules and those with a
   weak organizational framework which do not operate according
   to a system of binding rules. This variable contains two dimensions:
   the degree of organizational complexity and the existence of
   formal rules of operation.
6. *Relation to the national center*, which distinguishes between
   subcenters with direct ties to the national center and those whose
   contacts with the center are mediated by parties or other
   subcenters. Furthermore we may distinguish between subcenters
   that maintain direct but informal ties to the national center and
   those formally defined as agencies of the center but which possess
   sufficient autonomy to justify their separate existence. These
   relationships can be ranked on a scale of ascending importance:
   no relationship, indirect, direct-informal, direct-formal.

A comparison of the various subcenters according to the variables
outlined above brings into focus some of the major characteristics of
these subcenters and the differences among them.

The subcenters in the Labor sector were more numerous than those of other sectors but, more important, they were intertwined in the framework of the Histadrut. The latter served as an umbrella organization with the power to coordinate, mediate, and arbitrate not only among the subcenters that were its executive agencies, but also among the "movement" subcenters such as the various federations of kibbutzim and Moshavim, as well as youth movements, affiliated to the parties. The organizational components of the Histadrut were ramified, intersecting, and at times overlapping, with many subcenters connected simultaneously to different functional spheres and levels of the Histadrut. Membership in organizations such as settlement movements affiliated to the Histadrut was conditional on membership in the Histadrut itself, so the same membership criteria applied in both cases (see Table 5).

Table 5
Subcenters by Type of Membership and
Relation to Parties

Sector	N	Type of Membership			Relations to Parties			
		Individual	Federative	Irrelevant	Multiparty	Single-party	Quasi-party	Non-partisan
Labor	25	11	10	4	18	5	1	1
Ezrahim and religious parties	20	18	1	1	2	8	6	4
Extreme Orthodox groups	7	5	1	1	—	3	—	4
Transsectoral	22	13	1	8	7	—	—	15

NOTE: The type of membership is not relevant for subcenters where there is no question of registration, for example, in educational institutions or economic enterprises managed directly by the Histadrut.

Another characteristic of the Histadrut subcenters was the close connections with and pervasive influence of political parties. Almost without exception, the Histadrut subcenters were either single-party or multiparty in composition (see Table 5). The only exception was the Hagana of the 1920s (when it was under Histadrut control), which was a nonpartisan organization open to all, even those not members of the Histadrut or any party. The distinction between single-party subcenters and multiparty subcenters usually paralleled the distinction between "movement" subcenters and subcenters belonging to the Histadrut as a whole.

The Histadrut sector, then, was characterized by varied subcenter components linked into one system, which in turn formed a subsystem of the Yishuv. This subsystem was integrated by a central organization that regulated the relations of its subcenter components with frameworks outside the Histadrut subsystem, especially the national center. As an example, conflicts over resource allocation emerged periodically among the different settlement movements within the Histadrut. These conflicts were first settled within the framework of the Histadrut, which then empowered the Histadrut's Agricultural Center to negotiate in its name with the national institutions.

The subcenters of the Ezrahim lacked a comprehensive organization to unite and coordinate them. There was in fact practically no interlinkage among the subcenters of this sector. The establishment of Ha-Ihud Haezrahi as a federative framework uniting the Ezrahim subcenters was an attempt to remedy this situation, which arose from conflicting interests within this sector; from a perception of the political sphere as secondary in importance, particularly in relation to the economic sphere; and from the absence of a common ideological outlook bridging the gap between the religious and secular groups of the right wing of Zionism. The tendency to give priority to economic rather than political activity was reflected in the relatively large number of quasiparty subcenters, such as the economic organizations that participated frequently in elections (see Table 5).

The absence of a multifunctional comprehensive organization for the Ezrahim sector as a whole was not compensated for on the level of the subcenters. In other words, there were few subcenters that engaged in a wide range of activity (see Table 6). In contrast to the medium to high levels of institutionalization in the Histadrut sector, the average level of institutionalization in the Ezrahim sector ranged from medium to low (see Table 7).

The distinguishing feature of the ultraorthodox subcenters, in contrast to their Histadrut and Ezrahim counterparts, was precisely their lack of ties with the national center. This required the ultraorthodox community to build alternative institutions which provided not only

Table 6
Subcenters by Range of Activities

Sector	Number of Spheres of Activity			
	1	2	3	4
Labor	7a	5	7	6b
Ezrahim and religious groups	2	10c	5	3d
Extreme Orthodox groups	—	1	5	1
"Transsectoral"	4	16	2	—

a. All are economic enterprises of the Histadrut.
b. All are "movement" subcenters, such as the
   kibbutzim federations and youth movements.
c. Seven out of the ten are of the goal attainment and adaptive-instrumental type.
d. All represent political parties.

those services supplied by other subcenters, but also those supplied by
the national center. It is no surprise, then, to find that the level of
institutionalization of the ultraorthodox subcenters ranged from medium
to high, and that most tended to perform a wide range of functions.

The last group of subcenters is the transsectoral ones, such as the
Medical Association, Writers Association and other professional associations. These subcenters were not interlinked nor were they united under
one organization; partial exceptions were those subcenters which served
as semiautonomous agencies of the national center. By their very nature,
the transsectoral subcenters cannot be placed in the single-party category. This does not mean that they were all nonpartisan. There were
some transsectoral subcenters whose governing bodies were composed
according to a "party key" or through elections on a political party basis.

The Growth of the Political Power
of the Labor Movement

The major differences between the Labor movement and the Ezrahim
sector that have emerged through this comparison of the structural
characteristics of parties and subcenters help explain the shifts in the
distribution of power in the 1930s and 1940s, primarily the rise of the
Labor movement to its position as the national center's dominant elite.
As we stressed above, the impact of the structural characteristics of the

parties and subcenters on power relations within the Yishuv was indirect, through their effects on institution building and mobilization of manpower and resources.

While it is true that there was a greater degree of planning, coordination, and central direction in the institution-building process in the Labor movement, it should also be stressed that this process was at times motivated by short-run considerations and marked by trial and error rather than by deliberate planning. If in retrospect it appears as if the institutional network of the Labor movement emerged according to some master plan, it is well to recall that in fact the final results by no means reflected the intentions and desires of the founding fathers of the movement. Nevertheless, the degree of coordination and cohesion was not the product of random forces. These characteristics can be explained as adaptive responses made by this institutional network to various needs and challenges, and were determined by the presence of a political will to accept the authority of a common center.

The unique role of the Histadrut in the Yishuv's political system stemmed from its position astride a critical junction of channels of communication and resource flow. This position gave it control of transactions and communications between the national center and the subcenters affiliated to the Histadrut, between parties affiliated to the Histadrut and their members, between the Histadrut subcenters and the transsectoral subcenters, and among the various Histadrut subcenters themselves. The capacity of the Histadrut to regulate the activities of its subcenters was predicated, of course, on the willingness of the parties and movement subcenters that composed it to recognize its authority and accept it as a coordinating and mediating framework. This willingness had its limits, however, and the history of the Histadrut was marked by a continual process of defining and redefining the division of labor between the parties and the Histadrut.

The 1920s were marked by the ascendancy of the Histadrut in relation to the parties, but the late 1920s and early 1930s saw a reversal of this trend. The parties, or rather *the* party, Mapai, was able to regain its position as the directing political force behind the Histadrut and to reassert its authority over its members in the Histadrut apparatus. This trend toward concentrating more power and authority in the parties increased in the 1930s after Mapai abandoned the idea of making the Histadrut the nucleus of an autonomous workers' society and replaced it with the new political strategy of "from class to nation." The internal

Table 7
Subcenters by Geographical Scope, Level of
Institutionalization, and Relation to the National
Center

		Geographical Scope	
Sector	N	Country-wide	Local
Labor	25	24	1
Ezrahim and religious parties	20	16	4
Extreme Orthodox groups	7	3	4
Transsectoral	22	17	5

struggles within the Histadrut which accompanied the historic split of 1944 gave further impetus to the trend of moving key decision-making forums from the Histadrut to Mapai.

The institution-building process influenced the capacity to mobilize manpower, political loyalty, and material resources. The party members who manned the Histadrut apparatus, whether they served as elected representatives or salaried functionaries, made up a cadre of activists available for political mobilization. Moreover, they were economically dependent as well as ideologically committed to their parties. In addition, the Labor movement had at its disposal a permanent reservoir of available manpower mobilized in the collectivist movement subcenters, *kibbutzim*, and training groups. The conclusion is ineluctable, then, that the Labor movement enjoyed a major advantage over the non-Histadrut sectors in respect to its capacity for effective mobilization of manpower.

The mobilization capacity of a political framework depends not only on logistic aspects, but also on the commitment it inspires in its members and supporters. Political organization and political loyalty are inseparable aspects of the same phenomenon. Politically conscious people are more readily available for political mobilization, while those organized

Level of Insti-tutionalization			Relation to the National Center			
High	Medium	Low	Indirect	Direct	No Connection	Not Relevant
10	11	4	18	7	—	—
4	8	8	6	10	4	—
2	5	—	1	—	6	—
4	9	9	—	19	—	3a

NOTE: a. For professional organizations such as the Medical Association, the Authors Association, and the Association of Engineers and Architects, the institutionalized relations to the national center were irrelevant in the fulfillment of their specific roles.

in political movements are more available for indoctrination that strengthens their previous commitments. The Labor movement maintained an entire network of organizations devoted to political socialization, such as youth movements, the Labor school system, various ideological "seminars," and the like, whose tasks were to inculcate the values of the Labor movement and to foster intensive commitment to it. Some of these organizations, such as the Labor-sponsored school system, were concerned with indoctrinating "basic" movement values. Others, such as the youth movements, were based on more elitist premises and were concerned with producing cadres capable of interpreting and transmitting values. The ideological seminars in which movement activists participated were especially of this elitist bent. Membership in collectivist movement subcenters such as *kibbutzim* implied constant immersion in intensive socialization. The political indoctrination in these organizations was successful in creating high levels of ideological commitment and produced many of the Labor movement activists.

The Labor movement also had a number of advantages over most of its political rivals in its capacity for mobilizing material resources. Institution building provided the logistic base for resource mobilization,

while the high level of consensus concerning the national importance
of the colonizing tasks undertaken by the Histadrut made it possible
to give symbolic meaning to this otherwise instrumental activity. The
term "pioneering" (*halutziut*) and the constructivist ideology of "practical Zionism" (see below, chap. 6, n. 8) conferred broad meaning and
national significance on the tasks carried out almost exclusively by the
groups and organizations of the Labor movement. The only other
movements which shared the "pioneer" designation were the Hapoel
Hamizrahi and Haoved Hatzioni, which performed similar tasks. Usually,
though, this term was monopolized by the Labor movement to such
an extent that the term "pioneering camp" was synonymous with the
Labor movement.[33]

The capacity of the Labor movement for building institutions and
mobilizing resources that was reflected in the development of the Labor
subcenters is even more outstanding when contrasted with the development of subcenters in the Ezrahim sector. The most important feature
in this respect was the absence of a common framework uniting and
coordinating the Ezrahim subcenters. The absence of such a framework
is surely related to the fact that the term "Ezrahim" was a somewhat
vague appellation; at times one could not be sure to what organizations
and groups it applied. Moreover, the Ezrahim subcenters usually represented narrow particularistic interests. There were organizations in the
Histadrut sector as well with particularistic orientations, but they were
part of a political subsystem with explicit, broad national and social
goals. The tendency of the Labor movement to identify its colonizing
tasks with the goals of the Zionist movement enabled the subcenters
of the Labor movement to nurture a belief in their "mission" even when
the substance of their activities advanced their own particularistic
interests.

In contrast, the particularistic subcenters of the Ezrahim sector were
not linked in a comprehensive framework that could direct their
activities toward attaining broad social goals. They were unable to
translate their particularistic interests into terms that could win recognition for their collective meaning. This absence of strong attachments
to broad collective goals anchored in a vision of the "good society"
also made it difficult, if not impossible, for the parties of the Ezrahim
to create the high level of individual and group commitment the movement subcenters of the Histadrut enjoyed. Consequently the Ezrahim
sector did not succeed in mobilizing even the economic resources
available to it or in translating these resources into political power.

In contrast to the collectivist orientation of the left, the prevailing economic orientation on the right was individualistic. This meant that the capital of the Ezrahim was dispersed among a large number of enterprises, mostly family-owned, and that the primary purpose of investment was to make profits for the owners. The result was a paradox in which the parties and subcenters of the "wealthy" right were more plagued by shortages of funds than were the parties and subcenters of the left, whose financial base was actually more limited. The right thus lagged behind the left in developing a capacity for mobilizing resources and manpower.

These differences between the Labor movement and the Ezrahim sector had their impact on the results of the elections to the Elected Assembly and the Zionist congresses. The data presented in Table 8

Table 8
Electoral Power of the Main Political
Sectors in the Elected Assembly (percentages)

Sector	Elections			
	1920	1925	1931	1944
Labor parties	37.0	36.5	42.3	59.1
Center and right-wing parties	19.7	42.1	32.4	21.0
Religious parties	20.3	8.8	7.0	16.6
Ethnic groups	23.0	12.6	18.3	3.3
Total	100.0	100.0	100.0	100.0

SOURCE: Adapted from M. Atias, *The Book of Documents of the National Council of Knesset Israel, 1918–48* (Jerusalem: R. H. Cohen, 1953).

and Figure 1 derived from the table indicate a consistent increase in the vote for the Labor bloc in the elections to the Elected Assembly. The upward trend for the Labor movement was even more apparent in the elections to the Zionist congresses until 1935. (see Table 9 and Figure 2). Thus the Labor movement succeeded in using the institutional networks it had created to secure the dominant positions in the national institutions.

The existence in the Yishuv of a complex system of institutionalized parties and subcenters organized according to bureaucratic patterns

Table 9
Elections to the Zionist Congresses (percentages)

	12th	13th
Sector	(1921)	(1923)
Labor parties	8.0	21.0
Center and right-wing parties	73.0	56.0
Religious parties	19.0	23.0
Total	100.0	100.0

characteristic of developed societies was something of an anomaly among nonindependent political systems. This phenomenon is even more striking considered in relation to the absolute size of the Jewish population in Palestine—fewer than one hundred thousand in the early 1920s and about five hundred thousand in the 1940s—less than one-tenth of the population of London, Tokyo, or New York. The institutional network of the Yishuv thus resembled a large head placed on a tiny body. The development of an institutional system preceded population growth,

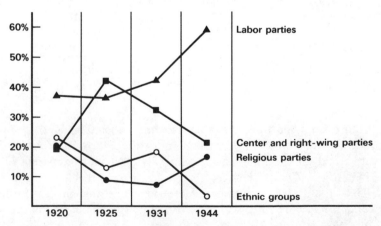

Figure 1
Changes in the Electoral Power of the Main
Political Sectors in the Elected Assembly

14th	15th	16th	17th	18th	19th	20th	21st	22nd
(1925)	(1927)	(1929)	(1931)	(1933)	(1935)	(1937)	(1939)	(1946)
18.0	22.0	26.0	29.0	44.0	48.8	46.3	46.8	39.9
64.0	62.0	58.0	57.0	44.0	35.2	37.2	39.0	45.1
18.0	16.0	16.0	14.0	12.0	16.0	16.5	14.2	15.0
100.0	100.0	100.0	100.0	100.0	100.0	100.0	100.0	100.0

SOURCE: Compiled from the protocols of the
Zionist Congresses, the Zionist Archives in
Jerusalem.

since it was designed to serve an expected future immigration as well
as the existing population. It was also facilitated by the existence of an
external supply of resources by which the institutional system of the
Yishuv was maintained and for which it acted as an allocative agency.

Another important feature of the institutional system of the Yishuv
was the dispersal of authority. In this respect as well, the political

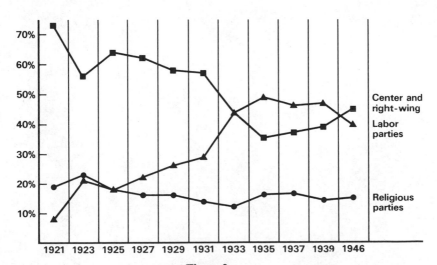

Figure 2
Changes in the Electoral Power of the Main
Political Sectors in the Elections to the Zionist
Congresses

system of the Yishuv resembled Western democratic systems, even though it was a nonsovereign ethnonational community at a relatively low level of economic development. The subcenters functioned both as foci of attraction and inspiration for members of various social enclaves and as agencies of the national center. However, the dispersal of authority did not prevent the national center from steadily increasing its authority in the political system. There was no contradiction between this trend and the ongoing process of institution building in the subcenters, since the more powerful subcenters supported the centripetal trends that led to the strengthening of the national center, which was, from the mid-thirties, actually controlled by Labor leaders. These leaders were members of an elite group characterized by a positive orientation to political power, collectivist values, and a future-oriented perspective.

5

Recruitment and Social Composition of the Political Elite

The Political Elites and Their Periphery

The connection between the process of institution building in the political system and the characteristics of the political and administrative elite who occupied the central positions in this system was dual. The institution-building process itself was an outcome of the elite's need to respond to economic, social, and cultural demands raised by various groups in the political system. Also, the extent to which the evolving national center responded to these demands was dependent (among other things) on the characteristics of the elite that occupied the national center and the subcenters of the various sectors. From this perspective, those groups led by an elite with high levels of personal commitment and aspiration for political power possessed distinct advantages in the political struggle. The elite which possessed these qualities was composed of professional politicians whose power was anchored in concrete group interests within the Yishuv.

This type of "anchorage" was not characteristic of most members of the senior elite group in the 1920s. For this reason this elite group found it difficult to establish a common ground with the new elite groups which drew their strength from representation of specific interests within the Yishuv. People such as Harry Sacher,

Henrietta Szold, and Col. Frederich Kisch were chosen by the Zionist
Executive in London to occupy the key positions on the Executive in
Jerusalem. They lacked a constituency in the Yishuv, nor did they have
a political base in those Eastern European countries from which most
of the immigrants of the 1920s came. The presence of this type of public
figure in key positions of the national center impeded the formation of
a coalitionary center composed of elite groups representing the various
party and movement subcenters. The change in the composition of the
Zionist elite in the 1930s reflected the rise of elite groups associated
with constituencies in the Yishuv, or with such constituencies among
potential Zionist immigrants to Palestine in their countries of origin.

The connection that developed in the thirties and forties between
political influence in the national center and ties to a "mobilized"
political base in the subcenters was expressed on three levels. On the
level of the national leadership, the change in the composition of the
Zionist Executive in the early 1930s ended the differences between the
recruitment patterns of the Zionist Executive and those of the National
Council Executive. On the level of intersectoral political struggle, in
this same period the Labor movement succeeded in consolidating its
position in the national center due to its stronger and more organized
political base. On the level of political development within the various
sectors, the positions of those leaders whose support was rooted in
groups within the Yishuv were strengthened. Thus the leaders of Ahdut
Ha'avoda, David Ben-Gurion and Berl Katznelson,[1] supplanted such
figures as Shlomo Kaplansky[2] whose position rested mainly on their
influence in the *Poalei Zion* World Union to which Ahdut Ha'avoda
was affiliated. In the same manner, even though Hamizrahi possessed
more influence in the Mizrahi World Organization, Hapoel Hamizrahi
gradually became the more powerful party. Similar trends appeared
on the right as well: Israel Rokach and Joseph Sapir became the
dominant leaders of the Ezrahim groups at the expense of General
Zionist leaders who were active mainly in the Diaspora, and veteran
Revisionist leaders from Jabotinsky's intimate circle lost their positions
and influence to the leaders of IZL.

The fact that the subcenters formed the political base of the Yishuv's
ruling elite was reflected in the coalitionary structure of the national
center. The impact of coalitionary rule was intensified due to the nonsovereign nature of the center; the option to withdraw from the organized

Yishuv made compromise imperative. In turn, the structure of the center influenced the nature of the political elite, which, as it was divided on the basis of association with relatively autonomous groups, could not become a "ruling elite" in the full sense of the term.[3] The model of a pyramidal political structure topped by a unified "power elite" controlling the sources of political and economic power is not appropriate for the political structure of the Yishuv. More apt is one based on the distribution of political power at the intermediate level similar to the "veto groups" model suggested for the United States. Policy-making processes in the center assumed the form of bargaining and compromise among representatives of sectors rather than the imposition of decisions from above. It can thus be said, in the absence of an extreme polarity between center and periphery, that the boundary between elite and non-elite, rulers and ruled, became blurred as well.

Studies point to two levels of criteria for elite recruitment. First were general criteria relating to such "qualifications" as ideological identification and membership in certain groups; second were those pertaining to personal abilities and qualities.[4] The qualifications for elite positions on the first level were much clearer within the Labor movement than within the elites of the Ezrahim. Ideological fitness in the Labor movement was determined by the extent of one's commitment to the movement, loyalty to its values, and willingness to carry out its instructions in respect to policy-making. In addition to these, the very existence of organized movement subcenters gave rise to demands for representation, thus ensuring that most elite positions would be occupied by those representing a specific political base. The base could be an association of settlements, trade unions, women's labor organizations, or even groups of immigrants with similar "movement" backgrounds in the Diaspora. This tendency for group representation had a different form within the elites of the Ezrahim, which put more emphasis on representation of economic interest groups, such as the Farmers Association. At times local authorities were also seen as units deserving specific representation in the Ezrahim sector. Intersectoral *landsmanschaften* groups within the Jewish community were at times also considered appropriate categories for group representation.

The second level of criteria for elite selection was the level of personal qualities. Here there were three main aspects: particular skills, style of behavior and appearance stemming from socialization in a particular social and cultural milieu, and what may be described as "personal merit." The important skills were not usually perceived as technical skills acquired in formal training for performing specific functions, but as more diffuse qualities, the most important of which were initiative, flexibility, and the ability to improvise. This perception facilitated horizontal rotation of positions and enabled an individual to hold several positions simultaneously. Role behavior among the elite was for the most part ad hoc and ad persona, i.e., particularistic in the sociological sense of the term, and patterns of hierarchical authority blurred to such an extent that they were frequently meaningless. Non- or even antibureaucratic patterns of behavior were so prevalent that political figures without a formally defined role in an organization could play an important part in shaping the policy of that organization.

The emphasis on flexibility, particularism, and capacity to improvise was understandable in light of the organizational characteristics of the political system. Institutions functioned on a broad interpretation of their responsibilities which often exceeded their formal authority. The necessity to adapt to constantly changing circumstances and the readiness of both elite and public opinion, in certain circumstances, to sanction extralegal activity of national and "movement" institutions prevented the crystallization of rigid organizational patterns based on fixed, obligatory rules of behavior. The Yishuv's small size too was conducive to an informal style.

The second criterion of selection for elite roles was a certain style of personal appearance, political rhetoric, and interpersonal relations. This style was related to the symbols, acquired through socialization within a "movement," which expressed the group's uniqueness. It included patterns of cultural consumption, particularly the use of leisure time; characteristic expressions and key words; style of dress and living accommodations; and, above all, certain forms of interpersonal relations in private as well as public roles. These characteristics make up what social psychologists call "role performance"[5] or in the words of E. Goffman, "the presentation of self in everyday life."[6] For example, a member of the Labor movement elite was supposed to behave in a conspicuously egalitarian manner in his relations with the rank and file, to profess his reluctance to assume public office, and to insist that he was not deliberately seeking the post, but simply agreeing to fulfill his duty to the movement. In addition, each political movement had its own rhetorical style and political lexicon.

The third personal criterion of selection for elite roles was the nature and amount of personal "merit" accumulated in the performance of pioneering tasks or in service to the movement. The Labor movement had two relevant types of past accomplishment: political activity on behalf of the movement, mainly before immigrating to Palestine, and a record of "personal realization" of the pioneering tasks. The first type was common to the Ezrahim sector as well, while the second was almost unique to the Labor movement. Some period of personal pioneering, whether long or short, was considered an essential component in the biography of outstanding politicians in the Labor movement. There were even examples of figures who lost most of their power and influence in the movement but, because of their past accomplishments, were rewarded with positions whose prestige exceeded their power. Thus "merit" accumulated in the past became a way to ensure one's "rights" in the present. The importance attributed to the accumulation of merit served as an ideological justification for the status conferred on the "founding fathers" of the Labor movement elite. Among the Ezrahim similar status was conferred entrepreneurs whose merits were accumulated by establishing economic enterprises that benefited the national interests.

The Labor movement did not consider political activity as a career—although it became a profession in many cases—but a "calling" or "mission" (*shelihut*). This conception had two facets: the first was that the relation between the person "called" to serve and those who charged him with his mission was one of mutual trust and loyalty; and second, in the perception of elite roles obligations and service to the collectivity took clear precedence over any desire for access to greater privileges. Over the years, the rewards connected with elite roles, whether power or material rewards, created a gap between the idea of "calling" for service and the actual life-style of the political elite. The official value system, however, refused to admit the existence of such a gap. As a result, various institutional arrangements developed to camouflage the benefits deriving from elite positions. Official salaries, for example, were relatively low and were often based on the principle of family size; instead the "public servants" received indirect material rewards such as expense accounts or trips abroad.

The criterion of personal merit did not play the same role in the Ezrahim sector as it did in the Labor movement. The pioneering era of the old *moshavot* actually ended in the last decades of the nineteenth century and the first decade of the twentieth century, so that during the period of the Mandate, the founding fathers of the Ezrahim elite had reached advanced age. Even so, veteran status did play some part as a criterion of elite selection among the Ezrahim and was seen to confer rights and privileges not only on the founding fathers' generation but also on their native-born sons. The young generation of the Ezrahim even attempted to convert this ascribed status into a basis of political organization: several organizations of "native born" were active in various periods.

The criteria of elite selection and recruitment were never articulated, although the scope of their application was wide indeed. Prevailing modes of election and appointment to elite positions offered extensive opportunities for applying particularistic considerations. Thus, the ruling elite was able to control the processes of expansion and turnover in its ranks. In other words, a large portion of the political elite was actually chosen through a system of cooptation.[7] There was little difference in this respect between roles defined as political that required their occupants to be formally elected and quasi-administrative roles based on appointment. For elective positions, the continuity of the existing elite was assured by the parties' "nominating committees" which prepared lists of candidates in deliberations closed to the public and then offered the result to the voters for ratification. For appointive positions, there were no rigid rules to delimit the size of executive and administrative staffs of organizations and no universal selection procedures or even formal definitions of the qualifications required for a particular position.

This description of the Yishuv's political elites points to a possible connection between the respective characteristics of the Labor movement's and bourgeois parties' elites and the subcenters of these two sectors. We venture the hypothesis that the broader conception of the political roles of subcenters of the Histadrut sector as compared with the Ezrahim sector was consistent with a tendency within the Histadrut sector to allow members of the elite to occupy several positions and fill several political roles simultaneously. The higher level of institutionalization characteristic of the parties and subcenters of the Labor movement was consistent with the tendency to professionalization among the elite and the de facto conversion of political activity into a career, in spite of its noncompatability with the ideological maxims.

The Social Background and Career
Patterns of the Labor and Ezrahim
Political Elites

The differences between the Labor movement elite and the elite of the
Ezrahim can be grasped through a comparison of their demographic
characteristics, professionalization, and career patterns. For some of
these characteristics there is little or no statistical data; the descriptions
given here are based on assertions made in the context of debates on
organizational issues which occurred frequently within parties and other
political bodies. For other characteristics partial data are available.

These data, appearing for the first time in this book, compare the
top leadership groups of the Labor movement and Ezrahim elites. For
the purposes of this chapter, the concept of "top elite" does not include
all the leading figures who participated in decision-making processes
in the parties or subcenters, but only the parties' representatives in the
executive bodies of the national institutions, i.e., the executives of the
Jewish Agency and the National Council. This restricted concept
facilitates comparison because it is limited to the institutional frameworks common to both sets of elites. The number of people included
in this framework is eighty-two, of whom fifty-six were from the
Ezrahim sector and twenty-six from the Histadrut sector.[8] Of the entire
group (eighty-two, sixty-two were members of the National Council
Executive, and only twenty-eight were members of the Agency Executive
(eight people were thus members of both bodies for various periods).
While these figures possibly permit a comparison between elites, most
of the additional statistical data referred to below pertains only to the
Labor movement elite, and only partially.

Just as the overwhelming majority of the Yishuv in the period of
the Mandate was of immigrant origin, most of the political elite were
foreign-born as well. Immigrants from Eastern Europe formed the
dominant component of the political elite just as they did of the
population as a whole (see Table 10).

The most outstanding difference apparent from the table is the greater
variety of countries of origin among the elite of the Ezrahim. The representatives of the Labor movement in the national institutions were all
of Eastern European origin. Among the Ezrahim elite, however, there
were members from Central Europe, Palestine, and the Middle East.

The Palestine and Middle East groups were composed of the children of members of the first wave of immigration, Ashkenazic and Sephardic members of the Old Yishuv, and others.[9] The difference in country of origin between the elites of the Labor movement and the Ezrahim reflects the different circumstances in which these elites crystallized. The Labor movement representatives in the national center were people who had risen to prominence within the parties formed to aid in the absorption of the Labor immigration. It is noteworthy that the Eastern European composition of the Labor movement elite remained constant even in the 1930s and 1940s, when the composition of the Yishuv in respect to country of origin changed. These changes were not reflected at the upper level of the Labor movement elite, but rather at the lower levels. For example, of the delegates to the Histadrut convention of 1944, 78 percent were of Eastern European origin, while 22 percent were from Central Europe, the Middle East, and Palestine.[10]

The representatives of the Ezrahim, on the other hand, were composed of two elements: one, called the "Yishuvist" group, that was active almost exclusively in the National Council and the local authorities; and the other politicians from the Diaspora who composed the entire Ezrahim delegation on the Agency Executive and part of its delegation to the National Council. Over the years there were fewer native-born political figures in the national center, as most of the "second generation" leaders tended to concentrate their activities in the municipal arena, the most prominent being the mayors of Tel Aviv and Petach Tikva.

Other characteristics of the two elites are reflected in their composition by age. The Labor movement elite began its career as a young group of leaders among the Labor immigrants of the second and third waves of immigration and continued to make up the nationwide leadership of the movement during the later waves as well. As a result, the average age of the Labor elite steadily increased. In 1920–21, *all* the Labor movement members of the executive bodies of the national center were below the age of forty-five, while in 1931, 40 percent were over forty-five; and in 1946, only 20 percent were below this age. There was comparable aging of the Ezrahim elite, though the process was less distinct and less consistent. In the early 1920s, the average age of the Ezrahim elite was higher than that of the Labor movement elite, as only half of its members were under forty-five. In the 1930s, the Ezrahim elite's average age was still higher than that of the Labor movement's. But in the late 1930s and early 1940s, there were leadership replacements among the Ezrahim, with the result that both elites were about the same average age, about half of the members of both elites on the national executives being below the age of fifty-five. A difference between the two elites appears also in regard to the data on age at the time of assuming a position in one of the national executives. Almost every member of the Labor elite reached such a position between the ages of thirty and fifty, whereas about half of the Ezrahim reached this position only when they were over fifty.

The age distribution indicates a low rate of turnover, as a result of which the elites continued to age. The same picture emerges when we compare the distribution of the two elites in respect to periods of immigration to Palestine (see Table 11). The data indicate a clear overrepresentation of members of the Second Immigration among the Labor movement elite. Representatives of the Ezrahim were much more balanced in respect to the relative share of the various waves of immigration and of the native-born.

The over-all picture that emerges from this comparison of the two elites indicates that the Labor elite was more homogeneous in country of origin, age distribution, period of immigration, age at time of immigration, and age upon accession to the elite. The profile of the average member of the Labor elite is of a person from Eastern Europe who came to Palestine during the second wave of immigration, when he was under twenty-five, and assumed a position on the national executives between the ages of thirty and fifty. Conversely, it is most difficult to construct such a clear-cut profile for members of the Ezrahim elite, because of the heterogeneous nature of this group expressed in the wide distribution of the data in relation to the median figures. Even so, those of Eastern European origin make up the majority, and while the presence of numbers of native-born is significant, those from other areas diminish this Eastern European dominance but do not cancel it entirely. Another important characteristic of the Ezrahim elite was a higher rate of turnover, as a result of which this elite was older than the Labor elite in the 1920s and 1930s and approximately the same average age in the 1940s.

The political roles in the institutional system of the Yishuv were occupied for the most part by figures for whom politics was their exclusive sphere of activity. The political elite of the Yishuv differed from the elites of "notables" in many developing countries for whom politics

Table 10
Political Elite by Place of Birth

Sector	Native-born	Eastern Europe
All the elite	7	59
	(8.5%)	(75.5%)
Labor movement	0	25
	0	(100%)
Ezrahim	7	34
	(13%)	(63%)

Table 11
Political Elite (1918–48) by Period of Immigration

Sector	Native-Born	First Immigration (1882–1903)
All the elite	7	7
	(9%)	(9%)
Ezrahim	7	7
	(13%)	(13%)
Labor	0	0
	0	0

Western and Central Europe	North and South America	Middle East	Others	Unknown	Total
7	1	4	1	3	82
(8.5%)	(1.2%)	(5%)	(1.2%)		
0	0	0	0	1	26
0	0	0	0	0	
7	1	4	1	2	56
(13%)	(1.7%)	(7.5%)	(1.7%)	0	

Second Immigration (1904–1918)	Third Immigration (1919–23)	Fourth Immigration (1924–29)	Fifth Immigration (1930–39)	1940+	Un-known	Total
25	13	14	10	2	4	82
(32%)	(16%)	(18%)	(13%)	(3%)	0	
13	10	6	8	2	3	56
(24%)	(19%)	(11%)	(19%)a	0	0	
12	3	8	2	0	1	26
(48%)	(11%)	(32%)	(8.5%)	0	0	

a. Also includes persons who immigrated to Palestine after 1940.

is an auxiliary sphere of their economic and cultural activity.[11] Of all the members of the national executives, only one-third occupied elite roles in the economic sphere; about 13 percent held elite positions in the cultural sphere as writers, teachers, etc., 59 percent did not fill any elite roles in other institutional spheres, though some did occupy roles in other spheres that were lower in status compared to their political roles.

The representatives of the Labor movement on the national executives were usually chosen from this stratum of professional politicians. Thus differences appear between the elites of the two sectors in regard to the tendency to make politics a career and the major source of livelihood. The average term of office of a representative of the Ezrahim on the national executives was six years, while it was eight years for a representative of the Labor sector. Twenty-seven percent of the Labor representatives served for periods of over fifteen years on the national executives, while only 9 percent of the Ezrahim did so. On the other hand, about half of the Ezrahim elite occupied their positions for less than three years, as opposed to 40 percent of the Labor elite.

The higher level of professionalization among the Labor elite was also expressed in the fact that the percentage of members of the Labor elite who earned their living in politics was double the comparable figure among the Ezrahim elite. Among the Ezrahim elite there was a larger proportion of members of the "liberal" professions, religious functionaries, teachers, businessmen, industrialists, and farmers. The Labor elite on the other hand was composed mainly of those without formal occupational training and those for whom politics was their only source of livelihood.

To complete the discussion of the role structure and the characteristics of the elite, it is necessary to examine the rate of mobility of the elite. We may distinguish between gradual ascent from position to position in the political hierarchy (53 percent of elite members followed this pattern) and rapid ascent that entailed skipping intermediate stages and arriving directly at the top. There were several variations of the pattern of rapid ascent. The "founding fathers" of an institution (22 percent of our elite group) would rise to prominence together with the institution. Nine percent moved from a prestigious position in the Diaspora to a political role in the Yishuv. Others (16 percent) directly acceded to a position in the elite without previously holding senior political positions below the top level.

The notion of "founding fathers" has a dual meaning. In this chapter, the concept is employed to describe the founders of specific institutions in the Yishuv, but it may also be applied in the context of the Yishuv as a whole and thus used to designate the early groups of immigrants who came to Palestine to build a new society. Since the community was new, the endurance of the evolving social structure was largely dependent on intergenerational continuity among the elite and in society at large. The first generation in Palestine rebelled against the society into which they were born and as a result of this rebellion created a new society. The second generation of the Yishuv was the first born into a social system created through this revolutionary process. The continuity of the creation was conditioned on assuring the conformity of the second generation to the values of its parents. The test of the Yishuv as a social system, then, was in its ability to institutionalize and stabilize the consequences of the revolutionary act. In the case of the labor elite, intergenerational relations became tension-ridden due to the contradictory expectations each generation held of the other. The ambivalence of the first generation toward the second was apparent on the ideological level: Zionist ideology strove for the "normalization" of the Jewish people, yet this desired state could be achieved only by revolutionary action on the part of a pioneering society. These contradictory demands were to be realized in the character of the second generation, who were supposed to conform to the revolutionary values of their parents while remaining faithful to the institutional frameworks they had created, and to be no less willing than their parents to work and sacrifice for collective goals, without challenging any of the conventions of the first generation. Consequently, the first generation, which developed a strong "in-group" consciousness and solidarity, desired to preserve its monopoly of the positions of leadership in the evolving political system.[12]

Thus, the obstacles in the way of the second generation were similar to those that blocked the political progress of the later waves of immigrants, who found the key positions in the political system already occupied and sought channels for their talents which had been neglected by the earlier waves of immigrants. For the second generation, the most obvious channel for their abilities was the military security sphere, which required intimate knowledge both of geography and terrain and of the Arab population. The increasing importance of security activity in the life of the Yishuv and the internal political implications of control of the security organizations enabled some of the younger generation with roles in the Hagana to rise to political leadership in the Labor movement. This trend undermined the political monopoly enjoyed by members of the "founding fathers" in the leadership of the Labor movement.

The problems facing the second generation of the Ezrahim elite were of a different character from those facing the second generation of the Labor movement. The most prominent group of native-born among the Ezrahim with strong political ambitions was the second generation of the *moshavot* and the children of the veteran Jewish neighborhoods of Jaffa and Jerusalem. The main opponents of this group in the struggle for political power in the Yishuv were the young immigrants of the Second and Third Immigrations who were of the same age group. The second generation among the Ezrahim were thus chronologically parallel to the "founding fathers" of the Labor movement. This fact deepened the estrangement between the two groups, which differed not only in their political and economic interests, but also in their social and cultural backgrounds. The path of public activity open to the children of the First Immigration veterans was mainly that of local municipal politics. Political activity in the veteran *moshavot* was practically a monopoly of this group, which was assisted by local electoral laws which restricted the voting rights of hired labor. This group also played a prominent role in municipal politics in Tel Aviv and the "mixed cities," where their generational counterparts among the old Sephardic population played similar roles.

The patterns of selection and mobility of the political elites of the Yishuv described above are quite different from the patterns of most political elites in societies undergoing revolutionary change, particularly in the dependence on institutionalized channels of personal mobility in the various stages of their careers and the relatively small importance of a charismatic affinity between leader and those led.[13] This was true despite the presence of political leaders with a charismatic potential, some of whom, such as the first prime minister of Israel, David Ben-Gurion, became typical charismatic leaders at a later stage in their careers. Patterns of political activity in the Yishuv were too institutionalized and organized, the distance between elite and nonelite too small, and the role of ideology in the leader-led relation too important for the rise of a leadership whose authority rested primarily on charisma. These same factors clearly helped strengthen integrative (as opposed to disintegrative) processes in the Yishuv. These integrative tendencies and the relatively balanced development of the various institutional spheres enabled the Yishuv to avoid most types of crises that create appropriate conditions for the rise of charismatic leadership. Moreover, as a new society composed largely of immigrants, the Yishuv was spared the crises that accompanied the transitions from traditional and posttraditional societies, or the post–World War I disintegration of Europe's middle classes. This meant that there was no widespread desire and hope for a great leader. The values of the Labor movement absolutely rejected the cult of the leader and thus were more compatible with the general attitude in the Yishuv, than was the political style of the Revisionists, which betrayed tendencies to idolize the leader.[14] In this sphere, as in others, ideology played an important role in shaping the political culture of the Yishuv.

6

The Ideological Dimension

In the study of the Zionist movement and the Yishuv, it is common to overemphasize the importance of ideological debates and of changes occurring over the years in the ideological positions of the various Zionist parties and movements. Thus, there is a tendency to reduce the history of Zionism to an account of the realization of ideology and tension between imperatives of ideology and the limitations imposed by reality. Although this approach results in a lopsided image of the history of Zionism, it is accurate in that it reflects the central position of ideology in the consciousness of the political elite of the Yishuv. The history of the Yishuv was indeed marked by intensive ideological controversies and debates, and idealistically inspired attitudes were actually conceived as legitimate criteria to assess the success or failure of political and social endeavors.

The preoccupation with ideological issues and controversies is related to the fact that the Yishuv as a society with its own distinct collective identity arose out of an ideological impulse. Zionist immigration to Palestine was propelled by ideological motivation. The tendency of the Yishuv to segregate itself to the point where it became an autonomous social entity also arose out of ideological imperatives. Even the common cultural basis of the Yishuv

—the Hebrew language—emerged as a modern spoken language not
through a gradual process of evolution, but through a deliberate process
of cultivation itself ideologically motivated. One definition of ideology
states it is a set of "ideas by which men posit, explain, and justify
ends and means of organized social action with the aim to preserve,
amend, uproot or rebuild a given reality."[1] If we accept this definition,
then the uniqueness of the Yishuv lies in that the fact that its very
existence was the outcome of "organized social action" aimed at a
deliberate transformation of reality.

This approach can also clarify the relation between ideology and the
institutional organization of the Yishuv. For the most part, this organization was not the product of the social and historical heritage of an
established community, but the outcome of conscious action on the
part of different movements which joined on a common ideological
basis. The most comprehensive ideological framework was the concept
of "Zionism" in its broadest sense: the drive to establish a national
center for the Jewish people in the Land of Israel through a process
of immigration and settlement, and to form an autonomous community
possessing its own political and cultural distinctiveness. Beyond this
broad consensus, Zionism split into a number of political and ideological
movements which differed from one another regarding "minimalist"
or "maximalist" approaches, different visions of the new Jewish society
to be created, and different views about the appropriate means for the
realization of Zionist goals. The fact that the fulfillment of Zionism
depended upon the construction of a new society made Zionism an
ideology of radical change, although its adherents included conservatives.
It also explains the importance of ideological factors in determining
the balance of political forces in the Yishuv and the extent to which
different groups in the Yishuv could be considered as central or
peripheral.

This connection may be further elaborated by applying the distinction
between two dimensions of ideology, the fundamental and the operative.
The fundamental dimension refers to the principles which determine
the final goals and grand vistas in which the ideology is to be realized,
while the operative dimension concerns the principles which guide concrete political action.[2] The creation of a new society from its very
foundations could not possibly have been guided by an ideology which
placed one-sided emphasis on the fundamental dimension. In this respect
Zionism differed from Messianic movements in Jewish history which

possessed the characteristics of millenarian movements.[3] Zionism, unlike such movements, was modern from its inception and placed a strong emphasis on the operative side. In fact, the New Yishuv owes its origins to the Hovevei Zion (Lovers of Zion) movement in Russia, whose major aim was to found Jewish agricultural colonies in Palestine without being concerned with the political dimension of Jewish independence. On the other hand, the operative dimension alone could not provide enough motivation to inspire immigration to Palestine, or to withstand the austere and difficult conditions of the pioneering way of life. In circumstances such as these, political success could be achieved only by those movements that possessed the capacity to develop a balanced ideology that did not put too much emphasis on either the fundamental or the operative dimensions. The impact on the emerging society of the Yishuv of the various ideological movements in Zionism was determined by their ideological orientations toward some fundamental attributes of social order and social action.

Ideological Orientations

The first of these fundamental attributes of ideology was the relation to *time*,[4] of which there were three major aspects: the attitude toward past, present, and future; the appropriate tempo of change in the context of social action; and the perception of timing.

The attitude toward past, present, and future was related to the problem of historical continuity, i.e., the extent to which each variation of Zionist ideology called for a break with the past or, on the contrary, rested on traditional legitimacy. The notions past, present, and future were also related to innovative or conservative orientations in ideologically inspired action. The combination of a break with the past and a demand for change is readily perceived as consistent, but it is also conceivable that a fundamental perspective resting on traditional legitimacy would have operative goals calling for change in certain spheres. Such a combination, for example, characterized the religious Zionist movement which sought to preserve the continuity of Jewish tradition, yet advocated such innovative endeavors as immigration and settlement in Palestine, which undoubtedly required a substantial future orientation.

By its very nature, Zionist ideology in all its variations implied a considerable emphasis on an active future orientation, since it called for the creation of a new political and social system in the future. Moreover, it emphasized activity in the present to prepare the way for the establishment of an autonomous Jewish society that would fulfill national, and perhaps even social aspirations in the future. The active future orientation was particularly apparent in the ideology of the Zionist Labor movement, which included both a departure from traditions associated with the Jewish past and a pronounced accent on promoting innovations in the present to determine the shape of the future. It should be noted that within the Labor movement there were disagreements concerning the degree of emphasis on a future orientation. However, even among the more radical component of the Labor movement, a degree of ambivalence toward the past could be discerned. For example, David Ben-Gurion shared many of the sentiments of the school of thought which developed a strongly negative evaluation of Jewish existence in the Diaspora; he was a bitter opponent of Yiddish and among the early advocates of the exclusive use of Hebrew. But he frequently employed symbols drawn from the more distant Biblical past which he associated with Jewish sovereignty in the Land of Israel.[5]

It was religious Zionism that faced the most fundamental problems in confronting the issue of a future orientation. The non-Zionist ultraorthodox circles subjected religious Zionism to intense criticism, charging that it was "forcing the end" or attempting to interfere in the "divinely ordained process of history."[6] According to the traditional conception strictly adhered to by the ultraorthodox, redemption will occur only with the coming of the Messiah. The religious Zionists replied that the modern "return to Zion" was actually the "beginning" of the period of redemption mentioned in traditional sources. This mixture of modernism and Messianism notwithstanding, religious Zionists continued to urge strict observance of the traditional religious way of life; the traditional legitimation was the basis of their Zionist activity. The non-Zionist ultraorthodox circles were in a better position to perceive the inevitable contradiction between participation in a basically secular nationalist movement and consistent observance of the traditional Jewish way of life.

In any case, insofar as ideological controversies within the Zionist movement were concerned (as opposed to those between Zionism and other ideological trends within Jewry), the core of the dispute in respect to the future was not the national question, but the shape of the Jewish society in Palestine. The Labor movement was unique in its comprehensive future orientation that called both for national and social change.

The various ideological movements within Zionism also differed in their conceptions about the pace or tempo of the changes each ideology desired. The problem of the pace of change is twofold: (*a*) does an ideology call for slow or rapid change; and (*b*) is change perceived as a gradual process or as something to be accomplished by the revolutionary approach of alternating rapid radical change and slower development? A revolutionary ideology emphasizes not the "average" rate of change but the "variance" in the rate of change.

The rate of change is also related to the time range of concrete political objectives. The debate in the Zionist movement on the definition of the "final goal" of Zionism reflected these problems. The Labor movement identified with the moderate approach of Chaim Weizmann, who opposed the definition of the final goal before political conditions were sufficiently ripe, whereas the Revisionists called for immediate definition of the final goal.[7] The decision to refrain from defining the final goal implied a willingness to accept slow and gradual progress while the realization of the more far-reaching goals of Zionist colonization were deferred until a distant future time.

Adherence to a policy of selective immigration and willingness to accept a slower rate of demographic growth for the Yishuv because of the limits of the country's economic absorptive capacity were consistent with the perception of Jewish colonization as an extended and gradual process. The Labor movement shared this gradual approach with the proponents of "practical Zionism" among the Ezrahim.[8] This approach of "one more acre, one more goat" was viewed with intense aversion by the Revisionists, as they advocated rapid change and revolutionary measures. The tendency to speed up the pace of development was reflected in the ideas of "transfer" or "evacuation," which called for the rapid immigration of hundreds of thousands of Jews from Europe in the shortest possible time.[9] The desire for revolutionary action to effect immediate change of the Palestine regime was expressed in the strong emphasis the Revisionists placed on the political and legalistic aspects of international recognition of the Jewish national home. This was in effect an extension of the Herzlian concept of "charter," which implied immediate action to establish a Jewish government in Palestine even before the emergence of an economic, demographic, and ecological infrastructure.[10]

The tendency of the Labor movement to strive for a gradual realization of objectives dictated by ideology applied not only to the national political sphere but also to the social sphere. This tendency was particularly evident among members of Hapoel Hatzair, who objected to the term "socialism" mainly because it appeared to them too grandiose, and an ultimate goal relevant only to the distant future.[11] The idea of socialism could not, they felt, serve as the basis of immediate objectives of the Labor movement in Palestine. Ahdut Ha'avoda's position was more ambitious, but the major ideologists of the party, in particular Berl Katznelson and Yitzhak Tabenkin, did not welcome the slogan coined by the Labor Brigade about an all-inclusive "workers' commune." Instead Ahdut Ha'avoda adopted "constructivist socialism," which implied the creation of a socialist workers' society through the gradual construction from the ground up of a workers' economy with the aid of national capital.[12] This gradual, constructivist approach to a large extent paralleled the constructivist approach of "practical Zionism." A different approach to the problem of pace was that of the left-wing Zionist movement. Hashomer Hatzair developed the doctrine of "stages," which called for gradual constructivism in the first stage to prepare for a second stage of radical revolutionary action. This approach was criticized for urging one "to act like Ahdut Ha'avoda while speaking of the future like the left wing of the Labor Brigade."[13]

The question of the pace of development was closely related to the question of timing of initiatives in political, economic, and other spheres. The question of timing in processes of social change in general, and in modernization in developing countries in particular, is essentially the question of synchronization of differential rates of development in various spheres.[14] The accumulated experience of social change in developed as well as developing countries indicates that there is no particular social institution whose rate of development exclusively determines the rate of development in other social institutions. This experience invalidates to a considerable extent the conception of an inevitable "spillover" of economic and technological change to the sphere of political development. Predictions based on this conception —which was rooted originally in Marxism, but has had a strong impact on recent functionalist theories of modernization and European integration—proved erroneous, mainly due to lags in the rate of development in different spheres.[15] It now seems evident that the different institutional spheres do not act in conformity with the economic-technological sphere that was once perceived as the "leading sector." Newer conceptions of social change generally attribute greater importance to the persisting influence of historical traditions, political structures, and cultural factors in speeding or slowing development.

However, in the case of the Yishuv, the impact of developmental lags originating in a lack of balance between institutional spheres at the outset of the development process was limited due to the absence of rigid traditions of premodern social and political patterns of organization. Thus the pace of Jewish nation-building in Palestine was subject to a considerable degree of ideologically directed control, and the problem of synchronization could be translated into operational concepts of timing. Policy decisions and institutional initiatives could be timed according to the image of the future held by political elites.

From this perspective the most important ideological controversy focused on the question of a balanced rate of development between the political sphere and the demographic and economic spheres. The major protagonists were the "practical Zionists," who focused on immigration and settlement, and the "political Zionists," who sought above all else progress toward political autonomy in Palestine. Even within "practical Zionism" the problem of balanced development arose between the rate of demographic growth determined by immigration and the rate of economic development measured by what was termed the "economic absorptive capacity of the country." The First Immigration, identified mainly with the Lovers of Zion movement, laid the foundations of "practical Zionism" in its most extreme sense. Later expressions, such as the colonization policies of Dr. Arthur Ruppin, articulated the same conception, i.e., that the development of the Yishuv was determined primarily by economic and settlement development. The opposing idea of "political Zionism" was authored by Herzl, but its most ardent advocates were Max Nordau and Vladimir Jabotinsky. They viewed the political sphere as the "leading sector" which would prepare a short cut in economic and settlement development. Jabotinsky, therefore, refused to scale down or obscure the ultimate goals of Zionism for reasons of political timing. He rejected the contention that it was useless to make demands that were not backed up by the demographic and economic assets of the Yishuv.[16]

A conception favoring a balance between spheres of development emerged in Weizmann's "synthetic Zionism," adopted by various Zionist circles, including the majority of the Labor movement. This concept implied not only parallel political and settlement development, but also mutual reinforcement between the two spheres. Ben-Gurion's preference for balance expressed itself in his tendency to subject the timing of adopting new objectives to the requirements of political strategy. For example, he opposed raising the demand for a Jewish state in the early 1930s[17] but supported partition in 1937; formulated the Biltmore Program calling for a Jewish state in all of Palestine in 1942; and in 1946 pressed for a formula which implied a renewed acceptance of partition. The ideology of "synthetic Zionism," sensitive to the requirements of synchronization in political and settlement activities, enabled the Zionist leadership to translate national political objectives into practical imperatives aimed at the balanced construction of economic, social, and political institutions. In this way, a realistic order of priorities was created which prevented the conversion of Zionist goals into a utopia.

This approach was alien to the Revisionist spirit. The point of departure for the Revisionist leaders was the political ideal and not the realities of economics, settlement, and immigration. The Revisionists and most of the other non-Labor Zionists were also opposed to the concept of simultaneous realization of national political objectives and social objectives inherent in the ideology of constructivist socialism. They contended that the struggle over the nature of the future Jewish society in Palestine should be postponed until the national political aims of Zionism were fulfilled. Paradoxically, this position paralleled the one adopted by the "orthodox" Marxist wing of Zionism represented by the left Poalei Zion party, which maintained that the emergent Jewish society would inevitably be capitalist and the transition to socialism should be achieved in the future by means of class struggle.[18]

However, the majority in the Labor movement aspired at a synthesis between action for the good of the workers and action for the benefit of the entire Yishuv. Thus the majority adopted a conception of the synchronized development of Zionism and socialism through colonization. The adoption of this concept and the attempts at its realization gave the Labor movement a strategic advantage. The Labor movement's political strategy in internal struggles—which combined the presentation of political demands to the national center with institution-building activities and the mobilization of political support—corresponded to the strategy of "synthetic Zionism" in the external struggles of the Yishuv.

Active and Passive Perceptions of
Man-Environment Relations

The various perceptions of history and of time as a factor in social action are related to another fundamental dilemma by which we may distinguish different belief systems: the difference between active and passive perceptions of man's relation to his social and natural environment. For example, a future orientation and a perception of controllable time are both compatible with an active attitude to the environment. Zionism intrinsically possessed the active orientation implied in the basic notion of "autoemancipation," but among the ideological trends within Zionism, there were different perceptions of the range of man's freedom to change his environment and mold his future through voluntary action. The question was which social and natural limitations were perceived as obstacles to be overcome and which were perceived as permanent constraints which man cannot challenge.

The distinction between active and passive relation to the environment did not correspond with the division between left and right in the Zionist movement. Thus both the Labor movement and the Revisionists manifested a dynamic, active approach to reality, while the more conservative part of the Ezrahim manifested a more passive approach. A characteristic expression of the active approach was the attitude of the "pioneering" sector of the Yishuv to opinions and forecasts of experts who cast doubt on the ability of the Zionist movement to overcome obstacles in economic development and settlement, and later, during the War of Independence, in the military sphere as well. The standard ideological response to the pessimistic emphasis on limitations of "economic absoptive capacity" was that it was possible to overcome such obstacles by sheer will power derived from high levels of motivation and identification with collective goals. In other words, the perception inherent in the notion of "pioneering" (*halutziut*) upheld the possibility of evolving forces within man that could enable him to prevail over seemingly insurmountable obstacles.

Another expression of the faith in voluntary action was the emphasis placed on the qualitative human factor as a counterweight to the chronic shortage of resources of manpower, land, capital, and even weapons and equipment in times of war. The constant repetition of Herzl's saying "If you will it, it is no dream" became part of the indoctrination process that enabled a numerically small community of settlers—at first thousands, later tens of thousands, never exceeding several hundreds of thousands—to have faith in the ability of few pioneers to act as a vanguard preparing the way for millions. This perception was apparent in the ideology of the BILU movement[19] of the First Immigration and was revived on a wider scale at the beginning of the Second Immigration. Some of its most outstanding expressions in later periods were in the ideology of the Labor Brigade in the Labor movement and the Brit Habiryonim among the Revisionists.[20] Nevertheless, there was a difference between the Revisionist variant of activism and the "pioneering" variant of the Labor movement. The central motifs of "pioneering" were elitism, service to the collective, asceticism, and a total commitment to goals set by ideology. But the mission-orientation of the Labor movement was translated into practical objectives which resulted in tempering the romantic-utopian components of Zionist ideology. By contrast, the symbolization of "the way of glory, romance, and death"[21] and the stress on "social austerity" made it difficult for the Revisionists to institutionalize their activist approach as the Labor movement did.[22]

In the course of various ideological controversies and especially in disputes about the "skepticism of the economists," Labor movement spokesmen, notably David Ben-Gurion, argued that "there are no 'laws' of economics."[23] This argument, however, usually referred to economic laws as generalizations depicting average "utilitarian" human behavior rather than to those expressing physical limitations stemming from an absolute deficiency of resources. The preoccupation of most Labor movement leaders with raising funds and creating appropriate organizational instruments, as well as their constructivist and gradualist approach, confirms their underlying recognition that voluntarism and activism have limitations. A practical approach of this kind was much less apparent among the Revisionists, and was conspicuously lacking in the extreme romantic wing of this movement whose major spokesmen were the poet Uri Zvi Greenberg and the historian Abba Ahimeir.[24] Their inspiration was apparent in the early ideological positions of IZL and LHI.[25]

The activist aspiration directed at changing the natural and social environment was shared only in a limited sense by the non-Labor and non-Revisionist bourgeois circles in the Yishuv. For them activism implied mainly the act of immigration and settlement, and their vision of the future Jewish society in Palestine was that of a "normal" society "like all other nations."[26] This "normalizing" approach did not demand the high levels of motivation required for mobilizing human resources beyond what appeared to be the "normal" level of other societies. The emphasis these circles placed on profitability as a cardinal criterion of investment was rooted in their assumption that the human will cannot be expected to compensate for the absence of capital or for non-profitability in competitive market economy. This approach was sharply criticized by Labor movement spokesmen, who stigmatized it as "petty bourgeois" and opposed to the virtures of pioneering. A strictly passive approach to the social environment appeared only among the non-Zionist ultraorthodox of the Old Yishuv, whose extremist wing viewed any active effort to change reality as heresy. For them, activism implied confounding the will of God, or as they put it, an "affront to Heaven." The world view that guided the extreme ultraorthodox elements was that the redemption of the Jewish people must await the advent of the Messiah; any attempt to "force the end" was heretical in essence.

Faith in man's ability to change reality through voluntary action doubtless contributed to the high motivation of those groups of people mobilized in social movements, whether these were pioneering movements or underground military organizations. This ideologically and politically committed minority succeeded in influencing the behavior of the majority in two ways. First, mainly in times of crisis, this minority acted as an avant-garde that set behavioral norms for society as a whole. Second, the pioneering minority increased the over-all capacity of the collectivity by making significant contributions through their own efforts. Phrasing our conclusions in economic terms, we may say that the high marginal increment of output contributed by the pioneering minority raised the average level of output of the community at large. And indeed the achievements of the Yishuv in the economic, military, and settlement spheres exceeded the predictions of most experts. Branches of the economy considered unprofitable eventually stabilized on a solid economic basis, and in the War of Independence military forces that were deficient in manpower and equipment frequently overcame superior forces.

However, the far-reaching conclusions sometimes presented by ideologues who idealized the supposed superiority of what Arlozoroff referred to critically as a "heroic economy" (as opposed to a "rational economy") are not substantiated by analysis of the economic data.[27] Some of the achievements attributed to high motivational levels may be explained as the result of high levels of investment of resources originating outside the system. It is also evident that faith in the power of voluntarism in the economic sphere was, in certain cases, carried to such an extreme that it was responsible for such economic practices as barren investments, deficits, and bankruptcies. In attempting to place the faith in voluntarism in its proper perspective, it is appropriate to cite the American sociologist Talcott Parsons's response to Ben-Gurion's saying that there are no laws of economics: "The fact that a piece of paper floats in the air does not mean that the laws of gravity are invalid."[28]

Collectivistic and Individualistic Approaches

The activist approach shared by both the left and the nationalist radical right within the Zionist movement, implied a high level of commitment to ideological goals. Commitment was not a commitment to abstract values, but a sense of service and dedication to a collectivity. This type of commitment was expressed on two levels: on the fundamental level, the collectivity was the frame of reference of the ideology —"nation," "class," or both; on the operative level, it was the movement itself that embodied the goals and needs of the collectivity as interpreted by the movement elite. From this perspective, there arises another basic dichotomy, associated with that between activity and passivity but not identical with it: the choice of collectivism versus individualism.

The perception of the individual as a bearer of collective ideals whose commitment to these ideals makes him or her subordinate to their imperatives was characteristic of both the pioneering ideology and the ideology of the national radical right. In its own way each of these movements called on the individual to sacrifice private interests and to place him or herself at the disposal of a movement that purported to serve collective goals and interests. In the Labor movement, the individual was mobilized in the service of two collectivities, nation and class. The most extreme expression of this mobilization was the Labor Brigade, which sought to prevent the formation of group interests within the collective by advocating a general "commune" for all Jewish workers in Palestine.[29] Other collectivist movements recognized the existence of subunits to mediate between the individual and the collectivity— such as the *kibbutzim*, which accepted the authority of the movement's umbrella organization and extended aid when necessary to other subunits.[30] The ceremony in which new members were inducted into the Hagana also emphasized the idea of the subordination of the individual to the authority of the collective framework: new recruits were inducted with an oath of allegiance which stated that each member becomes a party to a covenant between himself and the organization "for life."[31]

The Revisionist ideology in particular was noted for its collectivistic emphasis. The constitution of the New Zionist Organization stated that "the mission of Zionism . . . has priority over the interests of the individual and the group and class."[32] Even more extreme was the LHI position. Its founder and leader, Abraham Stern ("Yair"),[33] wrote that "we have enlisted in the cause of our entire lives; only death can release us from the ranks."[34]

In contrast to this collectivistic approach, the ideology of the parties of the center such as the General Zionists called for building the land through private initiative and political organization on the basis of common interests, rather than subordination of collective ideals. This approach was advocated in the 1920s by the "Brandeis group" of American Zionists[35] and by the Ezrahim in the 1930s and 1940s, especially the Farmers Association and other organizations of the private economic sector. The contrast between the ideological orientations of the Ezrahim groups and those of the left and the radical right help to explain the tendency among the Ezrahim to focus their public activities on the municipal or local plane. While the left and the nationalist right adopted comprehensive nationwide symbols of collective solidarity, the frameworks of solidarity of the second- and third-generation settlers in the *moshavot* and urban neighborhoods founded in the First Immigration were mostly local units.

Thus in regard to the collectivism-individualism dichotomy, as in the case of the active-passive dichotomy, there was a greater resemblance between the Revisionists and the Labor movement than between either one of them and the non-Revisionist Ezrahim. This similarity, however, concerned primarily the intensity of the commitment of the individual to the collectivity and not the scope of this commitment. In regard to the scope of commitment there was a clear-cut difference between the Labor movement and the Revisionist movement. The ideology of Revisionism was marked by a purely political and national emphasis without the intrusion of other components, such as the socioeconomic component of socialism in the Labor movement. Therefore, Revisionism tended to restrict the individual's scope of commitment to the collective to activities designated to achieve political goals. The Labor movement, on the other hand, strove in various ways to enlarge the scope of the individual's commitment to the collective, extending it to the individual's entire way of life, including spheres of activity not directly connected with the attainment of political goals. Thus the difference between Revisionism and the Ezrahim was that while both saw allegiance to the nation as superior to any other group allegiance, the Ezrahim viewed the commitment deriving from this allegiance as much less intense.

The Labor movement, on the other hand, developed an ideology of dual commitment—to nation and to class. The two commitments were considered complementary, since it was maintained that the organized "working class" was also the nation's vanguard. Thus, the Labor movement came to be perceived as mediating between the collectivity, for whose ultimate good it strove, and the individual, who was summoned to place himself at the collective's service. Allegiance to the movement per se became increasingly important from the time Mapai sought to participate in the national center. Later, when Mapai expanded its political recruitment and sought support among middle-class circles and professionals, allegiance to the movement tended to become in itself a criterion of affiliation to the pioneering sector of the Yishuv, which led to a partial shift in the meaning of pioneering roles. While at the outset these roles were perceived as open to all who wished to contribute to the common effort, with the institutionalization of the movement there was an increasing tendency to condition access to these roles (which conferred elite status on their occupants) on allegiance to the movement, so that membership in some movement umbrella organization became an almost essential requirement for occupying roles that were defined as "pioneering." In sociological terms, the shift was one from a pure universalistic achievement orientation to an orientation containing ascriptive-particularistic elements.

Territorial Boundaries and National Identity

As we have seen above, the definition of the relation of the individual to particularistic collectivities within the over-all national collectivity was a subject of controversy in the Yishuv. A firm consensus existed, however, concerning the commitment of the individual to the national collectivity, at least as far as the Zionist parties were concerned. The

question then arose as to how it was possible to maintain commitment
to a national collectivity whose territorial boundaries were not clearly
defined. The serious implications of this question are clear when we
recall that from its inception one of the points of departure for Zionist
ideology was the existence of a bond between a nation and its territory.
The Zionist movement was constantly engaged in disputes with movements advocating Jewish autonomy in the Diaspora over the possibility
of maintaining the autonomous institutional existence of a minority
group in societies which have become secularized in the wake of the
industrial and national revolutions.[36] Another controversy occurred with
the territorialist movement, which advocated a Jewish territorial concentration but not necessarily in the Land of Israel. Zionism responded
with fundamental arguments concerning the bond between the Jewish
people and the Land of Israel and operational arguments to the effect
that it would not be possible to attract Jews to a land other than Israel.[37]
The efforts to create a territorial concentration and a sovereign Jewish
society in the Land of Israel did not solve the ideological problem of
defining the territorial boundaries of the national collectivity while this
process was going on. Moreover, the concept of the unity of the Jewish
people itself implied a nonterritorial definition of the boundaries of the
collectivity.

This contradiction between the efforts to create an identity between
nationality and territory and the recognition of the existence of a nation
without a territory led to the emergence of several ideological trends
that claimed that a new "Hebrew" nation was coming into being in the
Land of Israel that was not identical with the Jewish nation in the
Diaspora. Such a trend was the "Canaanite" movement, a marginal
group whose literary and cultural impact was far more extensive than
its political impact.

A problem no less critical in the fundamental sense and with more
far-reaching implications in the operative sense was the existence of
two national communities in Palestine. The problem of the existence
of the Arab majority in Palestine became a dispute over the limits of
territorial flexibility in regard to the fulfillment of Zionist goals. Until
the idea of partition was broached in the 1930s, the territorial dispersion
of Zionist settlement was determined by economic and other considerations related to the availability of land and not to the problem of determining the future borders of a Jewish state, the establishment of which
was not deemed possible in the near future. Only in 1937 when the
idea of partition was raised did the issue of territorial flexibility of

Zionism become an actual controversy, with two alternatives: *more sovereignty in less territory, or more territory at the cost of sovereignty.*

In the controversy over territorial flexibility four positions crystallized. The fundamentalist position advocated full Jewish sovereignty in the "Land of Israel" on both sides of the Jordan River. This position rested mainly on the conception that the Jewish people's historical and religious rights to the "heritage of their fathers" were incontrovertible. Support for this position came mainly from the Revisionists and the Mizrahi, but it had some support in the Labor movement as well.[38] The second position, which was the province of a minority in the Zionist movement, preferred a large territorial framework rather than exclusive Jewish sovereignty. This position, known as "binationalism," was first upheld by Brit Shalom,[39] and later received its most important support from Hashomer Hatzair. The third position, which was advocated by Weizmann and Ben-Gurion in 1937, and ultimately adopted by the Zionist Organization in 1946, accepted territorial limitations on Zionist goals, at least temporarily, in order to establish a sovereign Jewish state in a part of Palestine. The supporters of this position did not entirely deny the bond between the Jewish people and the Land of Israel, but advocated flexibility in the operative goals of Zionism—at least in the short run.[40] The fourth position sought to postpone the decision on this ideological dilemma to a later time in order to permit the quantitative growth of the Yishuv to the point where a Jewish majority would exist in all of Palestine. The major political implication of this position was a perpetuation of foreign rule in Palestine until the Jews became a majority. Supporters of this position were found both in the Labor movement and among the Ezrahim.

The debate continued as long as the leadership of the Zionist movement could avoid making a final decision. However, in facing the United Nations debates of 1947, the Zionist movement could no longer evade a decision on the territorial dilemma—and it opted for partition. In the final analysis, after the establishment of the state and the flight of most of the Arab population, what emerged was a Jewish nation-state in a part of the Land of Israel.

The Ideological Debate

The intensive ideological activity in the Zionist movement involved a wide variety of issues, but a small number of master issues can be isolated: the national question; the social question, which centered on the nature of the desired social order; the question of democracy and political pluralism; and the status of religion in society.

Positions on these substantive issues can be classified according to three patterns. The first pattern is the single-issue ideology, which emphasizes one central issue. The second is the multi-issue ideology, which formulates a position on each substantive issue separately, so that a position on one issue is not necessarily connected to positions taken on other substantive issues. The third pattern is the comprehensive ideology, in which issues are treated and positions defined from the perspective of a uniform world view reflecting the pursuit of ideological coherence.

The tendency to construct comprehensive ideologies was most apparent in the Marxist wing of the Zionist movement. But this ideological trend encountered difficulties when it attempted to include its position on the national question in the comprehensive ideological framework of Marxism. In order to do this, Marxist Zionists relied on an interpretation of the national question that differed from the prevailing doctrines of "orthodox" Marxism. Hashomer Hatzair, for example, developed the formula of a "synthesis" between Zionism and "revolutionary socialism."[41] In adopting this position, they rejected the Communists' monistic approach, the cause of their negative attitude toward Zionist ideology.[42]

The extreme ultraorthodox groups outside the organized *Yishuv* also possessed a comprehensive ideology. These groups adopted the principle of deciding all issues on the basis of *halacha* (the Jewish religious law) as interpreted by their rabbinical leaders. The Agudat Israel party even institutionalized this practice by creating a body called the Council of Sages. As their political and ideological activity was also concentrated on the religious issue, Hamizrahi and Hapoel Hamizrahi were often vague on nonreligious issues because they were reluctant to depart entirely from the Zionist consensus by forming a distinctive view on issues other than the status of religion. Their political behavior thus resembled at times that of a single-issue party.

The party closest to a "pure" single-issue pattern was the Revisionist party. Jabotinsky, the Revisionist leader, described the tendency of his movement to deal only with the national issue while leaving decisions on other issues to the future as adherence to "one flag" only. Thus he rejected any ideological commitment beyond the nationalist one.[43]

The most typical representative of the multi-issue pattern was Mapai. Mapai had a broad ideological platform which dealt with the four major substantive issues mentioned above, though in respect to some of them its ideological formulations were vague or changed over the years. Since Mapai's ideological approach was related to its pragmatic and constructivist tendencies, its positions on the social and national issues were of a moderate-center nature. On every issue except one—the conception of the Jewish worker as the dominant element in the Zionist movement—Mapai's position was closer to the center of the spectrum of political opinion than to its extremes. A similar approach characterized a large part of the Ezrahim, which from their liberal standpoint strove for conciliation and cooperation between movements possessing different approaches to the problems of social order and religion. Like Mapai, the parties of the center and moderate right possessed distinctive positions of their own on each of the major substantive issues. They shunned the tendency to integrate these positions into an internally consistent ideological doctrine even more than did Mapai.

The "National Question"

Among the central issues of ideological debate in the Yishuv, the national question was particularly salient. The New Yishuv was a product of Zionist ideology and, except for the Communists, Canaanites, and the ultraorthodox, this ideology formed the common value basis of the entire Yishuv. The existence of a considerable degree of consensus concerning the final goal did not however prevent dispute over whether it was better to emphasize this by making it an explicit demand, or to soft-pedal it while concentrating on middle-range Zionist demands. The disputes concerned differences of approach on the operative rather than fundamental level. Yet, over the years, the debates on middle-range goals produced a feedback which eventually influenced, at least to some extent, the formulation of the ultimate goal.

The main source of both controversy and ideological change was the need to respond to what was called "the Arab problem." Since the basic premise of Zionist ideology was the desire to create a sovereign Jewish society in Palestine, at first the presence of the Arab population was perceived mainly as an obstacle to the fulfillment of Zionist goals which ought to be dealt with primarily on the operative level. But when the conflict with the Arab national movement and its "Palestinian" offshoot focused on the issue of rights to Palestine, the question of the Arab population was raised over and over again on the fundamental level as well. Even so, the overwhelming majority of the movement continued to believe in a distinction between the "right" of the Jewish people as a whole to Palestine and the "rights" of the Arab residents in Palestine.[44]

Two opposing evaluations of the Zionist response to the Arab problem are offered by students of the history of the Yishuv and the Zionist movement. According to one interpretation, there was a tendency among the founding fathers of the Yishuv to suppress the question, albeit not to the extreme of some of the early Zionist thinkers, such as Israel Zangwill, who spoke of "a land without a people for a people without a land."[45] In contrast to this interpretation, there is incontrovertible evidence that from the early period of Zionist settlement, the Arab question arose constantly in debates, which indicates that there was a clear awareness of its implications for the realization of the Zionist idea.[46] These two interpretations can be reconciled if we keep in mind the distinction between fundamental and operative ideology. On the fundamental level there was a tendency, at least until the late 1920s, to pay little attention to the question because it was perceived mainly as a constraint on the operative level. Thus, the debate in this period on issues associated with the "Arab problem" was almost entirely operative. The first organized expression of a revised treatment of the Arab question on the fundamental level was the appearance of the Brit Shalom group. The unique character of this group was its readiness to see the conflict in terms of two *subjective* claims or rights.

It is possible to indicate different levels of perception of the Arab-Jewish conflict in the development of Zionist ideology. The lowest level was the common perception at the turn of the century (before the rise of the organized Arab national movement) which treated the question as an essentially social problem on the local level and did not consider the Arabs a political community.[47] The next level of perception recognized the Arabs as a social entity with a political will of their own, but saw the nationalistic anti-Zionist stance as a distortion of the Arabs' true self-interest. This perception interpreted the Arab position as the outcome of intrigues fostered by British imperialism or incitement by the *effendi* class. This perception was widespread in the Labor movement mainly during the 1920s and thereafter in the Marxist wing of the Labor movement.[48]

The riots of 1929 and the revolt of 1936–39 strengthened a third level of perception about the Arabs, which was in many respects close to the Revisionist position. According to this view there was an inevitable confrontation between two national movements in Palestine and only the slightest chance for a peaceful resolution of the conflict. The Arabs were thus perceived as an opponent in a "zero-sum game," i.e., a contest in which gain for one side implies loss for the other. Jabotinsky gave a concise expression of this perception when he said that "any group of native-born, whether backward or cultured, sees its land as its own 'national home' in which it wishes to live and to remain the sole masters; such a nation will not voluntarily accept new masters nor will they accept any form of joint ownership."[49] The proponents of this opinion in the Labor movement were less explicit than Jabotinsky. They were aware of the contradiction between the national awakening among the Arabs and the Zionists' desire, out of ideological and social motives, to reach a modus vivendi with the Arabs as individuals. However, as long as the conflict continued to occupy center stage, the majority of the Labor movement sided with those who refused to condition Zionist activity on Arab consent, as Ben-Gurion had said: "We have come here and will continue to come here with or without a Jewish-Arab agreement on the matter."[50]

On the fourth level we discern the influence of the feedback effect from the operative aspects of the Arab problem onto the fundamental dimension of Zionist ideology. This approach was first expressed in the idea of the binational state, as for example in the words of Dr. Arthur Ruppin (a member of Brit Shalom) before the Zionist Congress of 1929: "We seek to rid ourselves of the mistaken notion that has ruled Europe for a hundred years and has caused a world war, to wit that a state can contain only one nation."[51] The perception of the conflict as a conflict between two rights found indirect expression in the readiness to accept the idea of partition. There were leaders, such as Ben-Gurion, who at first saw partition as one stage in the process of the ultimate fulfillment of Zionist goals in their entirety; yet a new perception began to crystallize that saw partition as a form of compromise between two just claims. The tendency to perceive the Arabs not as an object of Zionist activity but as subjects with legitimate claims of their own was apparent in Weizmann's speech before the Anglo-American Enquiry Commission in which he defined Zionist demands as "to move on the line of least injustice."[52]

The only element in the Yishuv that took an unequivocal position in relation to the Arab-Jewish conflict on both the fundamental and the operative levels was the Revisionist movement, which sought a one-sided resolution of the conflict through either force or British support. The Labor movement, the religious parties, and the General Zionists continued to grapple with the Arab question, with frequent differences of opinion occurring within these parties, as for example on partition, and with leading figures in these parties, such as Ben-Gurion, occasionally changing positions.[53]

Differences between moderates and extremists were also quite definite in positions adopted toward the British. Here there were no fundamental differences in approach, except between the LHI and the Communists on the one hand, and all the other movements on the other. The LHI and the Communists viewed Britain as an enemy because it was an imperialist ruler, while the parties of the organized Yishuv, the Revisionists, and even the IZL did not reject the British Mandate in principle, so long as its goals were compatible with Zionist goals (thus, the White Paper of 1939 was considered a betrayal of the Balfour Declaration by the British government). This approach was challenged by the LHI during World War II. Its leaders saw the British as an "enemy" and the Germans only as a "persecutor"; they not only insisted on continuing the struggle against the British, but also sought ways to establish contacts with the Axis Powers. Later, during the period of the postwar "struggle" against the British, the debate in the Yishuv and the Zionist movement took the form of a dispute between "activists" and "antiactivists" and revolved around issues of tactics and strategy, those groups who took a moderate stand on the Arab question adopting a less activist approach in relations with the British and vice versa.[54]

The "Social Question"

The point of departure for ideological debate in the social sphere was different from the departure point in the controversy over the national question. There was not even a basic consensus on the need to pursue a definitive ideological answer to the question of the desired social structure of Jewish society of the future. Among the Ezrahim and (even more) among the Revisionists, there was a tendency to deny the relevance of ideological debate over the nature of the ideal social order during the process of political realization of Zionism.[55] The dominant ideology on the Zionist left, however, stressed the mutual dependence between realizing Zionism and laying the foundation for a new and "just" society. This controversy was related to another about the place of class struggle in the Yishuv. Revisionism, for example, connected its opposition to the socialist ideology of the Labor movement with negation of the idea of class struggle. Jabotinsky described the use of the class struggle as a means to attain an equilibrium between wages and profits as "simply unthinkable since it is something that will destroy the Zionist enterprise."[56] This approach was further expressed in the efforts of the Revisionists to undermine the authority of the Histadrut, as when Jabotinsky published an inflammatory article calling on the workers to break strikes organized by the Histadrut.[57]

The issue of class struggle was also a subject of controversy in the Labor movement itself, even though most parties within the movement shared a common desire to combine the colonization process with an attempt to create a society based on equality in which organized workers would have a position of hegemony. While the extreme left—the Communists and Poalei Zion Smol—stressed the class struggle as the main path to the attainment of socialism, Mapai chose "constructivist socialism," although it did not abandon the trade union struggle as an expression of class conflict in a society where a private economic sector existed alongside the workers' sector. The experience of the Labor movement in the 1920s convinced the Mapai leaders that the controversies on the fundamental level over communism, socialism, and the class struggle, were irrelevant to the operative poblems faced by the workers in Palestine because the major problem was the creation of adequate conditions for the development of a Jewish working class.

This idea was formulated with great clarity by Chaim Arlozoroff, the brilliant young leader of the Labor movement who was assassinated in 1934. Arlozoroff contended that the three aspects of the class struggle —the political struggle for power, the social struggle over the prestige and a way of life, and the economic aspects of income distribution— did not apply in the social framework of the Yishuv. The struggle for power had no meaning in a binational society under colonial rule. The prestige aspect was irrelevant because the recognition in Zionist ideology of the need for productivization of the Jewish people and for transition to manual labor was sufficient to assure the prestige and status of the Jewish worker. The economic aspect was irrelevant because the tasks of social construction were based on external capital, in particular national capital, and this fact removed one of the class struggle's most potent motives, a redistribution of national income.[58] Even though

Mapai did not formally adopt Arlozoroff's theses in a literal sense, both Berl Katznelson's conception of "constructivist socialism" and Ben-Gurion's strategy of "from class to nation" were based on similar assumptions. Constructivism was predicated on the possibility of constructing an autonomous workers' economy by means of national capital raised through the national funds, while the strategy of "from class to nation" was based on the assumption that controlling the distribution of imported economic resources through the national institutions would do more to determine the workers' share of the national income than a class struggle or even a trade union struggle in the private economic sector.

The adoption of the "from class to nation" strategy resulted in a paradoxical shift in positions between the right and the left. In the 1920s the left was militant while the right and the center assumed a more conciliatory stance toward the workers. This posture stemmed from a mixture of paternalism and acceptance of the Zionist ideal of "productivization." In the 1930s, however, Mapai became increasingly moderate as it consolidated its leading position in the national center, while the right became more militant. This tendency was expressed in the strengthening of the Revisionist movement and radicalization of its position toward the Histadrut and the Labor movement. The shift between left and right in extent of radicalization created a situation where the positions that were dominant in the 1920s in each sector became the province of minorities. Within the Labor movement, Hashom er Hatzair became the major opposition group, stressing that "with the increasing development of the country, class conflicts will become more prominent while national solidarity will steadily diminish."[59] Among the non-Labor Zionists, Weizmann and the "A" General Zionists continued to view the workers' sector as a pioneer in the building of the country.

To the extent that debate on the "social question" centered on the issue of ownership of the means of production, a common approach crystallized among the moderate wings of both the socialist and the nonsocialist camps. This was the acceptance of a pluralistic economy in which a private sector established with private capital and initiative would exist alongside a workers' sector composed of Histadrut-owned enterprises and cooperatives of all types including the settlement movements affiliated to the Histadrut.[60] Besides the private and the Histadrut sectors, there was also a public sector in the Yishuv which included companies wholly or partially owned by the national institutions.

The prevailing support in the Labor movement for building a new society and a national home through the creation of a workers' economy caused a series of ideological disputes connected with the economic and social organization of that economy. The first centered on the choice between different organizational principles for the workers' economy: the cooperative system versus the administrative system. The "administrative system" referred to economic enterprises owned by the Histadrut or one of its subsidiaries whose managers were appointed by the central institutions of the Histadrut and whose workers were actually wage-earners whose position regarding control of the enterprise was no different from that of other Histadrut members who worked in the private or public sector. Under the cooperative system, on the other hand, the workers of an enterprise owned the means of production or leased them, in the case of land. The advantages of the administrative system were that the enterprises could be directed to serve the general interest and that the large scale of these enterprises permitted a more rational use of resources. On the other hand, there were those who argued that this system would eventually degenerate into "bureaucratism." The major advantage of the cooperative system was said to be the greater motivation and involvement of the workers, while a counter argument was raised that the cooperative system would create a tendency for the small units to attempt to free themselves from the control of the community. The position eventually adopted by the Labor movement permitted the parallel existence of both systems.

The second ideological dispute pertained only to the cooperative system and focused on the extent of cooperation in ownership and consumption in cooperative frameworks as a whole and in the Labor movement settlements in particular. Three organizational patterns prevailed in communal agricultural settlements: the *kibbutz* (and *kevutza*), the *moshav*, and the *moshav shitufi*. The issue was primarily between the first two, which were the dominant patterns. While the *kibbutz* embodied the maximum level of cooperation in production as well as consumption, the *moshav* was based on individual or family consumption with only very limited cooperation in production. The orientation of the *moshav* to the ideology of the Labor movement was expressed mainly in adherence to the idea of self-labor, and cooperation was confined almost entirely to marketing. Advocates of the *kibbutz* approach saw it as a higher level of fulfillment of socialist ideals, a more efficient instrument for the performance of pioneering tasks, and a more rational system of work organization. Partisans of the *moshav*, on the other hand, argued that the latter gave more freedom to the individual, increased the motivation to work, and strengthened the family unit— in this case the nuclear family—not only in the spheres of consumption and socialization but also in the sphere of production.[61] The wide gap between these two forms of settlement would seem to call for an intermediate type based on full cooperation in the sphere of production with consumption based on the individual and family unit, and indeed the *moshav shitufi* developed from the other two patterns, but the number of these settlements remained small. It is characteristic of the "constructivist" orientation of the workers' economy that a fourth possible type of cooperative framework did not take root in the Labor movement, the idea of "communes" based on full cooperation in consumption with the income of the group derived from the earnings of members working outside the communal framework. The Labor Brigade adopted this system in part but eventually disbanded, and subsequent efforts to establish urban "communes" on a permanent basis failed.

The third ideological dispute concerned equality of rewards. At the outset the *moshav* did not establish equality in income and consumption, but rather limited it to equality of opportunity in respect to the amount of land allotted to each family and the size of the initial investment in equipment, seed, and so on. Inequality stemming from differential productivity of units of production was recognized as legitimate. The *kibbutz*, on the other hand, instituted full equality between members in respect to economic and other instrumental rewards. Efforts were made to reduce inequality of symbolic rewards, such as prestige, by instituting the principle of rotation among occupational and administrative positions. But these attempts contradicted the need for specialization that eventually became more important as the economy and the means of production reached a higher level of development.

The fourth dispute concerned the ideal size of the socioeconomic unit, and had two facets. In the twenties, the Labor Brigade called for the creation of a "general commune" to encompass all Jewish workers in Palestine and abolish inequality not only within units of production (such as the *kibbutz*) but also between units of production. The debate on this issue ended with the disintegration of the Labor Brigade in the mid-twenties. Debate persisted, however, concerning the desired size of the communal socioeconomic unit. The advocates of large units (the "large *kibbutz*") based their arguments on economic efficiency and greater absorptive capacity, while the advocates of small units (the "small *kevutza*") emphasized the more favorable setting for interpersonal relations that would result from a smaller, more intimate group.

The Question of Democracy

A high level of ideological commitment is apt to create a favorable climate for ideological fanaticism, particularly when the ideologies concerned are radical. Adherents of radical ideologies are inclined to present their doctrines of a priori truths and to depict their rivals' doctrines as the embodiment of iniquity and falsehood. But in a political system whose center lacked the sanctions available to a sovereign state, the only possibility for creating effective political institutions lay in the willingness of all parties to establish a pluralistic political structure based on compromise. In these conditions the issue of democracy posed both an ideological and an institutional challenge to the political movements in the Yishuv. Ideological radicalism of one kind or another was characteristic of some of the Labor movement and of the Revisionist nationalist right wing and the underground military organizations which emerged from it. Within the Labor movement the first step toward pluralism was the founding of the Histadrut. It involved a compromise between the totalistic orientation of Ahdut Ha'avoda, which sought to concentrate all the functions of the parties in the Histadrut, and the desire of the minority, headed by Hapoel Hatzair, to maintain a degree of autonomy for the various political parties of the movement. Thus, Ahdut Ha'avoda abandoned its original position and came to accept political pluralism within the Histadrut,[62] while Hapoel Hatzair complied with the idea that the Histadrut would not confine itself to purely instrumental functions. Hapoel Hatzair, however, favored the coexistence of various political and ideological trends and opposed the application of the principle of majority rule, referring to it as "majoritarianism."[63] In contrast, Ahdut Ha'avoda called for the creation of centralized institutions as the "true" expression of the concentrated will of the collectivity.

In the 1930s, as the Labor movement became increasingly integrated into the institutional frameworks of the Yishuv and the Zionist movement, there was a greater tendency within Mapai to assume a more explicit ideological stance favoring pluralistic democracy. However, the acceptance of a pluralistic political structure and democratic procedure and the emphasis on the principle of "one man, one vote" were primarily products of operative considerations, rather than of fundamental beliefs. Even by the 1940s, there remained on the fundamental level a strong residue of belief in the movement's right to resort to coercion when necessary to realize its goals, as Ben-Gurion had said: "I would not hesitate to employ coercion to realize the goals of Zionism or socialism, but there is no way for us to compel either the Yishuv or the Jewish people. We must find the way through men's hearts . . . and through agreement."[64] The conception of democracy held by the Labor movement was therefore not based on unconditional compliance with democratic "rules of the game."

As Mapai became more willing to recognize the legitimacy of political pluralism, opposition, and the presence of conflict, the opposite occurred in Hashomer Hatzair, which changed from a nonpolitical youth movement into the major spokesman of the Marxist left in the Labor Zionist camp. Hashomer Hatzair continued to participate in the institutional frameworks of the Yishuv and the Zionist movement, as well as the Histadrut; its totalistic tendencies were turned inward. The outcome was the concept of "ideological collectivism," which rejected political and ideological divisions within what was seen as the "organic" entity of its *kibbutz* movement.[65] The "doctrine of stages" developed by Hashomer Hatzair enabled it to accept democratic rules of the game within the national movement and its political institutions while the political goals of Zionism were in the process of realization. The "dictatorship of the proletariat" and all this implied for political conflict would be postponed until Zionism had achieved its political goals, when the class struggle would become the dominant factor in political life.

For the Revisionists, the question of democracy was expressed in the problem of the role of leadership. This problem was twofold. On one hand, the movement itself was perceived as a kind of political order or fraternity, based on a quasi-military discipline. On the other, in regard to the Zionist movement as a whole, the Revisionists felt that their kind of radical nationalism qualified them for exclusive leadership of the Jewish national movement. Thus, one may detect certain anti-democratic overtones in Revisionism characteristic of the European radical right in the interwar period. This tone led Labor movement spokesmen to identify Revisionism as an expression of fascism.[66] The leadership principle was indeed explicit in the code of the Revisionist youth movement, Betar, which stated that "discipline implies the submission of the masses to the authority of a leader."[67] Jabotinsky himself remained a liberal with elitist leanings who believed that leadership should mobilize the will of the masses, not through coercion, but in the manner of a "conductor who is entrusted in good faith with the command of an orchestra."[68] The antidemocratic tone was expressed by the ideological mentor of the radical Brit Habiryonim, who stated flatly that a "harmonious" society dedicated to a particular ideal does not feel the absence of freedom just as the healthy person does not notice the presence of the air he breathes and does not uphold unrestricted freedom of speech.[69] The lack of clarity within Revisionism in respect to democracy continued to be reflected within the military organizations that emerged from Revisionism, the IZL and the LHI. LHI's approach was based on denial of the democratic principle of majority rule and substitution of a revolutionary right which would be free of any conventional restraints.[70] The IZL too was prepared to defy the will of the majority during a period of nationalist struggle, but justified this mainly on the grounds that the national institutions operated on a voluntary basis. This problem arose once again in the period of transition from Yishuv to state, when Menachem Begin decided, contrary to the opinion of some of his close associates, in favor of limiting IZL activity, after the establishment of a sovereign Jewish state, to legitimate political opposition according to democratic "rules of the game."[71]

Unlike the Revisionists and the Labor movement, the parties of the center and the moderate right were free of the radicalism that made it difficult to cooperate with other parties in the framework of common institutions. However, while all the Ezrahim accepted the liberal principle of political and ideological pluralism, there were some groups among them which did not accept the principle of democratic representation according to the formula of one man, one vote. The spokesmen for part of the Ezrahim sector, particularly the leaders of the farmers of the *moshavot*, sought to create political institutions based on group representation that would reflect "qualitative" as well as quantitative considerations. Moshe Smilansky, a leader of the *moshavot* farmers, expressed the view of this group when he argued that a way should be found "to take into account not only the ballot cast by the voter but also the weight of his contribution to society." Smilansky also expressed a preference for bargaining and compromise over strict majority decision: "why should we choose to defeat instead of to persuade?"[72] he asked, expressing a position compatible with the pattern of consociational democracy.

We see, then, that the democratic element in the ideologies of most movements within the Yishuv was mainly on the operative level, while on the fundamental level most parties carried traces of a predemocratic or even undemocratic position. On the operational level, the parties were facing the problem of how to combine coalescent politics based on mutual cooperation and compromise with a desire to make a decisive impact on the shape of society as a whole. In trying to solve this problem, the Zionist Labor parties adopted the formula of "hegemony" of the Labor movement in the Yishuv. This formula served to justify the efforts of the Labor movement to attain the key positions within political institutions while preserving their coalitionary structure.

The Status of Religion

The capacity of the political system of the Yishuv to exist as a pluralistic system was tested over the issue of religion and its role in the evolving Jewish society in Palestine. In spite of the identity between religion and nationality in Judaism, which received legal expression in the organization of the Yishuv as a religious community, the overwhelming majority of the Zionist movement was secular. Moreover, the ideologies of some of the groups within Zionism in general and the Zionist Labor movement in particular, had distinctly anticlerical overtones. These trends were the combined result of a socialist outlook and a negative attitude to the traditional Jewish way of life in the Diaspora. Even those secular ideological currents that did not wish to sever all ties with Jewish tradition found it impossible to make their ideology consistent with a religious world view—on the fundamental level, at any rate.

The point of departure of religious Zionism, which distinguished it from Agudat Israel, was the perception of the return of the Jewish people to its homeland as an act of religious significance.[73] In this sense there was more to the approach of religious Zionism than the desire to establish a society that lived according to the halacha. However, religious Zionism, as opposed to its secular counterparts, held, that a religious world view does not allow an authority higher than the *halacha*, which meant that acceptance of any political authority would remain conditional. Religious Zionism faced the difficulty of striving to obtain autonomy for the religious sector of the community and to create the optimal conditions for the observance of the *halacha* by individuals, while at the same time seeking to impose a religious character on the public life of the Yishuv as a whole. Religious Zionism chose to give priority to the second goal, thus distinguishing itself from Agudat Israel and the extreme ultraorthodox who tended to concentrate on developing a religious way of life for their own closed circles.

The issue of religion and its place in the political system did not assume high operative significance in the period of the Yishuv, since the absence of sovereignty relieved Zionism and the organized Yishuv of the need to reach decisions on most of the problems connected with the social role of religion. The existence of an external non-Jewish authority that recognized religious pluralism was a convenient arrangement. The legal framework of the Mandate provided positive institutional autonomy for the Jewish community in the religious sphere, expressed mainly in the assignment of all matters connected with personal status to the jurisdiction of the religious courts. This system was supported by the overwhelming majority of the Jewish community, who saw it as a factor strengthening the autonomy of Knesset Israel. The binational nature of Mandatory Palestine reduced to a minimum the possibilities of religious legislation in matters other than personal status.

The absence of a sovereign political framework meant, therefore, that the ideological conflicts over the status of religion on the fundamental level were expressed only partially on the operative level. In the Labor movement, for example, opposing opinions on the religious question never reached the stage of open confrontation since they were not connected with the actual political issues of the day. However, Labor leaders often voiced different opinions on the religious issues. While Berl Katznelson maintained that "a generation that creates and innovates does not throw the heritage of previous generations on the rubbish heap . . . but may keep the tradition by adding to it,"[74] other Labor leaders who received their political education in the Marxist atmosphere of Russian socialism tended to adopt militantly anticlerical positions. A variety of approaches to religion also characterized the Revisionist movement. Though Jabotinsky's opinions were thoroughly secularist and he was willing to accept only the national and social aspects of the Jewish

tradition,[75] there were others in his movement who possessed a religious
outlook, and some of them were even observant. There was a common
ideological tendency among parts of the Labor movement and the Revisionists to secularize certain symbols derived originally from the religious conceptions of Messianism and redemption and to fit them into
a nonreligious world view. This approach was characteristic of Ben-
Gurion in the Labor movement[76] and Abba Ahimeir of the radical
Revisionists. The latter, for example, spoke on the one hand of the
"spiritual health" of a "harmonious religious society," and on the other
of "Zionism that in its most basic sense is a secular antitheological
phenomenon."[77] Similar differences in approach to the question of religion and tradition were present among the General Zionists and other
Ezrahim groups, though the question of religion was not the center of
their ideological concern.

Universal and Jewish Ideological Influences

The variety and complexity of ideological positions in the Yishuv
and the intensity with which ideological debate was conducted were
to a large extent products of the intellectual climate in the Diaspora in
which Zionism arose and developed. The Jewish society in Europe of
the late nineteenth and early twentieth centuries had been exposed for
at least several decades to the intense influence of ideologies and trends
of thought from the non-Jewish environment. This was a period of
widespread political and ideological ferment, particularly in the areas
in which Zionism emerged—Central and Eastern Europe. Thus both
from a chronological and geographical point of view, Zionism began
at a crossroads where ideological and political movements met and
clashed within the Jewish society and the wider society of which it was
a part. The ideologies that animated political movements in Europe
served as a source of ideas and models for the ideologies emergent in
European Jewish society of the nineteenth century. Indeed, nearly all
of the important ideologies in the non-Jewish environment found a
parallel in Jewish society or the Zionist movement, with a stress on the
particular Jewish aspect for interpretation of these conceptions.

The first ideological model with a wide impact on Jewish society was
modern nationalism.[78] This model provided a common denominator not
only for the various brands of Zionist ideology, but also for the territorialist and autonomist trends within Jewish society. The influence of

non-Jewish nationalist movements was selective and differential; for example, the Revisionist political and ideological style was most heavily influenced by the Polish national movement and the Italian *risorgimento*.[79] The Zionist Labor movement, on the other hand, attempted to find its way to a conception of nationalism through the maze of current definitions among the left of Central and Eastern Europe. Its Marxist wing adopted a conception of Jewish nationalism based on the teachings of the Marxist-Zionist thinker, Dov Ber Borochov.[80] The nationality problems of the multinational Austro-Hungarian Empire influenced the development of Zionism, if only for the fact that many of the founders of the World Zionist Organization, chief among them Theodor Herzl and Max Nordau, were citizens of Austria-Hungry. In Eastern Europe, however, populist influences were more prevalent. Many Eastern European Zionists regarded ties to the land, to territory, as the key to nationality. This approach was reflected in the philosophy of the founders of Hovevei Zion, the most prominent of whom was the philosopher and author of "Autoemancipation," Dr. Leon Pinsker.[81] Later this approach was apparent in the stress placed on "redeeming the land," a motif that appeared in the Labor movement as well as among non-socialists from Eastern Europe, such as Menahem Ussishkin. In contrast, the conception of nationalism of Ahad Ha'am (the pseudonym of Asher Ginsberg)[82] was drawn, despite his Eastern-European origins, from Western European and especially English sources, evident in the special emphasis he placed on the cultural dimensions of national identity.

The second ideological model that had a deep impact on the Zionist movement was socialism. Marxian socialism in its two main variants—revolutionary and reformist— was reflected in the ideology of the non-Zionist Bund and the Zionist Poalei Zion at the turn of the century. It is also characteristic that the split in the international socialist movement after World War I between the reformist social-democratic wing and the "orthodox" revolutionary wing was replicated subsequently in a split in the Poalei Zion movement. The doctrinaire character of "orthodox" communist Marxist and the anti-Zionist attitudes of its leading exponents considerably weakened its Zionist parallel, and the majority of Poalei Zion and its affiliated party in Palestine, Ahdut Ha'avoda, gradually adopted a moderate social democratic interpretation of socialism. Ahdut Ha'avoda later adopted the concept of constructivist socialism shared by the other major workers' party, Hapoel Hatzair, whose inspiration was not Marxian socialism, but populist socialism.[83]

Populism, in its Eastern European version, was the third major ideological movement to influence Zionism. The populism of the social revolutionaries[84] and the "Narodnaya Volya"[85] which preceded them inspired the goal of skipping the stage of capitalist development in creating a productive workers' society in Palestine based on agricultural cooperatives. The social revolutionaries' influence was also felt in the ideals of voluntarism, personal example, and service to the collectivity integrated into the conception of "pioneering" (*halutziut*). From this point of view, the development of Hashomer Hatzair in the Labor movement in Palestine was exceptional, since at its outset it was closer to the populist approach and to Hapoel Hatzair, while later in the twenties it adopted a Marxist position closer to the intermediate groups between the social-democratic Second International and the communist Third International.

The fourth ideological model, which shared some traits with populism and which also influenced movements within Zionism, was a right-wing radicalism rooted in historical romanticism. The link with populism was the common feeling of revulsion and rejection of modern capitalism and its cultural side effects, such as the alienation from nature and the soil. In contrast to the socialist populism of East Europe, the radical right emphasized the racial and communal bases of the national collectivity and was more amenable to elitist sentiments. This ideological model influenced a trend within Revisionism whose major spokesmen were the historian Abba Ahimeir and the poet Uri Zvi Greenberg; there was an affinity between Brit Habiryonim and the European radical right, including its fascist offspring.[86] The racist elements of the radical right, which became sharply anti-Semitic with the rise of the Nazi movement, increasingly led Zionists to reject the romantic nationalist conception. Even so, traces of this ideology continued to appear in the poetry of Uri Zvi Greenberg, in the initial ideological concepts of the LHI, and in the "Canaanite" teachings of the poet Yonathan Ratosh.

A fifth ideological model that had a wide, although differential, influence on movements within Zionism was liberalism. Its impact was greatest in the English-speaking countries and in Central Europe, but thinkers such as Ahad Ha'am also drew some inspiration from it.

Besides the ideological models that originated in the non-Jewish world, intellectual and cultural currents within Judaism also had an important influence on the ideological development of Zionism and the

Yishuv. These ideas can be viewed partly as ideological models, but substantively speaking most of them were cultural rather than political. The first of these influences relevant in this context was the Jewish Enlightenment (Haskala) movement.[87] Although Zionism emerged as a reaction to that aspect of the Enlightenment movement which implied integration into non-Jewish society, Zionism, or at least its secular wing, adopted many of the social and cultural conceptions that originated with the Haskala: the attitude of intellectual openness toward the world at large, the quest for liberation from the bonds of tradition, the rejection of the ghetto mentality, and the striving for normalization and productivization. The major difference between Zionism and the Jewish Enlightenment was that Zionism rejected the call for integration into the non-Jewish society, advocating instead the building of an autonomous Jewish society in Palestine parallel to the national societies of other peoples. This aim of Zionism soon met with the obstacle of a binational reality in Palestine, where the Yishuv was a minority. Searching for a solution to this problem, all the ideological currents within Zionism drew inspiration from the ideological and cultural model that advocated autonomous Jewish organization, based on the Jewish communal structure, even within the framework of non-Jewish rule. Both Knesset Israel and the Jewish municipal frameworks within the Yishuv reflected the influence of autonomous Jewish communal organization, mainly as it existed in Poland.[88]

While the Jewish Enlightenment and autonomism had a wide impact on Zionism, the influence of cultural and ideological currents within traditional Judaism on groups and individuals in the Zionist movement and the Yishuv was more selective. The influence of Hassidism, for example, was actually less apparent in religious Zionism, whose standing among traditional Jewry was impaired by the opposition many Hassidic rabbis voiced to Zionism,[89] than in secular Zionist circles where there was a tendency of romanticize and idealize Hassidism stemming from the perception of Hassidism as a *popular* movement. This, at any rate, was the image prevalent among historians and scholars of Hassidism such as Samuel Horodetzky, Ben-Zion Dinur, and Raphael Mahler.[90] The image these writers created of the popular nature of Hassidism, its simplicity and directness, and the devotion of its adherents was absorbed by segments of the Labor movement; even a strictly secularist movement such as Hashomer Hatzair, which eventually turned Marxist, perserved a sentimental image of Hassidism. The other movement of importance

among East European Jewry, the Mitnagdim, whose center of activity
was in the *yeshivot* (rabbinical schools), influenced Zionism through
individuals, many of whom were educated in the Volozhin *yeshiva*. This
yeshiva was exceptional because of its Zionist-nationalistic outlook for
a certain period. German Orthodoxy, the third major movement in
traditional Judaism, was also predominantly anti-Zionist. But several
individuals with a strong Zionist orientation emerged from this movement and took part in molding the Mizrahi and Hapoel Hamizrahi
movements.

Ideology and Social Action:
The Fundamental and Operative
Dimensions of Ideology

Our examination of the sources of ideological influence on the political
movements in the Yishuv and Zionism has shown that these movements
were influenced primarily by ideological models from the non-Jewish
environment. Aspects of the political culture and political style of individuals and groups were influenced heavily by ideological and cultural
models originating in the Jewish society of the Diaspora, primarily
Eastern Europe. The specific contribution of the social and political
system of the Yishuv itself was to translate the general principles of
ideology into norms of action and means of implementation. Moreover,
feedback from the attempts to implement ideologically inspired goals
eventually influenced substantive aspects of the ideologies themselves.
An important example of this trend was the conception of constructivist
socialism, which departed from its ideological beginnings in populism
and socialism. A more extreme example was the Canaanite ideology,
which although it bore traces of populist and radical right ideologies,
was primarily an intellectual effort to come to terms with the new
cultural and national reality the Yishuv created. A completely different
example of feedback effect on ideology was connected to Zionism's
traumatic encounter with the facts of Arab hostility. One of the responses to this unexpected reality was the theme presented by official
Zionist spokesmen which emphasized Zionism's positive role in bringing
progress to a backward area. This contention has an obvious parallel
to the paternalistic imperialist ideologies that stressed the "white man's
burden." This parallel, however, did not derive from the direct influence
of these ideologies, but from the attempt to confront the political and

symbolic problem of a conflict of interests between two nations engaged
in a struggle over the future of the same land. It is noteworthy that this
land was ruled by an imperial power which itself assumed a paternalistic
stance on numerous occasions.

Ideological consciousness played a central role as a motivating factor
in immigration to Palestine and in the intensive participation in political
movements. Also, ideology provided models of the ideal social order.
The impact of such images was particularly strong on those movements
in the Yishuv that developed ideologies with activist, collectivist, and
future-oriented characteristics. The ideological currents that combined
these characteristics, i.e., subordination of the present to the requirements of future goals and giving preference to collective needs over
individual needs, also served to legitimate the political and social status
of certain groups. The "pioneering" sector was viewed as an elect group
worthy not only of general esteem, but also of positions of social and
political leadership. The positions attained through the inspiration of
this ideology were soon converted into a source of rewards such as
power, prestige, and to a lesser extent material advantage.[91] Notwithstanding this, the future-oriented collectivist ideology created sufficient
social and political pressure, in the sense of internal motivation and
external social pressure, to mobilize the resources of the Yishuv and
the Diaspora for efforts beyond those common to less ideologically
oriented societies. Its utopian elements inspired several unique forms
of social organization that became the trademarks of the Yishuv, such
as the Histadrut, the *kibbutz*, and the ramified network of national institutions operating on a voluntary basis. In the final analysis, however,
utopian elements of a fundamental nature could not be translated into
operational imperatives except through a process of transformation in
which some of their features would be abandoned or compromised.
Contradictions naturally emerged between the original ideological demands and their practical political and social applications. The "pure"
ideals and goals of fundamental ideology meanwhile continued to play
an important role in the process of political socialization and as a focus
for political identification. As a result, the political elites tended to
continue paying homage to components of the original ideology that
had been greatly modified or abandoned.

Two characteristic tendencies thus emerged. One was the tendency
to sanctify institutional frameworks and organizational forms originally
designated to represent and embody ideological values. The paradoxical

but familiar phenomenon of "conservative revolutionaries" emerged. Successful in institutionalizing the values contained in their ideologies, those who effected the revolution inherent in the fulfillment of Zionist goals became increasingly concerned with the maintenance and preservation of the institutional frameworks they had created. The second tendency, related directly to the first, was expressed in a growing dissociation between these institutions and the values they were supposed to represent. As the gap steadily widened between the "pure" values of fundamental ideology and the operational values guiding social and political action, the tendency to seek ideological justifications for the distribution of individual and group rewards and for activity motivated by particularistic interests and short-term expediency grew. This gap between word and deed, ideal and reality, was the outcome not only of pressures created in the process of institutionalization, but also of compromises among parties to the exchange process which took place in the political markets of the "state in the making."

7

Authority and Exchange

The emergence of the Yishuv as a semi-autonomous political system, a state within a state, involved the development of rules of the game that regulated the interrelations between the political system and its environment and between the national center and the subcenters. These rules stemmed from the nature of the political system as *field of authority* and as *network of exchange*.[1] The first aspect deals with the status of the various foci of authority in a political system, while the second is concerned with the networks of exchange and resource flow within the system and between the system and its environment, the media of exchange being material, symbolic, or power resources. There is a reciprocal relation between the two aspects. The exchange network is not an independent market composed of buyers and sellers freely interacting on the basis of supply and demand; rules and institutional arrangements for regulating exchange originate in centers of authority. In contrast, the position of an authority center as a regulating agency is influenced by its position as a party to exchange transactions. However, in a nonsovereign system such as the Yishuv, the distinction between the status of the center as a focus of authority and its status as a party to transactions governed by the law of supply and demand tends to blur. Inevitably, the authority of the center of a "state in the making" is rather limited, and limited authority is conductive to the formation of competing elite groups and subcenters, each with its own resource base and each attempting to preserve its autonomy vis-à-vis the center. In addition, the national center had to contend with external centers—the Mandatory government and the Zionist movement in the Diaspora—and it was also affected by relations with the Arab population in Palestine.

The interactions between the Jewish population and the external systems were controlled by the national center only in part. At times the periphery of the Yishuv maintained direct contacts with the peripheries and/or centers of the external systems; and the interrelations of the national center with external systems at times descended from the level of center-to-center to involve direct contacts between the national center and other "external" peripheries. The status of the national center as a source of authority was determined not only by the extent to which it controlled its relationships with the environment, but also by the extent of the autonomy of its subcenters. While the autonomy of the subcenters was related to their independent role in the creation of values, it was also based on the subcenters' role in mediating between the periphery and the center and between the periphery and external systems. Two questions arise: to what extent were center-periphery relations mediated by the subcenters, And to what extent did the subcenters mediate between the periphery and external systems without the involvement of the center?

One of the unique features of the political system of the Yishuv was the unusually large amount of resources channeled into the system from external sources and the related fact that most of these resources were controlled by the evolving national center. The impossibility of extracting resources on a large scale from the Yishuv, both because of the low level of resources in the system and because of the absence of compulsory extractive mechanisms, meant that the major share of the development and institution-building processes had to be borne by imported capital. We may view external sources of capital as a necessary but not sufficient condition for the consolidation of a strong central authority over a community that was part of a binational territorial framework. These external sources of capital not only permitted the existence of such a national center, but facilitated the promotion of political pluralism in a quasi-parliamentary framework. The center could respond positively to various demands for resources without having recourse to coercive mechanisms—in any case unavailable.

The capacity of the national institutions to accumulate power by manipulating economic resources was facilitated by the different preferences of various groups for different types of rewards. The demands various groups raised did not all focus on the same type of resource, and thus the pressure on the supply of resources available for distribution was reduced. In this respect, the Yishuv differed from most developing societies, where demands tend to focus on one resource—land—creating a situation where conflicting claims can be resolved only by expropriation or, in other words, taking from one group to give to another. The Yishuv was spared the bitter conflicts that usually accompany agrarian reforms in developing countries.[2] It should be mentioned, however, that while the scarcity of land was not a factor in internal social conflicts, it was of greatest relevance in the nationalist struggle between Arab and Jews. In fact, because the struggle for land was a basic characteristic of the latter conflict, it indirectly helped to unite the Jewish community itself and to strengthen the political system of the Yishuv.[3]

The different evaluation of rewards by different groups meant that differential rates of exchange operated in transactions between the national center and the various subcenters. These differential rates reflected the particularistic nature of political exchange, where, in contrast to economic exchange, there is no universal standard for evaluating commodities. Thus bilateral or even multilateral transactions were possible between various groups, in which each group exchanged (subjectively) less valuable resources for (subjectively) more valuable resources. Such transactions occurred, for example, between the Labor and religious blocs, where Labor made concessions in the religious sphere (e.g., enacting a formal prohibition of Sabbath labor on lands owned by the Zionist funds) in return for the political support of the religious parties, support that enhanced Labor's control of economic resources; or in Labor's attempts to manipulate the allocation of immigration certificates in return for political support which secured its dominant position in the area of labor relations.[4] The national center itself was a party to such transactions. It sought to increase its political power and authority and thus to acquire the capacity to supervise the flow of economic, symbolic, and human resources from the external environment to the system and vice versa. Indeed, it exchanged the resources at its disposal for recognition and legitimation of its authority.

Regulation of Relationships with
External Groups

The national center's regulation of relations between Jews and Arabs in Palestine depended on the extent to which the center rather than the periphery was the party to the relations. The only contacts between the centers of the two communities were the secret conversations held in the 1930s between the heads of the Jewish Agency and certain Arab leaders with close connections to the Arab Higher Committee. All other contacts on the center-center level were indirect and conducted through a third party, usually the Mandatory government.[5] There was almost no contact between the Arab center and the Jewish periphery. The weakness of the Arab center on the one hand and the high level of cohesion within the Yishuv on the other reduced the occasions of such contacts to a minimum. The only exceptions were attempts on the part of marginal groups in the Yishuv, such as the Communists and Brit Shalom, to establish contacts with certain Arab leaders. Another example of such efforts was the activities of Jacob Israel DeHaan.[6] All these attempts were considered usurpations of the national center's authority and sanctions were applied against those responsible for them —sanctions which in the case of DeHaan ended in political assassination. Yet the Jewish center did initiate contacts with the Arab periphery which focused on the purchase of land. Because the sale of land to Jews violated the norms of the Arab community, the contacts of the Jewish center with the Arab periphery in regard to land in effect represented attempts to undermine the authority of the Arab national center.[7] The Jewish national center also sought to control the interrelations between the two peripheries so that they would be subject to collective Zionist interests. Nevertheless contacts did exist between the Arab and Jewish peripheries, as the long struggle for "Jewish labor only" indicates. The relations between the Arab and Jewish sectors are summarized schematically in Figure 3.

The lack of symmetry in Arab-Jewish relations was also reflected in the media of exchange involved in transactions between the two groups. At the material level, the Jewish sector transferred capital to the Arab

Jews

	Center	Periphery
Arabs — Center	Limited contacts mainly through nediation	No contacts excluding sporadic contacts with marginal groups
Periphery	Intensive exchange without normative legitimation from the Arab sector	Changing scope of exchange in different periods. No normative legitimation from both sides

Figure 3
Center-Periphery Relations between the
Jewish and Arab Sectors

sector in return for land, labor, and commodities for consumption. On the level of symbolic resources the Arabs were unwilling to accept or recognize the symbols of the Jewish claim to create an autonomous political entity in Palestine. On the Jewish side, however, the problem of recognizing Arab nationalism and its symbolic apparatus became a political issue. There were groups in the Yishuv who were willing to view Palestine as the common territory of two national groups, each with its own distinct identity. Even those groups which accepted the idea of partitioning Palestine into separate states or cantons implicitly recognized the collective national aspirations of the Arabs of Palestine. Other groups continued to pursue exclusive Jewish domination of Palestine.

Relations with the Mandatory Government

In comparison with both the Jewish and Arab communities, the Mandatory government represented a different type of political entity, since it was the authoritative agent of an imperial power. From this perspective it is possible to treat British public opinion as part of the periphery of the Mandatory center. Relations between the Yishuv and the Mandatory political system were conducted mainly on two levels: between centers and between the Mandatory center and the periphery of the Yishuv.

Because the Mandatory government was the legitimate sovereign in Palestine, one of the national institutions' central tasks was to represent the Yishuv vis-à-vis the Mandatory government. Conversely, the recognition of the Jewish Agency in the Mandate Charter and of the National Council of Knesset Israel in the Religious Communities Ordinance required the British to conduct some of their contacts with the Jewish population by means of these institutions. Of course, there were many other instances where the Mandatory government maintained direct contacts with the Jewish population. These were areas such as police, courts, public works, ports, trains, and supervision of local government, in which the Jewish national center was not involved, simply because it acknowledged that these areas were within the sphere of the Mandatory government's authority. On the other hand, the leadership of the organized Yishuv actively sought to regulate the contacts of the Jewish population with the Mandate in areas of explicit political importance. Problems arose on various occasions: Jabotinsky's order to the Betar movement in the Diaspora to apply for immigration certificates directly to British consulates and thus bypass the Jewish Agency; the intervention of the British district commissioner in local government when he appointed Israel Rokach as mayor of Tel Aviv;[8] direct appeals by mayors and heads of other local authorities to the British authorities, bypassing the national institutions;[9] and the temporary suspension of enlistments to the British army in World War II in the wake of a conflict between the national institutions and the Mandatory authorities over the status of enlistment centers operated by the Jewish Agency.[10] These occurrences usually aroused strenuous protests on the part of the organized Yishuv or concrete sanctions, as in the case of enlistment in World War II.

The most important resource involved in transactions between the Yishuv and the Mandatory government was legitimacy. In this respect the two bodies were involved in a reciprocal relationship. The national institutions as the legally recognized representative of the Yishuv looked to the Mandatory government for assistance in consolidating its authority, while the Mandatory government often worked through the national institutions in exercising its authority over the Yishuv. However, the policy of cooperation adopted by the national institutions in their relations with the British was conditional, as the national institutions constantly strove to reduce the dependence on Mandatory rule. In contrast to what befell the Arabs after the dissolution of the Arab Higher Committee, the British failed in their attempt in 1946 to undermine the authority of the national institutions by applying direct sanctions, apparently because the National Institutions rested on a firm recognized legal base.

The network of exchange between the Yishuv and the Mandatory authorities also involved transactions of capital and other material resources, such as labor and, to a small extent, land. The Yishuv's major monetary contribution to the Mandatory government at first consisted of indirect taxes, but in the later years of British rule it paid direct taxes as well. Until World War II, over 90 percent of the taxes collected by the government were indirect taxes, mainly customs duties.[11] Because the Jewish sector imported far more goods than the Arab sector, the Jewish contribution to government revenue from customs duties was correspondingly higher.[12] As for property taxes, the urban property tax was much higher than the rural taxes, and here too the Jewish sector paid more as its population was predominantly urban. When an income tax was inaugurated during World War II (1940–41) the Jewish share was also higher. Data from 1944 indicate that the total sum of taxes collected from the Jewish sector reached LP 1,742,000, or 73 percent of government revenue from taxes, which averaged 3 LP per capita. Arabs paid LP 410,000 (or 17 percent) in taxes, while LP 250,000 (10 percent) was paid by others, including foreigners who were not citizens of Palestine.[13]

The benefits received in return for these taxes, in the form of governmental support for or provision of services, were unevenly distributed: the Jewish sector received must less, proportionately, than the Arabs. The national institutions occasionally complained that while the Jews paid most of the taxes, the Arabs received most of the services provided by the government.[14] But because the government followed a *laissez-faire* policy, providing only essential services to the population, the share of the government budget in over-all national income was generally low, except during periods of political and military unrest. During the Arab revolt, for example, large deficits appeared in the government budget, and the question of who was to cover these extra expenses became an issue between the British authorities in London and Jerusalem. Finally it was decided that the Mandatory government should foot the bill, which meant that in the end the Yishuv would have to pay.[15] During World War II as well the Jewish contribution to government revenue increased.[16]

But if one considers the problem of economic relations in wartime from the broad perspective of the economies of Palestine and Britain, rather than the narrow perspective of the government budget, then a different picture emerges. During the war the capital inputs from Britain to the Jewish and Arab populations by far exceeded what Britain received from both groups together. The inputs into the Arab and Jewish economies were mainly in the form of income from the purchase of goods and services needed by the British army for the war effort. Britain thus amassed a debt to the residents of Palestine amounting to tens of millions of pounds sterling. These foreign currency reserves were gradually released after the war and transferred to Palestine. Most of the British inputs to the Jewish population were dispersed throughout the economy without being channeled by the national center. A major exception was the direct British contribution to the defense expenditures of the Yishuv during the period when an imminent German invasion of Palestine was feared.

In their desire for British recognition of the collective identity of the Yishuv, Jewish leadership and public opinion were not content with formal British recognition of the legitimacy of the national institutions. They also sought formal recognition of the symbols identifying the Jews of Palestine as a distinct national community. But the British were reluctant, and partial recognition was obtained only after a prolonged struggle. For instance, the British refused to allow the term "Eretz Israel" (the Land of Israel) to appear only in Hebrew on official documents as a description of the territory ruled by the Mandate, and as a compromise in 1924 they allowed only the term "Palestine (EI)." This so-called compromise did not satisfy Jewish public opinion. The use of the Hebrew language in government services such as telegrams also involved a conflict because of the importance attached to Hebrew as a symbol of collective identity. Another struggle occurred as a result of demands by Jewish soldiers in the British army for the right to display the Jewish national flag in their units.[17] This demand was granted only when the Jewish Brigade was established as a separate unit of Palestinian Jews and it adopted the symbols of the Yishuv as the official symbols of the unit.[18] In respect to the formal and informal symbols of British imperial rule, the Jewish public was largely apathetic. It should be mentioned that, in contrast to other colonial societies in the British Empire, the vast majority of the Jewish elite did not adopt the status symbols of the British colonial elite. This group simply did not serve as a reference group for the elite of the Yishuv.

Relations with the Diaspora

The Yishuv's political relations with the Diaspora were conducted mainly through the Zionist movement which, lacking the features of a political community, could not operate as a fully integrated system. In spite of its complex institutional network with branches in many countries, its authority and mobilization capacity varied from country to country and could not match those of the Yishuv. Several factors influenced the status of the Zionist movement in various countries: the extent to which the Jewish population was segregated or integrated into the population as a whole; the level of institutionalization of Jewish communal life; the type of political regime and its attitude to ethnic and religious minorities in general and to the Jews in particular; the extent of unity or division within the Jewish community; and the strength of the Zionist movement in relation to other Jewish movements.

During the 1920s the dominant center of Zionist activity was in the Diaspora; the members of the Zionist Executive who resided in Jerusalem acted as an arm of the World Zionist Organization. This situation gradually changed with the transfer of the political center of gravity from London to Jerusalem in the 1930s. In the 1940s, however, with the increasing importance of the American Zionist movement both as a source of capital and as a political pressure group in the United States, demands were once again raised to increase the involvement of Zionist leaders in the Diaspora in decisions affecting basic policies and the deployment of resources. At times such trends make it difficult to distinguish clearly between the national center of the Yishuv and the leaders and high-level institutions of the Zionist movement. Nevertheless, the differences between them may be grasped by viewing the leadership of the Zionist movement in the Diaspora as the center of the Zionist movement and the representatives of the Yishuv on the Zionist Executive as forming the main pillar of the national center of the Yishuv. In accordance with this conception, there were naturally intensive relations between the two centers and also relations between the two peripheries that were not necessarily mediated by the centers. For example, the political parties of the Yishuv, through their sister parties in the Diaspora, carried on programs of political socialization, recruitment, and fund-raising among the Jewish communities of the Diaspora. In turn, Diaspora political and economic organizations were

active in the Yishuv, not only in supporting roles to the national center
but also as independent actors—for instance, as investors in the Yishuv's
economy.

The exchange relations between the Yishuv and the Zionist movement in the Diaspora were asymmetrical. In material resources the flow
was virtually one-way. The Zionist movement provided funds to the
national institutions to further the specific goals of Zionism, but these
funds were also employed by the national institutions to bolster their
political authority. The manpower inputs of the Zionist movement into
the Yishuv were also much larger than the output of the Yishuv to the
Diaspora, the latter being mainly emissaries of the Yishuv who were
sent abroad for specified periods of time to participate in the educational, political, and fund-raising activities of the Zionist movement.

The asymmetry in the exchange of instrumental resources between
the Yishuv and the Zionist movement was surely compensated for in
terms of symbolic resources. The existence of the Yishuv and its achievements in Palestine were the *raison d'être* of the Zionist movement—and
its sole source of legitimacy. On the other hand, its ties to the Zionist
movement were only one of the Yishuv's bases of legitimacy as an
autonomous social entity. The collective identity of the Yishuv was also
shaped by other ties to pre-Zionist Jewish cultural and religious values.
Moreover, in the process of Jewish settlement in Palestine a new way
of life with its own ethos emerged which also served as a basis of
legitimacy for the Yishuv as an autonomous entity. In the exchange
of symbolic resources, the symbols of the Yishuv and Land of Israel
thus contributed more to the formation of Zionist identity in the
Diaspora than the symbols of Judaism in the Diaspora did to the formation of the identity of the Yishuv.

It should be mentioned here that not all Jews in the Diaspora
identified with Zionist activity in Palestine and its symbols. Ultraorthodox groups were almost exclusively concerned with the symbolic system
of traditional Judaism and its associated identity, while assimilationist
Jews identified with the national symbols of their lands of residence or
with the universal ideological and political symbols of such movements
as international socialism and communism. In Palestine there were also
Jewish groups which sought to create a new identity completely distinct
from the Jewish identity of the Diaspora. While the Canaanites were
almost the sole proponents of this trend, other groups such as the LHI

were influenced by this approach.[19] In a wider sense, the claim was occasionally made that the native-born in general tended to be alienated and even hostile to the Diaspora and its cultural heritage.

The Imposition of the Center's Authority over the Subcenters and the Periphery

The problems of the authority of the center and the incomplete character of the sociopolitical system of the Yishuv were reflected primarily in the relations between the national center and the subcenters.

The concept of the political system as an "authority field" surrounding the national center implies that the authority relations between the center and the subcenters can be analyzed in terms of distance from the center. Three variables indicate a subcenter's distance from the center: (1.) the degree of recognition it accords the authority of the center; (2.) its relative capacity to influence the center; and (3.) the nature of its commitment to the system and its institutions.

Groups in the Yishuv varied widely as to the degree of recognition they accorded the authority of the center. These differences could be expressed in willingness to recognize both national institutions, or only one of them, or in a refusal to recognize either of them. But even among those groups who recognized both institutions, there were differences in conceptions of the appropriate extent of their authority. Some wished to limit this authority to certain spheres of activity, while others sought to expand it. A group that recognized the authority of both national institutions could be considered closer to the center than one that recognized only the Knesset Israel (there were no groups that recognized only the Jewish Agency); while a group that recognized only the Knesset Israel was closer to the center than one that recognized neither of the national institutions. The same can be said of a group that sought to expand the authority of the center as opposed to one that sought to limit it.

The differences between the main political groups in the Yishuv in respect to this variable can be presented schematically to illustrate the actual distance from the center of each group (see Figure 4). The main conclusion to be drawn from this diagram is that the differences in regard to the extent of the authority of the center cut across all major

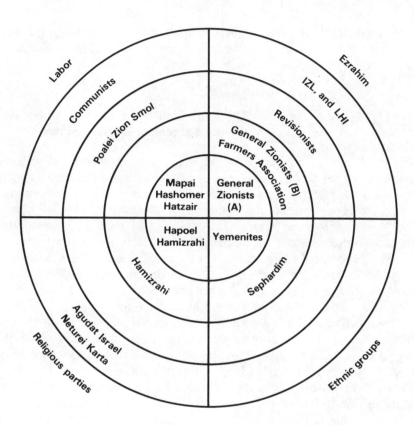

Figure 4
Parties' Distances from the Center Measured
by Recognition Accorded the Authority
of the Center

political groupings: left and right, religious and secular, organized on
an ethnic and on a nonethnic basis.

The various subcenters evinced different capacities for influencing the
center which stemmed from differences in mobilization capacity and
participation or nonparticipation in the ruling coalitions. There were
also groups in the Yishuv without political ties to the center and they
were naturally lacking in influence on the center.

There were numerous channels of influence on the center, most of them particularistic, uninstitutionalized, and informal. For purposes of this analysis influence on the center will be measured according to extent of direct participation of parties and political groups in the parliamentary and executive frameworks of the national institutions. A scale of participation can be constructed according to the following indexes: (1) participation in one or both of the national institutions; (2) participation in both executive and parliamentary bodies or only in parliamentary bodies; and (3) participation on a regular or an irregular basis. The possibility of nonparticipation for each of these variables also exists. Figure 5 summarizes the degree of participation of the various parties calculated on the basis of these three variables.

The parties in the innermost circle are those with the highest scores, that is, those with the greatest frequency of participation. The parties in the second circle had scores in the middle range, those in the third circle had the lowest scores, while those in the fourth circle had a score of zero since they did not participate at all. Comparing Figure 4 with Figure 5, we find a high degree of congruence between the positions of the parties in respect to recognition of the authority of the center and participation in the center (which serves as an index of influence on the center). There were certain exceptions to this trend, however. The Mizrahi party participated in all coalitions, yet also supported the Ezrahim in their attempts to restrict the scope of authority of the center. The Farmers Association and the Association of Sephardim gave full recognition to the national institutions, but since they were both oriented solely to the Yishuv they were not active in the Zionist Organization during the 1930s and 1940s. The Revisionists recognized and participated in the institutions of Knesset Israel, whereas their relations to the Zionist Organization varied in different periods. Their periodic participation in elections to the WZO meant that they were closer to the center in terms of participation than in recognition of the center's authority. The Communists participated only once in the elections to the Elected Assembly—after years of waging a bitter struggle against the organized Yishuv. This one-time act, which occurred in World War II, cannot therefore be considered to reflect recognition of the authority of the center. The IZL appears in the outermost circle in both diagrams even though one could argue for placing it with the Revisionists during the periods when it was formally connected to the party. (The IZL referred

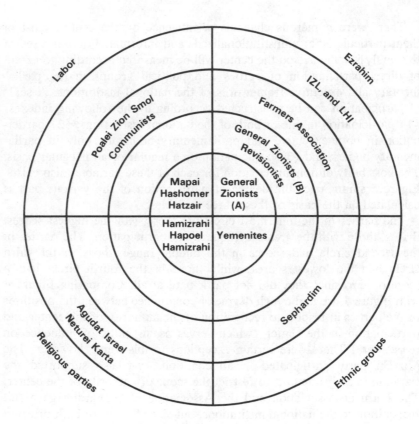

Figure 5
Parties' Distances from the Center Measured by
Participation in the Center

to here is the organization as it existed after 1937 and not the Hagana B group which was also called Ha-Irgun Hatzevai Haleumi.)

The third factor determining distance from the center was the nature of commitment toward the political system of the Yishuv. One can distinguish between different levels of commitment, presented here in descending order: commitment to the leadership of the Yishuv and its policies; commitment to the institutional framework of the organized Yishuv combined with an oppositionist stance toward the leadership and all or part of its policies; commitment to the central values and goals of the Zionist consensus combined with rejection of the policies and organizational frameworks designed to achieve these goals; and, last, a sense of Jewish identity with religious and national components or with only a religious component. It should be clear that the highest levels of commitment subsumed the lower levels, e.g., a commitment to the leadership of the Yishuv entailed a commitment to the basic Zionist consensus.

The distinction between the third and fourth levels of commitment reflects the problem of defining the boundaries of the Yishuv as a collectivity. From the perspective of the Mandatory power the Yishuv was primarily a religious community. But the nationalist consensus encompassing the vast majority of Jews in Palestine regarded the Yishuv as a nationalist movement with Zionism as its ideology. None of these implied commitment to the organized Yishuv as an institutional system. But it would have been impossible for a national center to crystallize without such a commitment on the part of most Jews in Palestine, including those in opposition to the leadership and its policies.

The position of the parties and political groups in respect to the variable of commitment is depicted in Figure 6. From a comparison of Figure 4 and Figure 6, differences emerge in respect to Hashomer Hatzair, IZL, and LHI. Hashomer Hatzair unconditionally accepted the authority of the leadership even though at times it intensely opposed its policies. The IZL and LHI rejected the authority of the national institutions while remaining faithful to the basic Zionist consensus.

A comparison of the position of parties and political groups on the continuum representing distance from the center according to the three dimensions of recognition of the authority of the center, participation in the national institutions, and the nature of commitment reveals a high degree of congruence among the three dimensions. Nevertheless they are not identical, and each dimension contributes in its own way to determining the distance of the parties from the center. For this reason it is difficult to provide clear-cut indicators of the boundaries of the system. It is likely that most definitions would exclude certain groups that were only vaguely oriented to the system on the fringe of the center's sphere of attraction.

Given these circumstances, the mechanisms through which the national center asserted its authority assume a special importance. The most important mechanism was the basic loyalty of individuals and groups

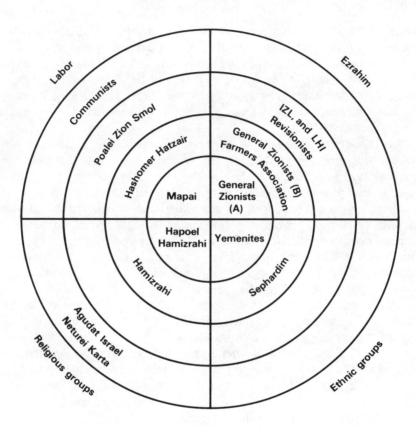

Figure 6
Parties' Distances from the Center Measured by
Commitment to the System

to the system and its central goals and symbols of identity. Second in importance was the bargaining process between the center and particularistic groups in which the position of the center was based on its control of the allocation of resources originating outside the system. The third mechanism was the exercise of the limited capacity of the center to enforce sanctions against groups and individuals. Given the nonsovereign nature of the political system of the Yishuv, the third mechanism was naturally the weakest. But the effectiveness of utilitarian bargaining mechanisms for the most part compensated the political system for the limited capacity of the center to employ direct coercive sanctions.

In the bargaining process, the capacity of the national center to extract resources from the Diaspora gave it extensive, though not unlimited flexibility in its transactions with the particularistic power centers in the Yishuv. Nevertheless the national center did not monopolize the resources from external sources. Separatist groups who were willing to forego the possibility of obtaining resources by way of the center set up their own mobilization machinery in the Diaspora in order to preserve their autonomy in the Yishuv. The classic example of such a group was the extreme ultraorthodox wing of the Yishuv. These groups continued to uphold the venerable tradition of the *halukka* (distribution of charity); contributions obtained from ultraorthodox groups in the Diaspora supported the network of religious, educational, and welfare institutions of the Old Yishuv. The *halukka* system was created long before the Zionist funds came into existence and it continued to exist during the Mandate and thereafter as well.

The most severe challenges to the national center's authority centered on problems of security related to the Arab-Jewish conflict. A monopoly on the use of organized force is typically regarded as an indispensable condition of political sovereignty. The very existence of an armed organization directed and controlled by the national institutions was an indication of the quasi-governmental nature of the national center. From an internal perspective, however, the problem of the authority of the national institutions centered on the existence of separatist military organizations which refused to accept the authority of the center and which operated under the inspiration of radical oppositionist groups.

The history of the Hagana illustrates the problems of external and internal authority which the national center faced. The Hagana was never accorded de jure recognition by the Mandatory government, which retained the view that responsibility for maintaining law and order was the sole province of the legitimate political sovereign in Palestine. Nevertheless, there were periods when the government accorded the Hagana de facto recognition and collaborated with it. The Jewish Settlement Police, for example, was formally subordinate to the Mandatory government, but its ranks were composed of Hagana members whose primary loyalty was focused on their underground movement.[20] The British commanders of the JSP accepted this situation in practice, though of course not in theory. Meanwhile, the changes in the political orientation of the Hagana discussed elsewhere, culminating in the 1930 transfer of control to the national institutions, reflected the crystallization of the national institutions as a focus of authority recognized by most subcenters in the Yishuv.

The main test of the authority of the national center as a state within a state, at least in the area of the use of force, occurred later, in the 1930s and 1940s. At that time security issues centering on authority and secession were at the heart of the internal conflicts in the Yishuv. The problem of splinter organizations was viewed by the leadership of the Yishuv both as a test of its authority and as a potentially disruptive factor in the conduct of the Yishuv's "foreign policy" in relation to the British and the Arabs. The leadership therefore made repeated attempts to eliminate the separatist organizations, primarily the IZL, or at least to assert some control over them. The most important attempt to solve the problem of separatism through the application of sanctions was the Sezon.[21] Other efforts to control the activities of the IZL and LHI involved negotiations rather than the application of sanctions. Whatever their success, these attempts also served to expose the weakness of the center's authority.

In the framework of the Jewish Resistance Movement in 1946 the IZL and LHI received partial recognition and legitimacy as junior partners in exchange for the commitment to submit their military plans to a joint military command for approval. However, after several months the Resistance Movement fell apart following the breakdown of the coordinating mechanisms when the IZL blew up British governmental headquarters based in the King David Hotel in Jerusalem.[22]

In the network of political exchange relations the national center held a strategic position at the intersection of the channels of resource flow from the Diaspora and the Mandatory government into the Yishuv. The power accumulated by the center can thus be viewed as a levy put on users of resources allocated by the national institution. In the exchange relations between the national center and the subcenters and among the subcenters themselves the following resources were transferred: factors of production, such as capital, land, and manpower; political resources, such as legitimacy; and symbolic resources related to the creation of different ways of life of groups in the Yishuv and their social and ideological needs. Legitimacy was directly connected to the problem of authority. Submission to authority which is not based on coercion implies that this authority is recognized as legitimate. The weakness of the coercive bases of authority in the Yishuv's political system served to increase the importance of legitimacy as a source of authority of the national center. The system of authority described at the outset of this chapter was thus based on the legitimacy accorded the national center by the subcenters and the periphery. In return for the provision of various services to the subcenters, the center expected the subcenters to recognize its position at the top of the internal pyramid of authority and its exclusive power to represent the Yishuv vis-à-vis external political elements.

Exchange Relations with the Subcenters

The phenomenon of a nonsovereign center of authority which serves as a focus of attraction for a national, religious, or linguistic group and bases its authority largely on normative resources was not unique to the Yishuv. Such centers have emerged in nationalist movements striving for independence or in separatist movements in multinational and multi-lingual states. What was unique about the national center of the Yishuv was the extent of the utilitarian resources at its disposal and the ways in which the center employed them. One type of such resources can be termed "capital," which includes money, tools of production, and land; the other type refers to manpower, which had to be mobilized in the Diaspora, transferred to Palestine, and provided with employment.

A common feature of all utilitarian resources was their constant scarcity, which created a gap between the goals the Zionist movement set for itself and the means available to attain these goals. Mobilization of manpower for immigration depended in part on the situation of the Jews in the Diaspora and even more on the number of immigration certificates the Mandatory government was willing to allot. This created a situation where the number of those wishing to immigrate was always larger than the number permitted to enter Palestine. The chronic lack of funds, an issue constantly on the agenda of the Zionist congresses, set the pace of land acquisition and determined the availability of employment for immigrants. The concomitant gap between demands and available resources increased the pressure on the allocative machinery of the Zionist movement and intensified internal conflicts and disputes. This was especially true of periods of severe shortages such as the later 1920s.[23] These internal conflicts and pressures were relaxed somewhat in periods when more resources were available, such as the period of the Fifth Immigration after Hitler's rise to power.

The Labor movement demanded a share of the budget larger than its electoral strength. Labor argued that the private sector had its own capital at its disposal while the labor immigrants were practically penniless. Moreover, it contended, the labor immigrants were performing critical pioneering tasks for the Zionist movement, and their demands for funds were not dictated by class or partisan interests but by the national interest.[24]

A related conflict centered on whether Zionist funds should be invested only in profitable economic enterprises or whether these funds should be employed to create a political and demographic basis for the entire colonization effort—regardless of strict economic considerations of profit and loss. The Labor leaders were aware of the unprofitable character of most of the Histadrut settlements and economic enterprises, and they naturally tended to place purely economic considerations on a lower level of importance in comparison to the colonization efforts as a whole. Ben-Gurion justified this position by saying that the hegemony of the Labor movement in Zionism did not rest on the fact that Labor was more effective or more honest than other sectors—but that it was more "Zionist."

The Labor movement's rise to dominance in the Zionist movement in the 1930s did not change the criteria of allocation among the various sectors, but it did change the position of the Labor movement in the framework that determined these allocations. The Labor elite, and especially Ben-Gurion, understood that their newly won control of the Zionist budgets would serve as an incentive for other groups to participate with them in a coalition despite ideological differences.[25] The conversion of capital resources to political power assumed truly significant proportions during World War II when the relations between private and public capital imports changed and became equal.[26] By the end of World War II the power of the Labor elite in the national center reached a new peak due in part to the increase in the amount of public funds at the disposal of the center.

In addition to the conflict between Labor and the Ezrahim over the criteria for allocating public funds, conflicts over the internal allocation of resources arose within the Labor movement. These conflicts pitted the heads of the settlement movements against the chiefs of the Histadrut's nonagricultural economic enterprises and the various settlement

movements against each other. The conflicts among the settlement movements were especially intense concerning that scarce but essential resource—land.[27] The main conflicts over land allocations took place
among the settlement movements organized in the framework of the
Histadrut's Agricultural Center, and focused on the sequence in which
land and funds were allotted to prospective settlement groups which
usually had to wait several years for their turn. The most intensive
competition in this respect was between the two forms of Labor settlement, *kibbutz* and *moshav*. These recurring conflicts between *kibbutzim*
and *moshavim* and among the *kibbutzim* themselves gave rise to attempts to institutionalize the allocation process and the criteria for determining priority for settlement. Two criteria were devised that were not
always consistent. The first was based on the length of the period of
preparation and training for permanent settlement. The second was the
"movement key," which determined priority according to political movement affiliation. The first criterion was supposedly dominant, but political pressure and the greater number of *kibbutzim* from a particular
movement awaiting their turn also influenced the sequence of allocation.

The Control of Manpower

The notion of "manpower," though placed for analytical reasons in the
category of utilitarian resources, was not simply a means to an end in
the sense that capital and land were. Manpower was also an end in
itself. Through their efforts to immigrate and settle in Palestine, Jewish
men and women were acting subjects fulfilling the Zionist goals of the
redemption of the Jewish people. Manpower naturally had a political
meaning as well. By recruiting, training, and indoctrinating manpower
in the Diaspora and by organizing the process of immigration and absorption, the parties and movements were in effect creating their own
constituencies in Palestine, the social bases of their political power. For
this reason political struggles concerning immigration certificates and
employment opportunities were far more intense than those over the
allocation of financial resources and land.

The process of mobilizing manpower comprised a number of stages:
initial recruitment, in which the prospective immigrant joined a youth
movement or political movement vocational training, usually in agriculture; political socialization prior to immigration; immigration, which
required obtaining an immigration certificate or making other arrange-

ments in the case of illegal immigration; absorption into a group in
Palestine, which could be a comprehensive social setting such as a
kibbutz or *moshav* or a more limited framework such as a political party
or trade union. Naturally not all immigrants passed through each of
these stages and there were also those who joined the stream of labor
immigration as individuals. The most important stage was of course
immigration itself. It was also this stage where most of the bottlenecks
occurred, at least in the 1930s and 1940s.

Immigration was a central political factor in the struggle between
the Yishuv and the Arabs of Palestine and in the internal struggles of
the Yishuv as well. During the Ottoman period immigration was not a
legitimate activity and most of the immigrants of this period entered
the country on the pretext that they had no intention of settling. The
Balfour Declaration and the British Mandate gave a fresh impetus to
immigration, which had halted during World War I. In the period of
the Mandate, immigration was legally recognized by the British authorities and the League of Nations as part of the right of the Jewish people
to build its national home in Palestine. Nevertheless there was never
unrestricted immigration during any period of the Mandate; the number
of immigration certificates issued by the Mandatory government was
(at least in the 1930s and 1940s) usually less than the number of those
seeking to immigrate. The flow of immigration was regulated by quotas
determined in negotiations between the British authorities and the
Zionist Executive. By 1920 quotas were set that distinguished between
those who did not need ordinary certificates and those who did.

The system for classifying immigrants was regularized in 1921. It
was based on several major types, bearing in mind the absorbtive
capacity of the country:[28] persons in possession of capital; handicraftsmen; students; relatives of residents of Palestine; persons of religious
occupation; and persons who had assured sources of income. These
restrictions turned the question of immigration certificates in a focus
of political struggle between the Labor movement, which sought to give
priority to pioneering elements, and the Ezrahim, who opposed this.

Preference for pioneering immigration implied a policy of selective
immigration, that is, prior selection of immigrants based on the principle
of the economic absorptive capacity of the country. The procedure of
selection was an inevitable consequence of the British policy of restricting immigration, but it could be interpreted also as a sign of compliance
with this policy. At any rate, the policy of selective immigration was a

controversial issue in the Yishuv. In this controversy the position of the
Labor movement was somewhat ambivalent. Until the late 1930s the
Labor movement and its allies among the General Zionists such as
Chaim Weizmann actually implemented a policy of selective immigration
and did not press for indiscriminate mass immigration,[29] as they should
have done according to their manifest Zionist position.

In order to institutionalize the recruitment and training of potential
pioneering immigrants, in 1923 the Hechalutz (Pioneer) sector of the
Labor movement created a central committee that was located first in
Berlin and later in Warsaw. A year later the Histadrut established an
Immigration Center whose major task was to increase the immigration
of pioneering elements from the Diaspora. These steps served to aug-
ment the political power of Hechalutz by forming a central organization
for the recruitment and training of youth, some of whom had no prior
movement socialization. By the end of 1925 the Labor movement had
convinced the WZO of the importance of increasing the pioneer immigration. This recognition was translated into a decision of the Zionist
Executive to allot 75 percent of the immigration certificates at its disposal to the labor immigration and two-thirds of this number to those
who had received prior vocational training, with priority going to
members of Hechalutz[30] (see Table 12). This policy was the first institutionalized expression of the allocative principle called the "party
key," which allocated resources, in this case immigration certificates, in
order to preserve a certain political balance between the various political
movements and parties.

Decisions affecting the internal composition of the labor immigration
could not prevent the strengthening of the Ezrahim as a result of the
Fourth Immigration, since middle-class immigration was in part a
separate category comprising those in possession of at least £1000.
The middle-class immigration encouraged initial political organization
among the Ezrahim sector. In 1924 the General Zionists began organizing, and in 1925 the Palestine branch of the new Revisionist party was
established. Opposed to the extensive influence of the Labor movement
in Zionism, the Revisionists called for nonselective immigration and
accused the immigration offices of the Jewish Agency of giving unfair
preference to leftist elements in the allocation of immigration certificates.
The economic crisis and emigration that occurred after the Fourth
Immigration intensified the internal conflicts in the Yishuv; the non-
Labor parties increased their strength, drawing on the reservoir of

Table 12
Immigrants by Type of Certificate

Year	Capitalists N	%
1920–21	—	—
1922	1,365	17.4
1923	1,002	13.4
1924	5,319	41.3
1925	11,923	35.9
1926	1,636	12.8
1927	414	15.2
1928	792	36.4
1929	739	13.9
1930	479	9.8
1931	609	14.9
1932	1,623	16.9
1933	7,202	23.7
1934	11,552	27.0
1935	15,551	25.2
1936	7,164	24.0
1937	2,558	24.2
1938	3,537	27.4
1939	6,179	37.8
1940	2,100	46.8
1941	838	22.9
1942	265	12.0
1943	394	4.6
1944	459	3.1
1945	85	0.6

newly arrived middle-class elements, and in addition some unorganized workers in the private sector began to leave the ranks of the Labor movement.

The Fifth Immigration of the 1930s was the largest in the period of the Mandate. An estimated two hundred seventy-seven thousand immigrants arrived in the period of 1932–44,[31] with sixty-two thousand arriving in the peak year of 1935. Most of the immigrants came from Germany and Poland, and the size of labor immigration decreased in proportion to the number in the capital-possessing category. In that

Students		Labor		Dependents		Unspecified		
N	%	N	%	N	%	N	%	Total
—	—	—	—	—	—	14,663	100.0	14,663
—	—	3,310	42.2	3,169	40.4	—	—	7,844
—	—	4,371	59.0	2,048	27.5	—	—	7,421
—	—	5,343	41.3	2,194	17.4	—	—	12,856
—	—	16,161	48.6	5,717	15.5	—	—	33,801
105	0.8	9,102	69.5	2,198	16.9	—	—	13,081
45	1.3	1,311	48.2	943	35.3	—	—	2,713
53	2.4	708	32.5	625	28.7	—	—	2,178
71	1.1	3,585	68.8	854	16.2	—	—	5,249
64	1.2	3,436	69.5	965	19.5	—	—	4,944
66	1.6	2,172	53.5	813	19.9	415	10.1	4,075
169	1.7	3,708	38.7	1,227	12.9	2,826	29.8	9,553
391	1.2	18,953	62.8	2,846	9.3	935	3.0	30,327
1,893	4.4	22,035	52.0	6,879	16.6	—	—	42,356
1,964	3.1	27,729	44.9	16,610	26.8	—	—	61,854
1,541	5.1	11,477	39.0	9,495	31.9	—	—	29,677
1,043	9.9	3,151	29.9	3,784	36.0	—	—	10,536
2,531	19.9	4,235	32.8	2,565	19.9	—	—	12,868
3,850	23.4	2,960	18.0	3,416	20.8	—	—	16,405
1,144	25.1	868	10.3	435	17.8	—	—	4,547
1,516	41.5	975	26.7	318	8.9	—	—	3,647
75	3.4	1,724	78.7	130	5.9	—	—	2,194
1,639	19.2	6,145	72.4	329	3.5	—	—	8,507
1,804	12.4	11,594	80.3	607	4.2	—	—	14,464
2,106	16.4	9,073	71.4	1,487	11.6	—	—	12,751

SOURCE: A. Gertz, ed., *Statistical Handbook of Jewish Palestine, 1947* (Jerusalem: Jewish Agency, Department of Statistics, 1947), p. 103.

period a new element was added to the list of organizations for preparation and immigration: Youth Immigration. This organization supervised the immigration of youth up to the age of seventeen from Germany, Austria, and Czechoslovakia, and facilitated their absorption in *kibbutzim, moshavim,* and educational institutions.[32] Immigration declined during the Arab revolt of 1936–39, and reached its nadir after the publication of the White Paper of 1939, with the result that from April 1940 to March 1947 only seventy-five thousand immigrants reached Palestine.

The allocative principle of the party key was institutionalized in repeated decisions of the Zionist Actions Committee. These decisions
also gave preference to potential immigrants who worked for or contributed to the Zionist funds, to those in organized preparatory groups,
and to professionals who had been members of Zionist organizations
for at least a year.[33] The Jewish Agency offices in the Diaspora in
charge of immigration were also composed according to a party key
representing the balance of political forces within each country according to the latest elections to the Zionist congress.

The problem of allocating immigration certificates became a political
problem of the first order after the secession of the Revisionists from
the WZO. The conflict with the Revisionists on this issue began even
before their secession and was the major cause of Jabotinsky's refusal
to regard the Zionist Organization as a "state without citizenship."
Jabotinsky issued an order to members of Betar to bypass the offices
of the Jewish Agency and apply directly to British consulates for immigration certificates.[34] In response the Zionist movement suspended all
certificates intended for Betar members and as a counter sanction Jabotinsky ordered Betar to boycott the Zionist funds. The Agency Executive
remained willing, however, to allot certificates to members of Betar
who applied on an individual basis. The Revisionists seceded from the
Zionist Organization in 1935 and their quota was utterly revoked. This
act led the Revisionists to organize a movement of illegal immigration
to Palestine.[35]

Until 1938 the Zionist Organization tended to oppose all illegal immigration, not only that organized by the Revisionists but also that sponsored by groups within Hebalutz. Internal differences within the Labor
movement on this question came to a head in the affair of the illegal
immigrant ship *Velos* organized by members of *kibbutz* movements and
the Hagana.[36] Ben-Gurion and others opposed these groups, fearing
that this approach would harm legal immigration and undermine the
principle of control by national institutions. Only in 1938, faced with
increased pressure for immigration from the Diaspora and the Mandatory government's reduction of immigration quotas, did the Zionist
Organization change its official policy and encourage illegal immigration
organized by Hehalutz and the Hagana. After the publication of the
1939 White Paper, the Mandatory government continued to allow immigration at the rate of fifteen thousand per year for a period of five

years, but most of this quota went to cover those illegal immigrants apprehended by the Mandatory government.

In the first stage of illegal immigration before the publication of the White Paper of 1939, the Revisionists had a quantitative advantage over the organized Yishuv. After 1939 the Hagana organized a larger portion of the illegal immigration than the Revisionists and private operators, and after World War II its numerical superiority in this effort became overwhelming. The "party key" principle was a major criterion for selection of candidates for illegal immigration among the refugees in displaced persons camps in Europe, many of whom organized in groups affiliated to political movements.[37]

In the struggle over the sociopolitical composition of immigration, the Labor movement had a distinct advantage in political and organizational aspects of the mobilization and absorption of the immigrants. The establishment of the Immigration Center in the Histadrut, the organization and training of groups of potential immigrants in the Diaspora, and the extensive work done by the emissaries sent abroad by the various groups within the Labor movement, all combined to enable the Labor movement to increase the share of its members and supporters among the immigrants.

While the competition for manpower in the Diaspora focused chiefly on the allocation of immigration certificates, the struggles connected with the initial absorption of the immigrants focused on jobs. Given the connection established by the quota system between immigration and the absorptive capacity of the country, one of the Histadrut's first activities was the establishment of a public works department that was instrumental in creating employment opportunities for thousands of new immigrants. There were three aspects to the process of allocating jobs: the problem of assuring a monopoly for the Jewish worker in the Jewish labor market in the face of competition from cheap Arab labor; the problem of regulating supply and demand in the labor market, or as the Labor movement put it, the struggle for "organized labor"; and the efforts of the Histadrut to attain a monopolistic or at least dominant position among the various labor organizations in the Yishuv.

The problem of dominance in these three areas gave rise to more intensive conflicts than problems of wages and working conditions. The latter two were more or less determined by supply and demand and by the extent of unemployment. Those employers who agreed to hire only

"organized labor" paid higher wages than those current in the unorganized labor market. The issue of organized labor focused on the
institution referred to as the "labor exchange." The Labor movement
opposed the existence of numerous labor exchanges each organized by
a separate labor organization and each competing with the others to
provide jobs. However, the Histadrut was willing to compromise with
other labor organizations and to cooperate with them in the framework
of joint labor exchanges. Labor organizations were in fact divided along
political rather than functional lines and each organization was active
in organizing workers in different branches and places of work. For this
reason, "labor organization" and "labor federation" are more appropriate terms in this context than the more narrowly conceived "trade
union." The only functional division of major importance in labor
relations was the division between labor organizations and employers.
But even here the distinction was blurred by the existence of Histadrut-
controlled enterprises that employed thousands of workers.[38]

The struggles that occurred in the area of labor relations focused on
three types of resources: utilitarian resources, such as capital and manpower, political resources, and resources of solidarity and allegiance
to the various parties and movements. The utilitarian resources included
not only employment opportunities for the existing labor force but also
the means to create new employment opportunities and to train additional workers. Naturally the increase in the job supply influenced the
conditions of exchange throughout the labor market. Political resources
included different types of pressure mobilized by the various sides in
labor conflicts to assure the attainment of their goals. The political
mobilization undertaken by the Histadrut in the fruit-packing disputes
between 1928 and 1935 serves as a major example. Workers were
mobilized for picketing the orchards in order to keep out Arab workers
and to protest against their employment. Resources of solidarity were
involved in labor relations because the organizations concerned with
providing jobs and other related services also engaged in political and
cultural socialization. The possibility of converting one type of resource
for another influenced political conflicts in the sphere of labor relations,
largely determining the bargaining positions of the various groups active
in the labor market. The private farmers, for instance, could not exploit
their economic power to the fullest since it was difficult for them to
convert it to political power. In contrast, the Histadrut succeeded in
utilizing its political resources in the economic struggle over Jewish

labor. Thus the Histadrut was able to assure its members jobs by ideological pressure and by wielding its superior capacity for political mobilization.

The conflict over the control of the labor market thus reflected the two facets of manpower as a resource. While other resources are simply means employed in mobilizing political support and in building political institutions, manpower active in the system is both a *resource* within the system and a *client* of the system. This explains the crucial contribution of immigration to the crystallization of the political system of the Yishuv. In societies not formed through a process of immigration, the amount of manpower available for the labor market and for political mobilization is a given of the system. In immigrant societies this amount changes constantly according to the dimensions of immigration. Therefore, control of the process in which manpower is introduced and absorbed into the system may change the balance of political forces in the system. Moreover the immigrant's dependence on the absorbing framework facilitates political socialization, which is of even greater importance in the case where the absorbing framework represents a political and ideological movement and the motives for immigrating are themselves ideological. The political elites of the Yishuv whose power rested on a firm political base were successful in exploiting these conditions for political mobilization and institution building and for consolidating the power and authority of the national center. Their achievements in these spheres were of critical importance in the postwar struggle for independence from the British and in the struggle for existence against the Arabs in 1948—struggles which transformed the Yishuv from an autonomous political society to a sovereign state.

8

The State of Israel and the Political Heritage of the Yishuv

The political system of the Yishuv seems to have exhausted most of the possibilities for institution building in a nonsovereign system. Its unique characteristics were rooted in the particular conditions of the Zionist endeavor. Naturally these characteristics had an impact on the transition from nonsovereign community to full-fledged state. Officially, the State of Israel was established on 15 May 1948. Actually the transformation to statehood was a gradual process which took place in the course of the War of Independence and was affected by the specific conditions created by the British political and military withdrawal from Palestine.

The existence of a viable and authoritative political system made it possible to fill the vacuum created by the disorderly British exit and the departure of tens of thousands of Arabs from the territory. Moreover, this change took place under conditions of war; the military effort alone required the swift mobilization of manpower and other resources in order to survive the prolonged conflict against first the local Arab population and later the armies of the Arab states. It is clear that the existence of a prestate political system enabled the Jewish community in Palestine to adjust to the revolutionary change that occurred in 1948—and to survive. This was the

Yishuv's main advantage over the Arab majority, which failed to mobilize its resources effectively for the decisive campaign over Palestine's fate.

However, the Yishuv's institutional system also had certain limitations which originated in the conditions in which it crystallized, primarily the lack of sovereignty:

1. Until the establishment of the state, the central national institutions of the Yishuv could exercise authority only over those groups which recognized this authority, whereas afterwards the government had to extend its authority to dissident or separatist groups that were not part of the organized Yishuv.

2. Before the state was established, particularistic political groups and parties served as agencies of the organized Yishuv in performing various quasi-governmental functions. Afterwards, a conflict emerged between the aspiration of the particularistic groups to preserve their status and the attempt of the center (and especially Ben-Gurion) to transfer some of their functions to the state.

3. Until the establishment of the state, the institutional system of the Yishuv was exempted from responsibility for certain spheres dealt with by the Mandatory government. Afterwards, it was necessary to extend the system's scope of activity to those spheres too, a process which called for intensified mobilization of resources. Moreover, since the most important among these spheres was the judicial sphere, this change entailed the adoption of new norms for regulating governmental activity. Under the Mandate, the national institutions operated within a rather loose constitutional framework which afforded considerable flexibility since there were few legally binding patterns of activity; a tendency prevailed to solve problems in an ad hoc fashion. The state, however, incorporated the Mandatory laws and legal framework (except few politically loaded laws such as restricting Jewish Immigration and land purchases). This step implied the obligation to act in accordance with established legal norms as well as the possibility, in principle, of dissatisfied parties appealing government decisions that deviated from these norms.

4. The growth of the Yishuv was sustained by a population with a European cultural and social background that for the most part had been positively motivated to immigrate. Accordingly, it had little difficulty in adjusting to the norms of the political system.

The only differences—in the case of the German immigrants—
stemmed from the fact that these immigrants came from countries
which had reached a higher state of modernization than that of
the population originating in Eastern Europe. Following the
establishment of the state, however, the political system had to
absorb a population of unprecedented size,[1] a large part of which,
since it came from traditional or transitional societies in Asia
and Africa, had an entirely different cultural background. This
population lacked the cultural predispositions which would have
facilitated its integration into a developed political system like
that of the Yishuv.

The contrast between the patterns of activity of the Yishuv's political
and bureaucratic system and those of the State of Israel was responsible
for several crises and much friction during the transition period. These
difficulties all stemmed from the process of transforming political structures from one level of institutionalization to another.[2] The transition to
statehood necessitated action in spheres that were unfamiliar to the
center, and also demanded a considerable expansion of the scale of
governmental activity. Some of the characteristics of the Yishuv's political system eased this transformation while others created obstacles.
The transformation was accomplished without serious crises jeopardizing
the system's integrity only because most of the essential patterns of the
Yishuv's political system were maintained in the new setting.

Authority over Dissident and
Separatist Groups

The first problem faced by the new polity was that of absorbing the
groups and parties which had not participated in the organized Yishuv.
The Israeli government, as a sovereign state, could not be content with
the kind of qualified authority that existed during the time of the Yishuv.
However, the fact that an external struggle was being waged at the time
the state was established compelled its leadership to seek a way of
settling the question of authority on the basis of consensus rather than
coercion. This constraint led to temporary compromises, some of which
simply deferred the test of authority to a later date. Some arrangements
resulted from certain international conditions, for example, the arrangement which allowed IZL and LHI to maintain separate military forces
in Jerusalem, which had not been incorporated into the territory allotted

to the Jewish State by the United Nations Resolution of 29 November 1947. Other arrangements included the establishment of combat units within the Israeli army consisting mainly of recruits from IZL and LHI.[3]

These arrangements and the various interpretations given them, along with the residue of mutual suspicion, constituted the background of the *Altalena* affair. The *Altalena* was an IZL ship which brought arms and IZL soldiers to Israel during the first truce in June 1948. Although the provisional government was notified of the sailing of the ship from France, failures in coordination between the government and IZL regarding the date of its arrival and disputes over the allocation of arms brought by the ship caused an armed clash between the Israel Defense Forces (IDF) and IZL units. At a result of the clash, the ship was fired upon, several IZL people were killed, and the equipment on board was destroyed.[4]

The *Altalena* affair was significant on two planes: that of the balance of power between the rival political blocs, and that of the establishment of legitimate authority in a sovereign state. The use of force was aimed at breaking the military backbone of the only alternative focus of power capable of constituting a threat to the rule of the organized Yishuv parties and the dominant position of the parties of the Labor movement, above all Mapai.[5] But it was also a manifestation of the principle of the government's exclusive authority over all armed forces—in other words, the enforcement of the government's monopoly of the legitimate exercise of force in a sovereign state. The *Altalena* affair may also be regarded as a variation of a recurrent historical phenomenon associated with the institutionalization of national or social revolutions. Upon consolidating its rule, the leadership of a revolutionary movement is in many cases compelled to liquidate by force the most radical groups which constitute a potential threat to political stability and processes of institutionalization.

The New Delineation of the Center's Functions

The second problem which the political system had to deal with was the redefinition of the center's functions in relation to those of particularistic political groups. This problem arose in several areas. As already stated, the security sphere was the first in which a contradiction emerged between groups with long traditions of partial autonomy and the demand for central direction. This problem materialized in the political struggle over the disbandment of the Palmach. On the party-political plane, this struggle involved a contest between the two largest parties at the time—Mapai and Mapam—over positions of influence in the state and, first and foremost, in the defense establishment. Even though it was an arm of the Hagana and subordinate to the national institutions, the spirit of the Palmach arose from its Mapam-inspired command.[6] In this "youth movement in arms," as it was called,[7] the political indoctrination sometimes deviated from the positions of Ben-Gurion and his party, Mapai, who were dominant in the leadership of the organized Yishuv. Ben-Gurion regarded with particular severity Mapam's swing to the left, expressed in an increasing tendency to adopt the international positions of the communist movement.

The political contest between Mapai and Mapam thus became bound up with the practical issue of determining the character of the army. This dispute embraced a number of issues concerning organizational structure and values. Ben-Gurion wanted to stress professional values in building the army, and thus preferred veterans of the British army to former Hagana commanders. Mapam regarded the Palmach as an organization with political goals, especially in the sphere of settlement, and as an ultimate military guarantee against a rightist threat to the Labor movement's dominance. Mapam submitted the question of the disbandment of the Palmach to the executive committee of the Histadrut. Ben-Gurion demanded that the subject be taken off the agenda since authority in matters of security belonged exclusively to the government. The majority of the Histadrut accepted this position.[8]

The dispute over the *Palmach* thus became interrelated with the problem of distinguishing the government as a decision-making body from the actual leaders who occupied governmental positions and the political groups they represented. The antagonists on this issue were those upholding a "movement" orientation and those upholding a "state" orientation who advocated the primacy of *mamlachtiut* (statehood) as a value. The principle of *mamlachtiut* implied that the state existed as an abstract system independent of the movements or parties whose representatives occupy governmental positions at any given time. On the other hand, the movement orientation emphasized the intimate relationship between the Labor movement's hegemony in the government and the very legitimacy of the government. The state orientation regarded the legitimacy of the government as entirely independent of the groups constituting its political base of support, whereas the movement orientation may be interpreted as advocating conditional legitimacy. *Mamlach-tiut* was the more explicit of the two orientations, while the far-reaching significance of the movement orientation was only indirectly implied in the contentions of some of its leading spokesmen. But while in a way *mamlachtiut* favored the nonpoliticization of government, activities which were supposed to reflect this principle in fact also served the political interests of the prime minister and his party. The disbandment of the Palmach was only the first step toward removing Mapam members from key positions in the national security network and placing the army command in the hands of men who were either Mapai members or professionals without a definite political coloring.[9] But the political and personal aspects of Ben-Gurion's decision to disband the Palmach were secondary in importance to the creation of the norm of a unitary army—an army that possessed no social or political allegiance except to the government through the minister of defense.[10] The connection between the struggles for control of the defense establishment and the problem of legitimacy of the government was by no means coincidental. For it was in the sphere of security more than in any other sphere that the problem of defining the boundaries of the national collectivity emerged—in other words, defining Israeli identity.

According to one conception, the "Israeli" collectivity comprised all residents of the state, Arabs included, and was reflected in possession of equal rights for all citizens, including the right to participate in elections to the Knesset. The second or nationalist conception, on the other hand, was maintained in the Law of Return, which granted citizenship automatically to any Jew who immigrated to Israel,[11] and in the Security Service Law, which made military service compulsory for citizens and for permanent residents who were not citizens[12]—but did not extend this obligation to Arab residents. Participation in the defense of the state was therefore organized according to nationalist criteria, rather than criteria stemming from the basic rights and duties of citizenship; the conception of Israeli identity adopted in this sphere bore a greater resemblance to the collective identity of the Yishuv than it did to a conception defined according to formal criteria of citizenship. It can even be said that the act of participating in the defense of the state became an expression on one' affinity for or allegiance to the national center.

This interpretation is supported by two exceptions to the criterion of "Jewishness" for determining compulsory military service. Members of the Druze community at first volunteered and were later drafted for military service.[13] And various practical arrangements were made, such as the exemption of *yeshiva* students and religiously observant girls from military service, to release the extreme non-Zionist ultraorthodox minority from service in the army.[14] The security sphere was thus perceived as symbolizing linkage between the ideology of the Jewish national renaissance with the State of Israel as a political entity.

The differences between the state and movement orientations were expressed in other spheres as well, of which the most outstanding and problematic was education. Following the desire of ideological groups in the Yishuv to shape the entire way of life of their members, separate educational systems or "trends" were established reflecting these ideological divisions. This fragmentation of education on an ideological basis became a focus of controversy because it clashed with the principle of *mamlachtiut*. Ben-Gurion and a considerable part of Mapai's leadership claimed that education should not be left in the hands of political movements.[15] Advocates of separate trends within the Labor movement argued that the Labor movement was not just a political group struggling for power in a competitive democracy but a political force with a special pioneering mission. Labor's duty was to preserve the social base of the pioneering sector through a separate educational trend. Ben-Gurion's views eventually carried the day. He and his supporters were helped by the fact that Mapai constituted the backbone of the coalition and as such held the education portfolio. This blunted the edge of the argument that the abolition of trends was liable to increase the influence of the Labor movement's opponents.

Political considerations and principles were also involved in the status of the religious trend. The religious Zionist parties opposed the complete integration of the Mizrahi–Hapoel Hamizrahi educational trend into the general one with the concomitant elimination of the differences between them, claiming that traditionally inclined parents would not agree to send their children to schools of a secular nature. Since they could not impose a religious character on all schools, they wanted at least to preserve the possibility of choosing between schools of a religious and a nonreligious nature. The religious parties were aided by the fact that the coalition relied on a partnership between Mapai and the religious parties during the early years of the state's existence. This partnership enabled the religious parties to exert pressure to secure an arrangement according to which supervision of all schools was transferred to the government but separate curricula were drawn up for all the schools of the religious trend. The compromise contained the seeds of continual conflict and competing attempts to persuade parents to send their children to one trend or another. This rivalry reflected a deeply rooted conflict in cultural values. It was sustained by political interests and also, to some extent by the institutional interests of the secular and religious state educational systems, each of which aspired to maximum expansion. From time to time this issue created friction between the religious and secular partners of the coalition, and negotiations at a party level were required to resolve the differences.[16]

The state's appropriation of functions from the particularistic political organizations did not go so far as to deprive them of all their functions. These organizations, especially the Histadrut, remained among the main power bases of the dominant elite. For this reason, this elite was interested in the continued provision of services by particularistic organizations, since only through joining these organizations (and thus helping maintain the power base) could people benefit from these services. This applied primarily to the health services of the Histadrut, for many people the only health service available. Thus, paradoxically, the Labor movement was more inclined to forego direct control of a public service with a definite value content, such as education, than a public service which was neutral in values, such as health. In this respect Mapai, the dominant power in the Histadrut's approach to education and health, differed from the approach of the national institutions of the Yishuv. In the time of the Mandate, the national institutions did not assume certain instrumental functions on the assumption that the Mandatory authorities would deal with them, whereas it zealously observed the principle of control over functions with a value significance. A different approach arose during the political conflicts after the establishment of the state. Mapai's main political rival during the early years of the state was Mapam, which had considerable influence in the Histadrut and the settlement movements. The parties of the right, on the other hand, did not at that time constitute a serious political competitor. It appears that Mapai preferred to transfer to the state those services that were likely to weaken the left. On the other hand, it preferred to leave under Histadrut control those services which, organizationally, tied to it large sections of the population, especially new immigrants, thus preventing their exposure to political mobilization by other parties. Mapai regarded Mapam as a competitor for influence among native-born youth, while it was mainly the parties outside the Histadrut—the

religious parties on the one hand and Herut, the political party established by the leadership of the former IZL, on the other—that were its
main competitors for political support from the new immigrants.

During the late 1950s, following changes in the structure of the
economy and the expansion of the defense establishment, the power of
the state authorities grew in relation to that of the Histadrut. At that
time the question of the transfer of functions from the Histadrut to the
state became a subject of contention within Mapai itself. Whereas Ben-
Gurion advocated the continued transfer of functions from the Histadrut
to the state, the claim was made, principally by P. Lavon, the secretary
general of the Histadrut, that too large a concentration of power in the
hands of the state contained the danger of "statism."[17] According to this
argument, the extensive range of the Histadrut's activities constituted
a guarantee against the overcentralization of political power within one
institutional framework, that of the state. In contrast, Ben-Gurion and
his supporters argued that particularistic centers of power represent
vested interests and interfere with the formation of policy guided by a
comprehensive conception of the national interest.[18]

Alongside the problem of the relationship between the state and the
movement subcenters, the establishment of the State of Israel created
another problem: the Jewish Agency's transformation from nucleus of
the national center at the time of the Yishuv into a new subcenter after
the establishment of the state. This old-new subcenter had no connection
with any particular party or movement, but from an organizational and
budgetary point of view it constituted a separate framework alongside
the state framework. Moreover, the political power relationships within
the Jewish Agency were not identical to those in the state institutions.
On the one hand, the Jewish Agency was connected with the Zionist
organizations abroad, principally in the United States. On the other
hand, the ruling coalition in the Jewish Agency was wider than that
in the Israeli government and at times included parties in opposition in
Israel, such as Herut.[19]

The continued separate existence of the Jewish Agency stemmed from
the role it played in the mobilization of resources, especially in the
United States. The tax-deductible status of contributions to the Jewish
Agency (through the United Jewish Appeal) in the United States was
granted on condition that the funds be used for what could be defined
as philanthropic purposes and would not be transferred directly to a
foreign government. Since funds for immigration and settlement were

raised in the United States, the administration of these functions remained in the hands of the Jewish Agency. Furthermore, at the time of the mass immigration, the absorption and maintenance of immigrants also remained within the jurisdiction of the Jewish Agency, a fact which contributed to the continued involvement of political parties in the process of immigrant absorption.

New Functions of the National Center: Executive, Judicial, and Legislative

The third problem that faced the political center in the early years was the expansion of its sphere of activity as a consequence of the need to assume functions which the Yishuv's political center had not been obligated to perform. The State of Israel in fact arose in the midst of administrative chaos deliberately left behind by the British. This, together with the fact that few Jews had been employed as officials in the Mandate's service, forced the newly established state to set up an entirely new administrative system for most of the government.[20] The fact that the state was established in the midst of a war increased the scope of government's activities and its ability to mobilize resources through emergency measures. Manpower was mobilized for military service or at least confined to its place of employment. Control was imposed on exports, imports, and the allocation of goods; financial means were mobilized by a revenue administration that was set up overnight. These initial steps helped to expand the scope of the administration's activities and to deepen its penetration into various spheres far beyond the point that was accepted in Mandatory times, when governmental intervention in the economy was quite limited.

Success in organizing the military sphere was essential in its own right and for the very survival of the system as a whole. The strength of the regular armies of the Arab states—whose manpower resources were much greater than that of the IDF—could be counterbalanced only by maximum mobilization of Israel's population, which numbered approximately seven hundred thousand on 14 May 1948. The professional cadre of the Hagana was incapable of meeting the new requirements due to its small numbers and the unsuitability of some of the veteran Hagana commanders for posts of command under conditions of modern regular warfare, because of either their age or their lack of appropriate military training. As a result, the new cadre of young military per-

sonnel[21] who emerged rose rapidly in rank due to the expansion of the
military framework and the high rate of losses among commanders.

The same circumstances of war that led to the rapid development of
a military system efficient enough to secure victory in the War of Independence caused considerable difficulties for the development of civilian
administration in the absence of an orderly transfer of authority from
the Mandatory regime to the Israeli government. The civilian functions
could be performed at first only by appointing officials of the national
institutions and mobilizing additional employees for government service
from activists of the political parties, the Histadrut, and the Hagana.
Consequently, traces of the party-key system were most apparent in the
early stages of the civil service. Many posts in government ministries
were filled by members of the party to which the minister belonged. In
this respect, the emerging government administration may be said to
have adopted the operational patterns of the organized Yishuv. The
emerging state bureaucracy was thus not a "civil service" in the British
sense of the term. The dividing line between it and the political realm
was blurred. Considerations of party politics influenced government
policy; and the heads of the executive branch on both the bureaucratic
and the political levels preferred policies that gave them a wide range
of discretion. This naturally became a source of power, because the
possibility of allocating resources on a particularistic and ad hoc basis
could be translated into influence over the bureaucracy's clientele. The
tendency to permit wide discretion to the executive was one of the
legacies of the Yishuv period. The executive organs of the national institutions operated without systematic control based on binding legal
norms. Actually, there was a legal framework within which those
institutions operated, but illegal and semilegal activities were justified
if they served national interest.

The extreme flexibility which characterized the institutional system
of the organized Yishuv was inconsistent with the organizational patterns
characteristic of the executive branch in sovereign states in Western
democracies. The concept of orderly government in a sovereign democratic system, as it developed in Western Europe and North America,
implies a system of obligatory universalistic rules as well as the existence
of authorities to ensure the observance of these rules. The latter function
is usually given to the judiciary and, in certain cases, to the legislature.
The transformation of the "state in the making" into a sovereign state

immediately raised the question of determining binding legal norms that could not be manipulated by particularistic interests.

In the judicial sphere, in contrast to other spheres, the State of Israel adopted the British norms to which the legal profession was accustomed by training and experience. The character of the legal authority was molded from the start by these norms, and political considerations did not play any outstanding role in appointments to the bench. This trend was facilitated by the fact that the organized Yishuv had not possessed a legal system of its own and also by the character of the first minister of justice, Pinhas Rosen, who was distinguished by his zeal for the judiciary's independence. In these circumstances, the courts, particularly the Supreme Court, attained an independent status based on public recognition and professional norms. It was this status that enabled the Supreme Court to resist deviations from the law on the part of the executive branch and by so doing to become a defender of civil rights. Protection of civil rights was institutionalized in the Supreme Court's second role, that a high court of justice which could be appealed to in cases where the executive's actions were *ultra vires*. This function of the court, which originated in the British legal system, has been exploited to a greater extent than in Britain itself. The publicity given to this function had a cumulative effect on the conduct of the executive branch.

The judiciary embodied a principle of action which conflicted with the principle of electoral and political dominance upheld by the political elite which shaped the new Israeli regime. This elite favored a close association between party politics and decision-making in government and rationalized its approach on the basis of a formalistic democratic ideology which maintained that ultimate authority was reserved to representatives of democratic institutions alone. Accordingly, antagonism sometimes arose between this elite and those authorities, such as the judiciary, who sought to create an autonomous sphere from which party and political considerations were excluded. Despite this antagonism, however, the political elite generally accepted the verdict of the judiciary and reconciled itself to the restriction of its freedom of action by the legal norms applied by independent judicial bodies.[22]

Whereas the judiciary fully exploited the authority granted it and even tried to extend it, the legislature of Knesset—which from the start possessed extremely broad authority—avoided translating all this authority into political power vis-à-vis the executive branch. The Transition

Ordinance and afterwards the Basic Law: The Knesset granted the Knesset far-reaching authority in comparison with other parliaments.[23] First of all, the Knesset was established as the sole legislative body. Second, the Knesset was not restricted in the process of legislation except by its own rules of procedure. Since no other body was authorized to invalidate its laws as unconstitutional and since there was only one clause in one law the amendment of which required a special majority, a simple parliamentary majority could easily change any law.[24] Third, the Kenesset alone was entitled to dissolve itself before the date fixed by law. Fourth, the parliamentary immunity of Knesset members was most comprehensive and included unlimited protection against charges of slander in the case of statements made both inside and outside the Knesset. The immunity of a Knesset member may not be revoked even if the member consents.[25] Even revocation of immunity in the case of a criminal charge which has nothing to do with anything said by a Knesset member depends on a resolution of the plenum based on the recommendation of the Knesset House Committee.

The extensive authority of the Knesset is an extreme manifestation of the tendency to emphasize the ultimate sovereignty of this institution which symbolizes Israel's representative democracy and forms the link between the electoral process and policy-making. Paradoxically, it was this concept that eventually led to the Knesset's relative weakness vis-à-vis the executive, since it was responsible for shifting the center of political decision-making to the leadership of the parties. The parties and their machines constituted the main instrument for mobilizing the support of the voters who determine the strength of each party in the Knesset. The party institutions also determine the lists of candidates for the Knesset. Furthermore, party discipline is based on an ideological tradition which regards the person elected as a party delegate and expects him or her to give way to the party's opinion, except on questions regarded as "matters of conscience."

The tendency to shift the center of gravity in decision-making from the parliamentary party representatives to other party institutions was a consequence of the fact that these institutions served as a common forum for party representatives in governmental and other public institutions. The existence of foci of political power possessing quasi-governmental authority, such as the Jewish Agency and the Histadrut, resulted in a need to coordinate the policy of the party representatives in these institutions. This need was particularly felt in those parties such as

Mapai whose status in both the government and these institutions lent national significance to their policies. Accordingly, policy-making processes were concentrated in the hands of the parties' central leadership whose patterns of action were frequently ad hoc and informal.[26]

Another restriction on the authority of state institutions resulted from an act of the Knesset itself. By passing the Marriage and Divorce Law, the Knesset surrendered its right to legislate on matters of personal status. In this sphere, all inhabitants of Israel—whether Jews, Muslims, Druze, or Christians—are subject to the religious laws of their respective communities. As far as Jews are concerned, the right to perform marriage and divorce ceremonies was given to authorized rabbis employed by the religious councils.[27] Exclusive jurisdiction in matters of personal status was handed to the rabbinical courts, which render judgments only according to Jewish religious law. Similarly, jurisdiction over Muslims was granted to the Muslim religious courts, jurisdiction over Druze to Druze religious courts, while sole authority to perform marriages and divorces between Christians was given to the religious authorities of the recognized Christian communities. This decision of the Israeli legislature to continue the practice that prevailed in the period of the Mandate, according to which a person was subject to religious law in matters of personal status, was significant from the viewpoint not only of religious institutions' authority, but also of civil rights.[28]

The transfer of jurisdiction in personal status to other authorities which operate according to laws that cannot be changed by the Knesset was part of the wider question of the relationship between state and religion in Israel. This question, in fact, constituted the focus of a political value conflict from the moment the state was established. On the value level, the conflict was defined as one between a state ruled by civil law and a state ruled by *halacha* (religious law), while on the political level, the conflict was reflected in the controversy over the need to adopt a constitution for the state. The first Knesset was elected as a constituent assembly whose task was to pass a constitution and then resign. But at its first meeting it decided to become a parliament in the full meaning of the term and to change its name to the First Knesset. This was actually a reflection of the tendency to postpone a basic decision on the enactment of a constitution. The Knesset decided that the state's constitution would consist of different sections, each of which would constitute a separate "basic law." In this way, the Knesset made it possible to postpone legislation connected with the question of religion and state without having to delay constitutional legislation on other matters. The fact that the question of state and religion was left open was a source of crises in the government coalition and, in some cases, even led to the resignation of the religious parties from the coalition.[29] But the postponement of constitutional legislation made it possible to overcome crises by ad hoc arrangements lacking constitutional validity, such as the so-called status quo agreement on matters of state and religion which enabled the formation of coalitions after every election to the Knesset.

The Political Aspects of Immigrant Absorption

The fourth problem that faced the state was the absorption of new immigrants. In contrast to other new states established after the Second World War, the State of Israel experienced a change of population as well as a change of regime. Independence was accompanied not only by the creation of a new sovereign authority but also by the emergence of a new clientele for the political system. On the one hand, a considerable part of the Arab population fled during the War of Independence, while on the other hand, the state absorbed an immigration that doubled the Jewish population within less than four years—from seven hundred thousand in 1948 to over one million four hundred thousand in 1952. This demographic change involved both economic and social problems. Capital imports could not keep pace with immigration during the first years of the state's existence. This lag meant that the amount of capital mobilized by the state abroad was insufficient to meet the housing requirements of immigrants and to provide permanent employment for them through investment.[30] A large proportion of the immigrants thus continued to live in immigrant camps or temporary housing (ma'abarot). Only a minority of the immigrants were absorbed in agriculture, industry, or services, whereas the majority continued to exist on Jewish Agency allowances or from public works provided for them by the government.[31]

To these problems were added cultural and social problems. Of the two main sources of immigration, one was the remnant of European Jewry, who carried the traumatic memory of the Holocaust. These people had been uprooted from their homes, dispossessed of their property, and left without family; many of them were mentally or physically ill. The second source were the Jewry of Muslim countries in the Middle East and North Africa, whose cultural background was alien to the European cultural patterns of the Yishuv. Moreover, they were, for the most part, poorly educated, without means, and lacking the vocational training that would enable them to integrate into the economy. The dimensions and nature of the immigration created not only organizational problems connected with housing, livelihood, and education, but also problems of absorbing the immigrants into the social and political system without upsetting its stability or its cultural and political continuity.

The problem of preserving the dominant political culture arose from the difference between the new population and the veteran population of the Yishuv. Large sections of the new population were not acquainted with the rules of the political game in multiparty democratic societies and especially with the complicated network of relationships among movements, parties, and groups which had developed in the Yishuv. Nor had they undergone the political socialization typical of a large part of the European immigrants, whose motives for coming to the country were more ideological. Their ignorance of the Hebrew language caused immigrants difficulties in their contacts with the veteran population and the absorption administration. These characteristics of the new immigration intensified its dependence on the absorbing institutional system—a dependence characteristic of all immigration processes.

Also contributing to this dependence was the desire of the dominant elite to guide the new immigrants in order to ensure continuity of the existing political culture as well as this elite's positions of power. It is not surprising that the dominant elite, especially those organizations under the influence of Mapai, developed a paternalistic approach. The immigrant was conceived as an object of sociopolitical mobilization rather than as a subject with an autonomous will, aspirations, and expectations. The paternalistic approach expressed itself in the way the absorbing institutions interpreted the notion of the "integration of exiles": integration was to follow the model of a "melting pot" in which the immigrants abandoned their alien features in order to resemble the absorbing society. In the political sphere the paternalistic approach implied an effort on the part of the political parties to mobilize new immigrants into their ranks. This tendency was in line with the general conviction in Israel that new immigrants had the right to become full-fledged citizens im-

mediately on arrival; voting rights were granted to immigrants without
any restriction whatsoever, such as knowledge of the language or a
period of residence in the country.

The granting of full rights of political participation supposedly exposed the immigrants to free, unfettered competition in which the
parties could mobilize their support. Open competition in which the
parties could approach the new immigrants on equal terms could even
have changed the political balance of power. It was difficult, for
example, to assume that immigrants with a traditional background from
Asia and Africa would give their votes to Labor movement parties
whose ideology reflected European socialism in the late nineteenth
and early twentieth centuries and had absolutely nothing in common
with the immigrants' background. Parties such as the religious ones or
the nationalist Herut were likely to offer such immigrants alternatives
more suited to their cultural predispositions. Another hypothetical
possibility was the organization of new political frameworks for new
immigrants or immigrants from certain countries. These hypothetical
possibilities, however, were never realized. The results of the elections
to the Knesset in 1949 and in the fifties revealed that the division of
power among the party blocs—the Labor movement parties, the right-
wing and center parties, and the religious parties—had not essentially
changed in spite of the changes in the size and composition of the
population.[32] Nor did any new political force emerge outside the existing
parties. The only changes that did occur affected the internal balance
within the main political blocs and were caused partly by mergers and
splits among the parties themselves. Furthermore, an analysis of the
election results in the 1950s shows that these changes originated mainly
in shifts among the votes of veteran residents, and not in the impact of
the new immigration's vote.[33]

This stability in the political system calls for an explanation. What
was the reason that the apparent exposure of new immigrants to competitive political mobilization did not create a large-scale floating votes?
The answer lies, among other things, in the gap between the immigrants'
de jure right to participate in the country's political life and the influence
of the informal mechanisms that regulated the de facto processes of their
integration. Constitutionally the openness of the system was optimal.
Moreover, the absorption machinery, unlike that at the time of the
Yishuv, was controlled by the state or the Jewish Agency and not by

movements or parties. Yet, the absorption institutions were only a formal façade behind which the party machines operated. On the practical level, various branches of the state administration operated as agencies of political bodies through the system of the party key. The absorption machinery, particularly that of the Jewish Agency, was manned by party representatives; groups of immigrants were directed by the absorption authorities to frameworks sponsored by political movements, in accordance with prior agreements. This phenomenon was particularly salient in the case of the immigrants directed to agricultural settlement, which had always possessed a clear ideological coloration. These patterns of deployment served to limit free competition for the political support of the new immigrants, including those who were eventually absorbed in the large cities.

For a considerable proportion of immigrants, the logistic organization of immigration began abroad. Immigrants from Europe and North Africa spent weeks and sometimes months in transit camps in Italy and France. The Jewish Agency's emissaries who operated in these camps were chosen on the party-key basis. They often cooperated with emissaries of their own parties and settlement movements in attempting to enlist the immigrants into their ranks. In immigrant camps in Israel, where immigrants remained until their transfer to another transit framework, the immigrants were entirely dependent for accommodation, food, clothing, health, and educational services on the absorption personnel. This dependence decreased only slightly when the immigrants were transferred to *ma'abarot*. Here they obtained temporary employment in public works for which they were paid a minimum wage. But they remained outside the more open economic and social system of the veteran Jewish community. No less important was the fact that the transition to the next stage in the absorption system—permanent residence in an agricultural settlement, development town, or urban district, and permanent employment—was also regulated by the absorption machinery which determined the order of departure from the *ma'abarot*.

This dependence exposed the immigrants during the first stage of their life in the country to the manipulations of the absorbing personnel, who, as we have stressed, were not apolitical bureaucrats. The principle of the party key in the main absorption organization—the Jewish Agency—received almost complete legitimation and was recognized de facto in the state administration, at least during the first years after the establishment of the state. Furthermore, services were supplied by frameworks which in practice were dominated by parties. Thus, for example, health services were provided to immigrants, in accordance with an agreement with the Jewish Agency, by the Histadrut, in which Mapai had an absolute majority. The major agency for the provision of religious services was the rabbinate and the ministry of religious affairs, which politically tended to act in a manner that served the interests of the religious parties. Even the transfer to permanent frameworks, which occurred in the mid- and late fifties, did not fully expose the immigrants to free competition by political parties. That part of the immigration which was absorbed in agricultural settlement remained linked to party frameworks through the settlement movements. The connection between the agricultural settlements and their respective umbrella organizations was reinforced by the economic and organizational sanctions which these bodies could impose on deviants, whether individuals or entire *moshavim*.[34] A greater degree of openness existed in the immigrant and development towns, but here too there were many possibilities for political manipulation. Political parties obtained influence by acting as intermediaries in procuring jobs, business licenses, housing credit, and so forth.[35] This phenomenon was particularly significant among immigrants with a traditional social background, such as those from Yemen and some of those from North Africa, who came to Israel organized in "extended families," a practice which facilitated the manipulation of entire kinship groups whose heads became agents of the parties and received various benefits in exchange.

The greatest exposure to free competition existed in the large cities where possibilities for party manipulation were more limited and opportunities for economic and social mobility for the individual were greater. Over the years, the relative openness of urban life exercised a certain influence on the immigrants' voting patterns. In the election campaigns of the 1960s, immigrants' votes showed noticeable signs of mobility away from Mapai toward opposition parties, principally to Herut. In this respect it is worth mentioning that most immigrants were finally absorbed in the large cities. Some of them arrived there not directly from the *ma'abarot* but only after an intermediate period spent in a *moshav* or immigrant town.[36] There was a high population turnover in the new agricultural settlements and immigrant towns, which was apparently politically significant. The immigrants who had spent some time in a *moshav* or even an immigrant town had, however, been subjected, during a critical period for the crystallization of their political identity, to the influence of selective political socialization, which in many instances left an imprint on their later voting patterns.

This pattern of absorption by the political system had far-reaching effects on the political culture and political stability in Israel. First and foremost, it created a contradiction between the official position of Israeli parties (the Labor parties in particular) in regard to the appropriate system of political mobilization and the actual methods employed by party members. While official positions stressed ideological affinity as the basis of party membership, party workers among the immigrants mobilized support by allocating benefits. However, this instrumental dimension of party affiliation could not serve as a complete substitute for ideological attachment. There was a need for a new basis for securing the identification of party members with the political frameworks they joined. Intellectual identification with sophisticated ideologies typical of the parties of the Yishuv was exchanged for simpler and even simplistic symbols aimed at provoking positive emotional reactions toward charismatic personalities and the concepts they were regarded as personifying. Much effort was expended attempting to identify the state's achievements with the personality of Ben-Gurion. At the other extreme of the political spectrum, there was a major effort to boost the personality of Herut leader Menachem Begin as the embodiment of militant nationalism. These changes in the methods of political mobilization and the symbols of political identification were not expressed in the official ideologies; the parties preferred to create a gap between theory and practice rather than modify their ideology.

In the course of time, these developments had a feedback effect, if not on the contents of the official ideology, at least on the role of ideology in the considerations and decisions of the dominant political elite. One may point to the mass immigration as one of the main factors responsible for the Israeli version of the "end of ideology." At the same time, it should be noted that the decline of ideological fervor did not occur to the same extent in all parties. In fact, those parties that lagged behind in the transition from ideological to pragmatic thinking, such as Mapam, were weakened due to the difficulties they encountered in enlisting support among the immigrants. These changes in the nature and function of ideology can also be seen as part of the process of "normalization," that is, the transformation of Israeli society from a pioneering to a "normal" society.[37] Another consequence of the patterns

of immigrant absorption in the political system was the strengthening
of the party machines, which consisted of a cadre of paid workers whose
main task was the manipulation of political power at the local level.[38]

It was the radical changes in the style of political activity that, paradoxically, helped to preserve the stability of Israel's political system.
The experience of other countries has shown that changes in the style
of political activity, such as the transformation of an elite party into
a mass party or the rise of a charismatic leader, often lead to the rise
of new elite groups. In Israel, the composition of the leadership was
preserved despite changes in the composition of the population and the
manner of political mobilization. The flexibility demonstrated by Israel's
political parties, above all by Mapai, in adapting their patterns of
activity to the new reality created by immigrant absorption enabled
them to undergo the transformation from Yishuv to state with a minimum of change in the personal composition and authority of the leadership. In addition to this continuity of political leadership, power
relationships among the principal party blocs remained stable as well,
so that the political sphere in general was distinguished by stability in
the period of demographic, economic, and social changes which marked
the first years following the state's establishment. The relative stability
of the political system enabled Israel's parliamentary democracy to observe the basic rules of the game of a pluralistic and competitive political
system. The paternalistic pattern of immigrant absorption restricted free
political competition between the various parties, but at the same time
it afforded each of them a certain amount of breathing space and thus
enabled pluralism to survive without presenting any serious threat to
the position of the veteran political elite. It may even be ventured that
had it not been for the success of this absorption pattern in perventing
a threat to the position of the elite and the vested interests of the veteran
population, the center would have had to choose between deviation from
the rules of parliamentary democracy and acceptance of political disintegration. Disintegration would have endangered not only the position
of the elite but also the capacity of the system to solve social, economic,
and security problems.

Political Parties in the Transition
from Yishuv to State

From the foregoing it is clear that the major social, political, and
organizational actors in the transition process from Yishuv to state were
the parties, since it was actually the parties that established the political

framework of the state in 1948. The capacity of the parties to adapt to
the new circumstances the emergence of the state created was determined largely by their previous structural characteristics and patterns
of action—particularly, the tendency to role expansion inherited from
the period of the Yishuv. This tendency was a prominent feature of all
Israeli parties, but the parties that were able to expand the scope of
their activities most were those whose key positions in the power
structure enabled them to control the allocation of resources through
government and public bureaucracies. Although all parties were to some
degree involved in the manipulation of nonpolitical resources for political purposes, the parties that were involved to the greatest extent were
the two major participants in the coalition—Mapai and the National
Religious Party (Mafdal), the successor of Mizrahi and Hapoel Hamizrahi. Even a strictly oppositionist party such as Herut was involved in
these activities, as seen from the fact that Herut maintained its own
health services and housing companies.[39]

Role expansion was less manifest in the left-wing parties of the
Histadrut, Mapam, and Hatnua La'Ahdut Ha'avoda, for the lines
dividing each party from its associated *kibbutz* movement were blurred.
In fact, the party acted as the political arm of the movement while
other nonpolitical functions were concentrated in the *kibbutz* movement. The *kibbutz* movements were naturally concerned with the
mobilization and allocation of resources and thus created an organizational apparatus which first served the needs of the *kibbutz* members
and to a lesser extent the needs of the active urban members of the
parties.

This role expansion of Israeli parties was more important during the
early years of the state than at a later period. As we mentioned above,
the parties played a central role in absorbing the mass immigration and
in recruiting manpower for the government bureaucracy in the early
years of the state. But after the late 1950s apparently the tendency to
role expansion gradually diminished. Most of the transit facilities and
makeshift camps for immigrants that had been intensively penetrated
by the parties disappeared, and most immigrants after the late 1950s
were absorbed directly into permanent urban settlements where direct
party influence was rather limited.

Other factors that reduced the dependence of new immigrants and
other groups on the party machines were the conditions of relative
prosperity and full employment and the development of universalistic
mechanisms under government auspices for the allocation of jobs and

social security benefits. An additional factor was the gradual professionalization of the civil service. As the tasks of the civil service became
more complex and as the need for expertise became more apparent,
the importance of political criteria in manpower recruitment decreased.

Nevertheless, the scope of activities engaged in by Israeli parties
remained rather broad in comparison with that of parties in other
democratic nations. Narrow particularistic parties such as the Farmers
Association disappeared as their members were absorbed into more
heterogeneous parties, such as the General Zionists. National ethnic
lists also gradually disappeared. Most parties began to broaden the
social basis of their electoral support, though differences continued to
exist in the relative amount of support received from different strata.
Here we may point to three characteristic types.

The first was the heterogeneous party. The party closest to this type
was the largest of all Israeli parties, Mapai, which later became the
dominant component of the Israel Labor party. The party closest to
Mapai in this respect was Mafdal, Mapai's main coalition partner
during the 1950s and 1960s. The votes of these two parties came from
both low- and high-income groups, manual labor and white-collar
workers, the salaried and the self-employed, rural and urban groups,
new immigrants and veteran residents, Oriental Jews and Jews of European origin, and from among those with high as well as low levels of
education. The distribution according to country of origin is of special
importance when we consider that in Israel there is a high correlation
between country of origin, level of education, occupation, and (at least
until the 1970s) level of income; and that Jews from countries of
African and Asian origin (i.e., Oriental Jews) tend to concentrate in
the lowest levels of the social hierarchy.[40]

The second type was the homogeneous party. Although there was
no such thing as a completely homogeneous party, Mapam and Hatnua
La'Ahdut Ha'avoda on the left, the Liberal party in the center, and
Agudat Israel of the religious parties were closest to this type. These
parties had one major characteristic in common: the predominance of
Jews of European origin among their leaders, rank and file, and voters.
The factor of social origin meant that few of their supporters were from
groups with low levels of income and education. There was, however, a
clear distinction between parties of the left and the Liberals in respect
to the number of their supporters among the self-employed and those
with high incomes. The left-wing parties mentioned drew their support

from the Labor movement settlements, skilled labor, white-collar workers, and professionals, while the supporters of the Liberals were mainly businessmen and industrialists with the addition of some professionals and senior white-collar workers.

The third type was the party characterized by a polarity in the social origins of party leaders and followers, with a leadership composed almost solely of those of European origin while members and supporters were largely of Oriental origin. The party closest to this type was the right-wing opposition party, Herut. In absolute terms the number of Oriental Jews who supported Herut was lower than the number who supported Mapai, but in relative terms the percentage of Orientals among Herut's voters was higher than the comparable figure for Mapai. In this context it should also be mentioned that the relative extent of support for Herut among the veteran Sephardic groups who settled in Palestine before 1948 was higher than the rate of support among Orientals who immigrated after 1948.[41] In the 1960s, Herut and the Liberals formed a common electoral and parliamentary bloc (not a full merger), and the distribution of voters for this bloc, called Gahal, was similar to the distribution for a heterogeneous party.[42]

Another change took place with regard to the frame of reference refers to the orientation of a party, either inward toward a solid nucleus of members and supporters, or outward toward the wider society. In this sphere as well there was a wide range of variation among Israeli parties, with the orientations that crystallized before the establishment of the state persisting thereafter, in a less decisive way. The parties whose pattern of action was closest to the sectarian type were Mapam within the Labor movement and Agudat Israel among the religious parties. These parties tended to concentrate first on serving the needs of their members both in the instrumental and value senses, even when this meant relinquishing opportunities to make an impact on the wider society.

The importance of the sectarian parties lies more in the existence of groups of people highly commited to their framework than in their influence on Israeli political life in general. The parties that have had the widest and most significant impact on political life were those with an external orientation, especially Mapai. Both organizationally and ideologically, this party was the opposite of a sectarian party. An intermediate type between the sectarian and the "catch-all" parties was Herut. On the one hand Herut sought support from a wide variety of groups, but on the other hand it maintained the organizational structure and policy-making procedures characteristic of a movement. The latter characteristics were particularly evident in the tendency to reject the incorporation in its leadership of any figure or group other than those belonging to the narrow inner circle of its leader, Begin, and his former comrades-in-arms in IZL. Nevertheless, Herut's willingness to join other parties in political blocs such as Gahal or the Likud is an indication of a strong external orientation existing parallel to—and sometimes at cross-purposes with—an internal orientation.

Examination of the changes that occurred in the structural features of the parties after 1948 shows that in the process of adapting to the political framework of the state, the structural differences between the parties narrowed. The parties moved in the direction of the example set by Mapai, which before the establishment of the state preceded the other parties in developing organizational frameworks for mobilizing resources and manpower on a broad scale.

The over-all power of Mapai can be attributed to the cumulative result of its achievements on three different planes: the electoral, the parliamentary, and the governmental. On the electoral plane, Mapai's power lay in its success in continually retaining the support of at least a third of the voters in elections over the years, despite the demographic, economic, and cultural changes in the electorate. This success can in turn be attributed to Mapai's structural and ideological characteristics. First Mapai's very size assured it control of a larger share of resources from the start, a fact which affected the election results. The allocation of resources accordance with the party-key principle turned power relationships in the *present* into the basis of resource allocation affecting power relationships in the *future*. The party-key principle was thus a mechanism that preserved the status quo in existing power relationships. But control of resources was not in itself sufficient. In order to derive electoral gains from these resources, it was necessary to exploit these resources for gaining the support of groups and individuals. Mapai's activity over a wide range of fields that were not always purely political created momentum for the efficient exploitation of the resources for Mapai's electoral needs. Both the continuity of Mapai's activities and the existence of a logistical network for mobilizing active supporters at election time helped Mapai to preserve its position among the voters between elections.

On the parliamentary plane, Mapai's power was determined not only by election results—which in the proportional system gave it a representation equal to its proportion of the total vote—but also by its pivotal location on a left-right ideological continuum. The impossibility of forming a coalition without Mapai, due to the unfeasibility of a coalition between the extremes of left and right, lent Mapai a stronger bargaining position than it deserved by virtue of its representation in the Knesset. Mapai's bargaining capacity on the parliamentary level also affected its power on the governmental level. First, it enabled Mapai to form a government in which it would have a majority of ministers; second, it enabled Mapai to distribute portfolios in such a manner that it would retain control of the key positions of prime minister, minister of foreign affairs, minister of finance, minister of education, and minister of defense. In these circumstances, Mapai's power in the coalition was even greater than its power in the Knesset, and this situation was reflected in decision-making within the coalition.

These features of Israel's political system influenced the political aims as well as the actual conduct of other parties besides Mapai. Mapam's leader, Meir Ya'ari, referred to parties aiming at being a "corrective" to Mapai in contrast to parties which seek to become an alternative to it. Actually most parties gave up attempting to replace Mapai as the ruling party, at least until the mid-sixties.

To summarize, then: the central phenomenon marking the transition from a "state in the making" to a sovereign state was political stability in circumstances of social change. This stability depended on the political center's ability to solve some major problems which it faced when independence was achieved: the imposition of authority on formerly dissident or separatist groups; the appropriation of quasi-governmental functions from particularistic political bodies; the assumption of new governmental functions and the enforcement of binding legal norms; and the absorption of the new immigration of the 1950s. Several factors helped the leadership of the Yishuv to cope successfully with these problems and to avoid crises that could have threatened the integrity of the entire system: the existence of rules of the game which had been accepted by the vast majority of political groups before the establishment of the state; the center's ability of mobilize resources in the Diaspora; and the circumstance of the state's establishment at the height of a military struggle which compelled all political bodies in the state to accept the decisions of the central government.

The government which came to grips with these problems was a coalition government, but this did not upset its stability because a strong central party provided the nucleus of the national leadership. This party also ensured the cooperation of other parties by permitting them a share, albeit unequal, of the resources controlled by the political center. Mapai received political support from its coalition partners and a commitment from the opposition parties to abide by the decisions of the government in exchange for access to economic, political, and symbolic resources. The democratic and parliamentary rules of the game that regulated these processes were expressed in the reshuffling of coalition partners rather than in changes in the ruling party, Mapai continuing to constitute the pivotal center of the party system. This ensured stability and continuity at the level of interparty relationships. At the same time, the parties were able to affect the demographic, economic, and cultural changes among the population by acting as agents for the distribution of resources and, to a great extent, as intermediaries between the citizen and the government, and by maintaining a wide range of activities that extended beyond the purely political sphere. One may hypothesize that this pattern of political party activities and government responsiveness to demands presented through the parties contributed to the government's stability, yet at the same time reduced its effectiveness, at least as far as domestic policy is concerned.

9

Conflict Regulation as a Test of Authority Without Sovereignty

Political Integration and Conflict Regulation

The assumption that "there is a distinct overlap between political integration and conflict regulation problems"[1] has become part of the basic approach of social scientists concerned with political integration both within and among political communities. This realization highlights the extent to which political systems are successful in defusing and mitigating conflicts in order to maintain a basic level of social consensus.[2] Essential in this context are rules of the game that prevent the unregulated and unauthorized use of violence and coercion and that permit common action by groups in spite of their conflicting interests. These rules may be based on compromise or on specific procedures for the resolution of issues. The capacity to deal with conflicting demands and interests can thus become a test of legitimate authority. Political conflicts pose a challenge to all political systems, and the challenge becomes more severe as the authority of the system's center is weaker.

We may distinguish four possible outcomes of political conflict that threatens the integrity of a political system. One possible outcome is the monopolization of political power by an elite group which resolves conflicts according to its own interests and values. The opposite of this is the fragmentation of the system to the point where centralized authority disappears and in its place separate centers of authority emerge around different elite groups; this second possibility implies the breakdown of the dominant center and the disintegration of the system. Between these two extremes are two intermediate possible outcomes based on recognition of the legitimate authority of a political center and a consensus concerning the way of dealing with conflicts. The first is the existence of rules of the game based on competition between different elite groups where conflicts of interest are resolved in institutional frameworks according to constitutional procedures. This system is characteristic of presidential or parliamentary democracies based on the interplay between a ruling party and the opposition party that serves as an alternative. The second intermediate system is one of cooperation between elite groups in a coalitionary structure based on bargaining and compromise. This system appears in what we have referred to as "consociational democracies," which are based on the creation of a cartel-like arrangement in the center of political authority.

The two intermediate systems which are both based on a plurality of elite groups are not necessarily mutually exclusive. The first one, of course, stresses controlled competition between rivals and defined procedures for determining the outcome of competition, while the second stresses bargaining and compromise. In the social reality of democratic regimes, however, both elements exist within a single system, and the differences between political systems are determined by the relative emphasis on the competitive or· the consociational element. Furthermore, mechanisms associated with the consociational system, such as bargaining and compromise, are employed to resolve conflicts between functional—although not necessarily political—interests manifested even in totalitarian regimes, where the political center is ruled by one dominant elite.[3] A typical mixed form encountered in democratic regimes is the existence of a coalition in which some but not all of the political elites participate while other elite groups remain in opposition.

Political conflicts may lead to any of the four possible results, including of course the second possibility of the disintegration of the political framework. But the probability that any particular outcome will occur varies in accordance with the nature and extent of social and political cleavages, the strength of the political center, the amount of resources at the disposal of the center, and the external pressures on the system. For example, it is reasonable to assume that an attempt by an elite to create a monopoly in a system in which allegiance to the center is mainly voluntary would result in the fragmentation of the system, as groups denied representation could exercise the option of secession. It is also reasonable to assume that such a system would evince a greater tendency than a sovereign system to adopt patterns of cooperation based on compromise and bargaining, rather than the pattern in which the minority is subjected to clear-cut decisions made by the majority. We may conclude, then, that the constraint implied by the absence of a compulsory constitutional framework is important in determining the systematic consequences of political conflicts. The options open to such a system appear to be between cooperation based on bargaining and compromise and the disintegration of the system as a whole.

The relationships discussed above between conflict resolution and political integration have a direct relevance for the political system of the Yishuv. It is clear that challenges to the political system posed by the internal conflicts in the Yishuv were of greater severity than those facing sovereign states with political centers resting on legitimate authority and a monopoly of the use of coercion. But the fact that the political system of the Yishuv was able to crystallize around a relatively authoritative national center and that this center steadily increased its authority over the years points to the presence of integrative factors which helped the system to overcome the obstacles stemming from the lack of sovereignty.

The growth and consolidation of the political and social system of the Yishuv involved three major dimensions, each of which contained the potential for conflict among the various social and political groups. The first focus of conflict was the legitimacy and scope of authority of the political center. Conflicts over this issue are found in both sovereign and nonsovereign political systems, though the latter are more vulnerable to their consequences. The second focus of conflict was the regulation of exchange and resource allocation. The third focus was ideological competition among images of the ideal future society advocated by different groups. From the moment that one elite group, the Labor movement, achieved a dominant position in the national institutions, it was faced with the problem of preventing the disintegration of the political framework as a result of these conflicts. The conditions imposed

by the nonsovereign political framework meant that the ruling elite
had to create mechanisms for making decisions binding on all parties
to the system while simultaneously dealing with opposing elites who
possessed the option of withdrawal from the system. Thus, the problem
of conflict regulation became the major challenge to the political leadership, a challenge that would determine the fate not only of the dominant
elite, but of the political system as a whole.

Relations between political elites were determined by the nature of
the conflicts among them and by the size of the gaps created by these
conflicts. Such gaps can be measured according to the number of
dimensions of the conflict and its intensity, which in Dahrendorf's words
can be described as the "energy expenditure and degree of involvement
of conflicting parties."[4] Our analysis suggests a direct relationship between the degree of involvement of parties in the conflict and the extent
to which the subject of the conflict was a central issue. The intensity of
conflict is also assumed to be related to the means used. As a struggle
becomes more intense, the tendency to resort to more extreme measures
increases. Therefore, as an indirect measure of the intensity of political
conflict, we may arrange the means used in political conflicts in a scale
of increasing severity, from persuasive means, through economic and
social sanctions, to violence. The intensity of a conflict is also reflected
in the frequency of contacts of a conflictual nature. For example, there
were groups in the Yishuv, such as Agudat Israel, whose contacts with
other groups were restricted to certain spheres, so that although expressions of conflict were intense, they were relatively infrequent. The
situation was reversed in the relations between Mapai and the Zionist
left wing within the Histadrut.

From the perspective of the national center, what counted most was
the size of the gap between the dominant elite in the center and the
other major elites. As we recall, after the mid-1930s, the leadership of
Mapai made up the nucleus of the dominant elite in the center. Therefore, practically speaking, the willingness of other elites to recognize
the authority of the center was dependent largely on the conflicts between the Mapai elite and other elites and the nature of their regulation.

Data indicating the extent of the gap between Mapai and the other
political elites are presented in Table 13, with the gap measured according to the intensity and number of dimensions of the conflict. The data
show that the dominant elite maintained a variety of political relation-

ships expressing different levels of conflict with other elite groups, both
within and without the organized Yishuv. The extent of the gap between
parties to a conflict varied according to the groups involved, so that
the efforts required to bridge this gap were different in each case.

Table 13
**Types of Conflicts between Mapai and Various
Elites and Groups, 1933–43**

Conflict between Mapai and	Dimensions[g]			Intensity	
	Legitimation of Authority	Resource Allocation	Image of Society	Means	Frequency
Revisionists	+	+	+	+	+
Right-wing Ezrahim and religious parties[a]	−	+	+	−	+
Liberal center[b]	−	+	+	−	−
Ethnic groups[c]	−	−	+	−	−
"Assimilating" elites[d]	+	−	−	−	−
Communists	+	−	+	+	+
Extreme Orthodox Jewry[e]	+	−	+	+	−
Zionist left-wing in the Histadrut[f]	−	+	−	−	+

a. Includes the right wing of the General Zionists, the Hamizrahi movement, and the Farmers Association.
b. Includes the left wing of the General Zionists.
c. Includes the Sephardic and Yemenite organizations.
d. Includes nonpolitical notables socially involved with the British and Arab officials and had reservations with regard to the organized Yishuv.
e. Includes Agudat Israel and other extreme Orthodox elements, especially in Jerusalem.
f. Includes Hashomer Hatzair, Poalei-Zion Smol, and after 1944 the Hatnua le-Ahdut Ha'avoda.
g. The symbol (+) indicates a high level of conflict. The symbol (−) indicates a low level of conflict.

Impeding and Facilitating Factors in
Conflict Regulation

The conflicts between the central elite and other elites posed a constant
threat to the existence of the organized Yishuv as a political system,
and there were a number of factors that impeded the capacity of the
center to regulate and possibly even resolve conflicts. The authority of
the center was weakened not only by the voluntary character of participation in the system, but also by the need to wage a constant struggle
for supremacy with the subcenters, which maintained a high degree of
autonomy. In the mid-1930s the assertive exercise of political power
on the part of the Labor movement and unwillingness to concede the
subcenters' autonomy led to the break with the Revisionist movement
and the creation of the dissident underground military organizations.
Ironically, it was the Labor movement itself that had created the
autonomous subcenter that served as a model for others—the Histadrut.
Even after Mapai adopted the approach of "class to nation" and its
leaders assumed key positions in the center, the Histadrut continued
to maintain its autonomy in spheres such as labor exchanges, settlement
policy, and education.

Another obstacle to the mitigation or reduction of conflict was the
"missionary" ideological approach that characterized at least several
of the political movements in the Yishuv. The process of building a
new society from the ground up meant that political decisions could
potentially help mold the basic character of the Jewish society of the
future. Bitter ideological struggles arose because practical decisions were
linked to abstract ideological viewpoints. The ideological basis of
political organization created a multiplicity of political parties (and
other types of subcenters) that congealed into rigid vested interests.

Still another impediment to the center's effective treatment of conflicts was the existence of external centers that served as complementary
centers in some spheres and competing centers in others. Both the
Mandatory government and the Jewish and Zionist frameworks in the
Diaspora served as alternative political authorities for those groups who
disagreed with the policy of the national center or who felt themselves
unjustly deprived of resources or influence in the center.

Paradoxically, some of the factors that impeded the effective resolution of conflicts in the Yishuv also created conditions that facilitated the
regulation and mitigation of conflicts. The restriction of authority

implied by the absence of sovereignty was compensated for in part by restriction of the responsibilities of the center. For example, this meant that the center did not have to resolve the question of the status of religion in society, a task which might have brought on *kulturkampf*.[5] Nor was it obligated to deal with the judicial sphere, which was the responsibility of the Mandatory government. Had the Yishuv desired to establish an independent judiciary system, this would have raised serious problems concerning the independence of a legal system in a political system characterized by extreme politicization.

At times, the existence of other Jewish "centers" in the Diaspora helped to mitigate internal conflicts in the Yishuv, since some of the activities that might have created a source of conflict were carried on abroad, primarily activities related to the mobilization and political socialization of manpower. On the other hand, the political mobilization of potential immigrants in the Diaspora meant that the national center had to determine the distribution of immigration permits among the various movements, which created conflict in another area—the allocation of manpower resources. The tendency for the focus of conflict to shift from mobilization of resources to their allocation was related to the position of the subcenters vis-à-vis the national center. The subcenters impeded the resolution of conflicts by detracting from the authority of the center, but facilitated their resolution by reducing the center's responsibilities. In this fashion the center assumed coalitionary structure. The subcenters functioned as agencies of the center for the performance of certain tasks, chiefly political mobilization, socialization, and interest articulation, while the national center became the institutional framework for the coordination of the common activity of sectors of the organized Yishuv in areas where such activity was considered both necessary and possible.

The variety of ideological movements in the Yishuv was another potential source of conflict, but here too there were mitigating factors which helped to reduce ideological tensions. The ideological and political division that reflected the whole range of economic, cultural, and political cleavages in the Yishuv tended to be cross-cutting. For example, there were right and left wings in both the religious and secular camps, there were "maximalists" and "minimalists" on the national and territorial questions within the right and the left; and in addition to the Histadrut, there were labor organizations affiliated with parties of the right and center, while the Histadrut itself often shared the ownership of economic enterprises with private investors.[6] Futhermore, the socio-economic characteristics of various groups did not correspond to the ideological divisions. The cross-cutting positions of parties on various issues often resulted in a partial overlapping; parties in disagreement on a particular issue were still able to cooperate on other issues, and in doing so reduced the severity of political conflicts in general.

A similar outcome was obtained from the varying preferences of political elites for rewards. These different preferences based on different orientations to resources, opened the door to a variety of patterns of "give and take" between the dominant elite and other elites. One of the characteristics of the Labor movement elite was an inclination to prefer rewards of power to status and economic rewards. Thus, for example, it was possible for Labor to allocate positions of high prestige but limited power to representatives of the Zionist movement in the Diaspora. The power orientation also eased the Labor elite's relationships with the bourgeois elites. The Ezrahim tended to concentrate on economic rather than political activities, and relinquished opportunities to translate their economic achievements into political power, content with a secondary role in the Yishuv's political leadership.

These diverse orientations facilitated limited cooperation between the Labor elite and the conservative Ezrahim elites but intensified the conflict between the Labor movement and the Revisionists. As the Revisionist movement was also power oriented, it openly challenged the Labor elite, preferring to appear as an alternative to the Labor elite rather than cooperate with it in exchange for access to the resources at its disposal. Hence their secession from the World Zionist Organization and establishment of a rival Zionist organization with an independent underground military organization. For these reasons, the conflict between Mapai and the Revisionists was far more intense than the conflict between Mapai and its Ezrahim opponents within the organized Yishuv. Thus, the coalition in the national center was composed of the parties of the Labor movement and the Zionist center, moderate right, and religious parties, while, because of their striving for political supremacy and their inability to play the role of a junior partner in the center, the Revisionists were excluded. Besides the Revisionists, other groups that remained outside the organized Yishuv were those which did not recognize the center's authority, were indifferent to the formation of a national center, or were without a distinct political identity. They included notables from the old Sephardic community who

enjoyed a high social status in the Ottoman period and who were more
involved than other Jewish or Zionist groups with Anglo-Arab elite
circles in Jerusalem during the period of the Mandate.[7] The preferences
for differential types of social rewards influenced various groups' orientation to the organized Yishuv. The relationship between differential
preferences for rewards and political orientation to the organized Yishuv
is presented schematically in Figure 7.

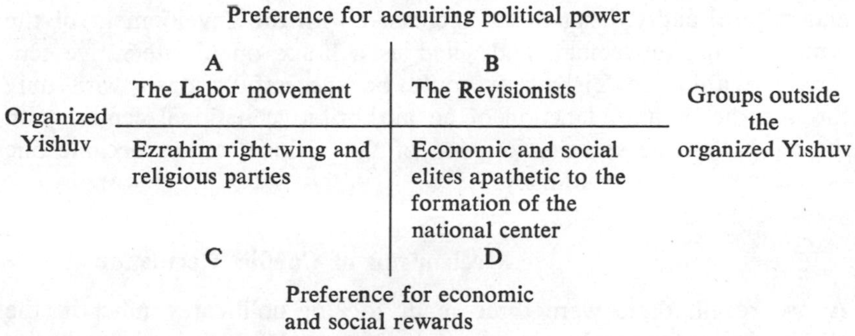

Preference for acquiring political power

	A The Labor movement	B The Revisionists	
Organized Yishuv			Groups outside the organized Yishuv
	Ezrahim right-wing and religious parties	Economic and social elites apathetic to the formation of the national center	
	C	D	

Preference for economic
and social rewards

Figure 7
Affiliation to the Organized Yishuv and
Reward Preferences

We may conclude, then, that the different orientations to resources
facilitated the reduction of potential conflict among the various groups
and contributed as well to the regulation of those conflicts that did not
involve the struggle for political supremacy.

Another factor facilitating conflict regulation in the Yishuv was the
role of the national center in allocating scarce resources. Since most of
these resources were mobilized from outside the Yishuv, whether from
the Diaspora or the Mandatory government, their mobilization was not
itself a focus of internal conflict; the center did not have to extract
resources from one sector of the Yishuv in order to allocate them to
another. Although these resources were indeed scarce, most of them
represented inputs to the system from its environment. Moreover, the
inputs to the system expanded in proportion to the system's expansion;
thus, in theory at any rate, it was possible to channel resources to all
sectors simultaneously.

The regulation of conflict in the Yishuv was thus promoted by a number of conditions which permitted conflicts to be mitigated and their resolution to be postponed for an indeterminate period. However, these conditions were insufficient to permit the institutionalized regulation of conflict. A major and essential condition for the resolution of conflicts was the willingness of most of the Yishuv to cooperate in the creation of an authoritative national center. This willingness stemmed from the consensus surrounding basic Zionist goals and from the recognition of an external threat to the existence of the Yishuv as a distinct political and cultural entity. That threat increased with the development of the Arab national movement, and acted as a brake on disintegrative tendencies within the Yishuv. It could be successfully dealt with only through the organized action of an authoritative national center, with the result that the security function of the national center became one of the bases of its legitimacy.

Mechanisms of Conflict Regulation

As we recall, there were three main foci of political conflict in the Yishuv for which regulatory mechanisms were developed: the authority of the national center, resource allocation, and ideological confrontations over the nature of the future society.

The regulation of conflicts concerning the authority of the national center was achieved through a combination of rules of the game predicated on democratic representation and a coalescent political culture stressing compromise and cooperation among political parties. The creation of a multiparty political system rejecting the idea of a political monopoly by one group was reflected in the coalitionary structure of the national institutions and in the presence of a number of institutionalized meeting points for the various elite groups not necessarily in the framework of the center.[8] For example, the local authorities served as a common political forum for left and right and included Revisionists and ultra-orthodox elements who did not participate in the institutions of the organized Yishuv. Further, both the left and the right maintained political frameworks in which groups who were not affiliated with the organized Yishuv participated. The Histadrut functioned as such a framework for the left including even Communists.[9] Likewise, there were right-wing economic organizations, such as the Industrialists Association and the Farmers Association, which were dominated politically by right-wing members of the organized Yishuv but which also included Revisionists, who had withdrawn from the organized Yishuv. The relations between ideological positions, attitudes toward coalescent tendencies in the Yishuv, and the exercise of institutionalized meeting points between various political groups in the Yishuv are presented in Figure 8.

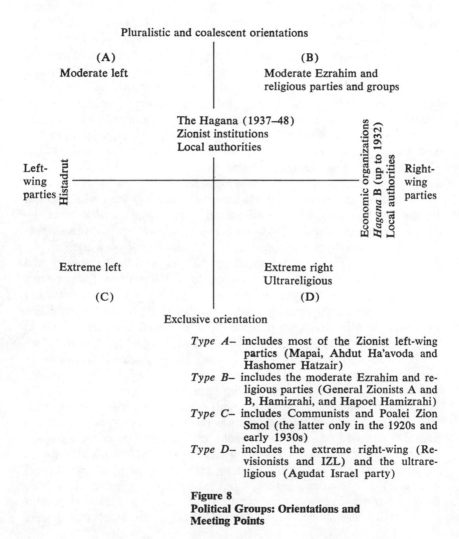

Type A– includes most of the Zionist left-wing parties (Mapai, Ahdut Ha'avoda and Hashomer Hatzair)

Type B– includes the moderate Ezrahim and religious parties (General Zionists A and B, Hamizrahi, and Hapoel Hamizrahi)

Type C– includes Communists and Poalei Zion Smol (the latter only in the 1920s and early 1930s)

Type D– includes the extreme right-wing (Revisionists and IZL) and the ultrareligious (Agudat Israel party)

Figure 8
Political Groups: Orientations and Meeting Points

As the diagram indicates, on both the left and right wings there were coalescent elements which accepted institutionalized pluralism as the basis for achieving consensus, or at least a modus vivendi, and there were also dissident elements which strove for party and sectoral exclusivity.

The institutionalized meeting points helped to bridge the gaps between political groups and reinforced the pattern of cross-cutting cleavages and partially overlapping positions of issues. Groups which shared some views in common could act as intermediaries between other groups poles apart from each other and thus help prevent severe confrontations. For example, on several occasions, members of the Ezrahim attached to the organized Yishuv mediated between the Hagana and the IZL.[10] Nevertheless there was a distinct difference between mechanisms for regulating conflicts among members of the organized Yishuv and mechanisms for dealing with conflicts between the organized Yishuv and groups outside it. Within the organized Yishuv the central mechanisms were the parliamentary frameworks of the national institutions, based on proportional representation, and the coalitionary structure of the executive institutions, which assured minority groups a role in decision-making and resource allocation. The resolution of conflicts by compromise applied mainly to those groups which recognized the authority of the national institutions, and not to dissident groups such as the Revisionists which were subjected to various social, economic, and political sanctions. There were attempts to negotiate with these groups over issues of great importance to the organized Yishuv leadership, but these attempts usually produced only partial, temporary compromises in which the dissident groups gave their qualified consent to refrain from activities deviating from the policy of the organized Yishuv. Both the sanctions and the compromises indicate the problems in dealing with conflicts inherent in a nonsovereign political system.

The coalescent orientations of most of the political groups in the Yishuv also facilitated the evolution of a quasi-federative political structure composed of subcenters cooperating in some areas of common national interest and acting as agencies of the center in other areas. In other words, the political system was based on a decentralization of authority with the secondary centers comprising political movements and social and economic organizations rather than territorial units. This detracted somewhat from the "centrality" of the center, in that part of its authority was delegated to particularistic institutional frameworks that exercised a considerable degree of autonomy in utilizing the resources at their disposal. As a result, the boundary separating center from periphery was blurred in many areas, which prevented mutual estrangement between center and subcenters.

The second focus of conflicts was the problem of the regulation of exchange processes and allocation of resources. The characteristic arrangement for allocating resources among those groups affiliated to the organized Yishuv was the party key. This system carried the principles of proportional representation and coalition to extreme.

The party key made the allocation of resources both within the Yishuv and within the Israeli polity authoritative. This is prevalent among small consociational democracies; other terms, such as "equal or proportional patronage,"[11] have been proposed to describe similar phenomena.

The balance of power between the parties, as reflected in political representation on quasi-parliamentary and executive bodies, was expressed in budgets, the granting of immigration certificates, and appointments to positions in the administration of national and public institutions. This method of allocating scarce resources facilitated conflict regulation by obviating unchecked competition for resources. The political parties were transformed into agencies for the allocation of resources, a function which they could then exploit in mobilizing political support. The party key thus helped to maintain the internal political status quo, since the ability to gain additional support depended to a large extent on the amount of resources at the disposal of the political parties, which, in turn, was a function of their power at the time. Moreover, the conversion of political parties into agencies controlling a more or less defined part of the resources distributed by the center tended to reduce the potential floating vote. The internal stability of the system encouraged individuals and groups to identify with some political party in order to benefit from the attendant advantages. Given their control over the allocation of administrative posts in the national institutions, for example, the party leadership could use cooptation, to absorb potential political activists and thus maintain control over the selection of persons for public positions. Because cooptation rather than selection according to universalistic criteria was the prevalent system of administrative recruitment, the particularistic trend in the institutional system of the Yishuv was strengthened.

The third dimension of conflict in the Yishuv was the ideological dimension. The fact that cooperation existed among various groups in spite of intensive ideological conflict calls for an explanation. Apparently, acceptance of ideological pluralism and tolerance was inconsistent with zealous adherence to ambitious ideological programs. Thus, the effective functioning of the central political institutions required the relief of ideological tensions among various political groups, each of which was pursuing its own path to the ideal social order. Three mechanisms in the political culture of the Yishuv made the mitigation of ideological conflicts possible:

1. There was a common denominator in the ideologies of all parties of the organized Yishuv and even of some dissident groups, such as the Revisionists, in the consensus over basic Zionist aims. Beyond the various ideological conceptions which split the Zionist movement into ideological currents and subcurrents, there was an overriding consensus that the national aims of Zionism took precedence over other social and political goals in the event of perceived conflicts. The attitude toward those movements that were not a part of this consensus was intolerant.

2. The national institutions tended to avoid ideological dilemmas in their discussions and decisions, concentrating on "practical issues" that could be resolved in a pragmatic spirit. Hence the avoidance of a definition of Zionism's final aim and the readiness to compromise on all matters relating to the status of religion in the public life of the Yishuv. Political decisions were taken on a tactical rather than a strategic level; the short- rather than long-term objective was emphasized. Over the years this pattern of behavior influenced the political mentality of the dominant elite, so that the over-all approach to problems emphasized pragmatic solutions to concrete problems, while ignoring some of the more far-reaching demands of the movement ideologies.

3. There was a tendency to channel the expressions of ideological zeal into movement subcenters or enclaves in which ideologically inspired social experiments could be conducted. Attempts to translate ideology into organized social action were usually made in the Histadrut, settlement and youth movements, organized religious bodies, and economic enterprises, rather than in the national center. The subcenters provided a wide latitude for autonomous social initiative and experimentation, and unique life-styles developed within them that were transmitted through institutionalized socialization to the younger generation or to new

adult members of the movement. It was under these circumstances that the social experiments which characterized the Yishuv, such as the *kibbutz*, *kevutza*, and *moshav* developed. However, within the ideologically oriented enclaves there often prevailed an atmosphere of intolerance toward political deviations that tended to be more intense than the antagonism between movements of different ideological coloration. Hence the tendency of movement frameworks to split as a result of ideological controversies.

The Yishuv's Pattern of Conflict
Regulation and the State of Israel

The modes of conflict regulation created in the Yishuv serve to highlight, perhaps more than many other features of the political system, the internal cohesion of the Yishuv as a social and political system. This achievement is all the more remarkable when we consider that the Yishuv was not a "normal" society but one intensively engaged in numerous "pioneering" social experiments and institution-building activities which increased its social diversity and compounded the problems of integration and regulation. What is more, the new forms of social organization produced by the Yishuv had an impact that often extended far beyond its rather limited demographic and territorial scope.

The full expression of these creative and innovative capacities was made possible by the openness of the political and social system of the Yishuv, which continued to expand with the inflow of human and material resources. The openness of the system made possible the establishment and coexistence of a variety of institutions, many of which were based on antithetical ideological premises, within the same social and political framework. Each wave of immigrants made its own contributions to these process of innovation and institution building. It is possible to draw a parallel between the Yishuv and the phenomenon of the "open frontier" in the period of expansion of colonizing societies, such as nineteenth-century American society. But in the Yishuv, the frontier had an institutional rather than a territorial meaning. Social innovation was facilitated by reduction of the potential areas of conflict among the various enterpreneurial groups and by the continuous increase in the flow of resources into the system. The ideological platforms of the various groups were seemingly rigid and uncompromising; nevertheless, patterns of political and social behavior were created that permitted most groups to advance simultaneously toward their goals. These patterns of behavior were in turn made possible by the openness of the system and by the different orders of priorities with respect to resources among political groups, which permitted the establishment of mutually beneficial exchange relations. The flow of external resources into the system provided the raw material for institution building and facilitated innovations in the system which at the same time created new demands for additional resources. The partial autonomy of the Yishuv was one of the factors that made possible the "openness" of the system. The innovative response of the Yishuv to the situation in which the mandatory government confined its activities to limited executive functions was to build autonomous political institutions which gradually attained characteristics of a quasi state.

Mutually beneficial exchange relations formed the foundation for a consociational pattern of democracy. Group relations were not based on a zero-sum conflict of interests, where mutual antagonisms may lead to attempts by groups to monopolize control of resource allocation. Most parties in the Yishuv recognized the mutual benefits to be obtained from bargaining and cooperation in a coalitionary system of government that mitigated the competitive aspects of the struggle for power. It is claimed by social scientists who developed the concept of consociational democracy that such a system serves the mutual interests of the political elites at the expense of the interests of the sectors they are supposed to represent. But it is also possible, as it happened in the case of the Yishuv, that the interests of the sectors and the elites that represent them are mutually reinforcing, and, what is more, that the interests of one sector are not perceived as inherently opposed to the interests of another due to the differential orientations to resources. A non–zero-sum approach is particularly applicable to cases of steady increase in the amount of resources available to a community from external sources. Naturally, at each stage the absolute amount of resources is limited and in that sense grounds for a zero-sum approach do exist. But when resources are imported without requiring any tangible return and do not have to be extracted from one group in order to be given to another, then the potential for antagonisms arising out of feelings of discrimination and deprivation decreases. These external resources help explain the tendency among most groups in the Yishuv to prefer rules of the game based on cooperation as opposed to competition. Not surprisingly, this tendency was more marked when available external resources

increased, while during periods when the level decreased, the rules of
the game tended to be modified in a competitive direction. It should be
noted that the model of consociation described above has particular
attributes which are absent in other consociational systems. The fragmentation in the Yishuv was political and ideological rather than ethnic,
religious, or cultural. The system of bargaining and cooperation among
the different elites and the groups they represented was primarily the
effect of the availability of resources and the lack of sovereignty.

The consociational approach eventually became an integral part of
the political culture of the Yishuv and left its imprint on the political
culture of the State of Israel. The tradition of preferring coalitions
based on broad participation, rather than conformity with the principle
of the "minimum winning coalition," was reflected in the composition
of most coalition governments in Israel. This tendency notwithstanding,
just as there were certain groups that remained outside the organized
Yishuv in the prestate period, there were also groups that remained
outside the coalitionary framework of the state, until the late 1960s
at any rate.

Consociational democracy in the State of Israel, however, was different in certain features from that of the Yishuv. Although the political
culture based on consensus and cooperation among political groups
persisted, increasingly it came to resemble consociational patterns in
countries where there is a certain degree of alienation between political
elites and the public they are supposed to represent. This tendency
toward oligarchy after the establishment of the state can be considered
one of the main causes of the decline of entrepreneurial and innovative
activity on the part of the subcenters in the post–1948 period. Another
cause of this decline was the change in orientation among the political
elites, who became more concerned with manipulative control of the
public than with activating it for new and creative tasks. These trends
were directly related to the absorption of masses of new immigrants in
the early years of the state. One of the most distinctive characteristics
of these immigrants was their willingness to acquiesce, if only for a short
time, in being an *object* of political mobilization by the established
elites, while consciously or unconsciously relinquishing the possibility
of being a *subject* actively participating in the formation of the national
center. The ruling elite was thus able to absorb this population into the
existing party and movement frameworks in a fashion that best served
its own interests.

Another process that helped to modify the consociational pattern arose from the transformation of the Yishuv into a sovereign state. The political system acquired a number of new functions characteristic of a state; the concomitant disappearance of the open frontiers meant that there was no way for the center to acquire new functions and authority except at the expense of the subcenters. This created the background for the struggle between the "movement" orientation, which sought to maintain the autonomous authority of the subcenters, and the "statehood" orientation, which upheld the primacy of the state as a focus of allegiance and as a source of values and entrepreneurial activity. This struggle during the early years of the state ended in a partial victory for the statehood orientation and a partial reduction of the authority of the subcenters.

Another basic condition for the maintenance of a political culture based on bargaining and compromise remained in force, however. The flow of material and human resources from abroad continued. The economic and demographic growth of Israeli society continued, frequently at a pace that exceeded the growth rate of the Yishuv. But although Israeli society continued to expand in quantitative terms, the level of its qualitative and innovative enterprise was considerably below that achieved in the period of the Yishuv.

The period of the Yishuv thus left a varied legacy of organizations, life-styles, and values that could potentially be adapted to new conditions—except that in the process of adaptation much of the creative dynamism that characterized the period of the Yishuv was lost. So, in the final analysis, Israeli society did not escape the fate of other revolutionary movements that became "routinized" in the process of institutionalization. Was this, then, a fulfillment or a betrayal of the vision of the Yishuv's founding fathers? Their vision, we recall, contained a paradoxical admixture of utopian pursuit of ideal social order and an earthy desire to "normalize" the conditions of life of the Jewish people. The attainment of sovereignty was followed by a gradual fading of utopian aspirations under the pressure of pragmatic necessities. However, this development only further accentuated the tendency of Israeli society to become more and more like all other nations.

Appendixes

Appendix 1

Palestine Population by Communities

Year	Date		Jews
1922	(23 X)	Census	83,790
1923	(30 VI.)		89,660
1924	"		94,945
1925	"		121,725
1926	"		149,500
1927	"		149,789
1928	"		151,656
1929	"		156,481
1930	"		164,796
1931	(18X1.)	Census	174,606
1932	(31.XII)		192,137
1933	"		234,967
1934	"		282,975
1935	"		335,157
1936	"		384,078
1937	"		395,836
1938	"		411,222
1939	"		445,457
1940	"		463,535
1941	"		474,102
1942	"		484,408
1943	"		502,912
1944	"		528,702
1945	"		554,329

			% of Jews			
Muslims	Christians	Others	Total Including Nomads	Total Excluding Nomads	Of Total Pop.	Pop. Settled Of
589,177	71,464	7,617	752,048	649,048	11.1	12.9
599,331	72,090	7,908	768,989	670,381	11.7	13.2
627,660	74,094	8,263	804,962	709,938	11.8	13.4
641,494	75,512	8,507	847,238	756,594	14.4	16.1
663,613	76,467	8,782	898,362	810,885	16.6	18.4
680,725	77,880	8,921	917,315	834,206	16.3	17.9
695,280	79,812	9,203	935,951	857,073	16.2	17.7
712,343	81,776	9,443	960,043	882,511	16.3	17.7
733,149	84,986	9,628	992,559	921,699	16.6	17.9
759,700	88,907	10,101	1,033,714	966,761	16.9	18.1
778,803	92,520	10,367	1,073,827	1,007,274	17.9	19.1
798,506	96,791	10,677	1,140,941	1,074,388	20.6	21.9
814,379	102,407	10,793	1,210,554	1,144,001	23.4	24.7
836,688	105,236	11,031	1,308,112	1,241,559	27.3	28.7
862,730	108,506	11,378	1,366,692	1,300,139	28.1	29.5
883,446	110,869	11,643	1,401,794	1,335,241	28.2	29.6
900,250	111,974	11,839	1,435,285	1,368,732	28.7	30.0
927,133	116,958	12,150	1,501,698	1,435,145	29.7	31.0
947,846	120,587	12,563	1,544,530	1,477,977	30.0	31.4
973,104	125,413	12,413	1,585,500	1,518,947	29.9	31.2
995,292	127,184	13,121	1,620,005	1,553,452	29.9	31.2
1,028,715	131,281	13,663	1,676,571	1,610,018	30.0	31.2
1,061,277	135,547	14,098	1,739,624	1,673,071	30.4	31.6
1,101,565	139,285	14,858	1,810,037	1,743,484	30.6	31.8

SOURCE: A. Gertz, ed., *Statistical Handbook of Jewish Palestine, 1947*. (Jerusalem: Jewish Agency, Department of Statistics, 1947), pp. 46–47.

Appendix 2

Summary of Jewish Immigration by Periods

Citizenship	1919–23
Austria	497
Bulgaria	328
Czechoslovakia	112
England	180
Germany	469
Greece	158
Hungary	291
Italy	37
Latvia	401
Lithuania	901
Poland	9,158
Romania	1,404
USSR	13,363
Yugoslavia	145
Iran	197
Iraq	171
Turkey	478
Yemen	184
USA	601
Other countries	886
Stateless	—
Unspecified	5,140
Total	35,101

1924–31	1932–39	1940–45	1919–45	%
294	5,623	892	7,306	2.2
1,127	948	2,257	4,660	1.4
363	4,779	1,181	6,435	1.9
173	806	89	1,248	0.4
660	35,980	2,022	39,131	11.7
696	5,280	797	6,931	3.1
230	1,107	1,297	2,925	0.9
57	556	559	1,209	0.4
858	3,212	86	4,557	1.4
3,014	5,208	180	9,303	2.8
37,387	83,847	6,833	137,225	40.9
3,739	9,548	6,474	21,165	6.3
14,636	2,473	634	30,836	9.2
136	702	746	1,729	0.5
865	489	176	1,727	0.5
2,617	124	627	3,539	1.0
1,140	1,455	3,537	6,610	2.0
2,317	6,416	5,537	14,454	4.3
1,158	4,621	16	6,396	1.9
882	6,704	2,037	10,449	3.1
—	4,132	4,616	8,748	2.6
1,146	2,087	110	8,483	2.5
73,435	186,097	40,433	335,066	100.0

SOURCE: A. Gertz, ed., *Statistical Handbook of Jewish Palestine, 1947*. (Jerusalem: Jewish Agency, Department of Statistics, 1947), p. 100.

Notes

Chapter 1

1. The "disturbances of 1929" broke out on 23 August 1929 and continued for about one week. The immediate background of these disturbances was a dispute over the right of Jews to pray at the Wailing Wall. The hostile attitude of the British administration toward Jewish self-defense efforts created a bitter crises between the national institutions and the Mandatory government. This crises was made even more severe as a result of the conclusions of the British parliamentary inquiry (Shaw Committee) into the background of the disturbances. The committee maintained that the Arabs were bitter because they had not been granted self-government while the Jews had received special status with the recognition of the Jewish Agency as a semiofficial body. For a detailed account of the disturbances see *History of the Hagana* Tel Aviv: Maarachot, 1964, vol. 2, pt. 1, chs. 19–25.

2. In accordance with the conclusions of the Shaw Committee and the Hope-Simpson Reports, which denied the feasibility of absorbing additional Jewish immigrants.

3. The total sum of private capital in Palestinian pounds in 1925 was LP 24.5 million, in 1930 LP 16 million, and in 1935 about LP 42.5 million. See A. Ulitzur, *National Capital and the Building of the Country* (Jerusalem: Keren Hayesod, 1939), ch. 10 (in Hebrew).

4. The Peel Commission, set up to report on the situation in Palestine following the dis-

turbances of 1936, recommended dividing the country into three parts: a Jewish state, an Arab state and an area of the British Mandate. The full report can be found in *Palestine Royal Commission Report*, Cmd. 5479 (July 1937).

5. The "Round Table Conference" (also referred to as the "London Conference" or the "St. James Conference") was convened following the Woodhead Commission Report in February, 1939 (which had recommended changing or rejecting the major recommendations of the Peel Report, and suggested a partition map much worse from the Jewish point of view; see *History of the Hagana*, 2, pt. 2: 785–88). In addition to the members of the Arab Higher Committee the representatives of five independent and semi-independent Arab states (Egypt, Iraq, Transjordan, Saudi Arabia, and Yemen) also participated in this conference. The Jewish delegation consisted of representatives of the Jewish Agency, the National Council, and a representative from the Orthodox community. At the conclusion of the conference, the British government proclaimed that the solution to the question of Palestine lay in declaring an end to the Mandate and in establishing an independent Palestinian state which would be allied with Britain. To the Jewish population, the implementation of such a plan would mean the nullification of the Balfour Declaration and the terms of the Mandate. For a discussion of the London Conference, see J. Bauer, *Diplomacy and Underground in Zionist Policy, 1939–1945* (Merchavia: Sifriat Poalim, 1966), pp. 21–39 (in Hebrew). See also *History of the Hagana*, 2, pt. 2: 788–91, and W. Z. Laqueur, *A History of Zionism* (London: Weidenfeld and Nicolson, 1972), pp. 523–27.

6. The White Paper of 1939 recommended (1) the granting of independence to Palestine within ten years, (2) a limit of 75,000 immigrants to Palestine over a five-year period (after which Jewish immigration was to be conditional on Arab approval), (3) a limit on acquiring and settling land in most parts of Palestine. See *History of the Hagana*, vol. 3, pt. 1, ch. 1; Bauer, *Diplomacy and Underground*, pp. 39–47; Laqueur, *History of Zionism*, pp. 528–33. The Land Transfer Regulations, intended to implement the recommendations of the White Paper, were published in 1940. They stated that the Arab sale of land to Jews would be allowed in certain areas only.

7. For an analysis of the interrelations between history and sociology, see S. M. Lipset, "History and Sociology: Some Methodological Considerations," in S. M. Lipset and R. Hofstadter, eds., *Sociology and History Methods* (New York: Basic Books, 1968), pp. 20–58.

8. For the issues concerned with comparative research, see R. T. Holt and J. E. Turner, eds., *The Methodology of Comparative Research* (New York: Free Press, 1970).

9. R. K. Merton, *Social Theory and Social Structure* (Glencoe, Ill.: Free Press, 1957), pp. 5–10.

10. T. S. Kuhn, *The Structure of Scientific Revolutions* (Chicago: University of Chicago Press, 1964). See also R. T. Holt and J. M. Richardson, Jr., "Competing Paradigms in Comparative Politics," in Holt and Turner, *Methodology*, pp. 23–29.

11. For a comprehensive analysis of this concept see: A. Lijphart, "Consociational Democracy," *World Politics*, 21, no. 2 (January 1969): 207–25; H. Daalder, "On Building Consociational Nations: The Cases of the Netherlands and Switzerland," *International Social Science Journal*, 23, no. 3 (1971): 355–70; H. Daalder, "The Consociational Democracy Theme," *World Politics*, 26, no. 4 (July 1974): 604–21; A. Lijphart, "Comparative Politics and the Comparative Method," *American Political Science Review* 65, no. 3 (September 1971): 691–93.

12. Lijphart, "Comparative Politics and the Comparative Method," p. 691.

13. For a critical analysis of the concept of boundaries of a political system, see J. P. Nettl, "The State as a Conceptual Variable," *World Politics*, 20, no. 4 (July 1968): 549–92.

14. See Edward Shils, "Center and Periphery," in Shils, *Center and Periphery: Essays in Macrosociology* (Chicago: University of Chicago Press, 1975).

15. For further discussion on the limitations of the center-periphery model, see ch. 3.

16. See for additional definitions G. Lehmbruch, "Consociational Democracy in the International System," *European Journal of Political Research*, 3, no. 4. (December 1975): 377–79.

Chapter 2

1. See, e.g., J. S. Coleman, "The Political System of the Developing Areas," in G. A. Almond and J. S. Coleman, eds., *The Politics of the Developing Areas* (Princeton, N.J.: Princeton University Press, 1960), pp. 532–76; C. Geertz, "The Integrative Revolution," in C. Geertz, ed., *Old Societies and New States* (New York: Free Press, 1963), pp. 105–57; S. N. Eisenstadt, "Sociological Aspects of Political Development in Underdeveloped Countries," *Economic Development and Cultural Change*, 5, no. 4 (July 1957): 289–307; S. P. Huntington, *Political Order in Changing Societies* (New Haven and London: Yale University Press, 1968), ch. 3.

2. See, e.g., L. Kuper and M. G. Smith, eds., *Pluralism in Africa* (Berkeley and Los Angeles: University of California Press, 1969).

3. In respect to the years 1922 and 1931 see *The History of the Hagana* (Tel Aviv: Maarachot, 1964–72) 2, pt. 3, tables A, B: 1388–89 (in He-

brew). Regarding all the years and the year 1939 see Government of Palestine, *A Survey of Palestine, 1945–1946* (Jerusalem: Government Printer, April 1946), 1: p. 141.

4. On the legislative council see: Y. Porath, *The Emergence of the Palestinian Arab National Movement, 1918–1929* (Jerusalem: Institute of African and Asian Studies, The Hebrew University, and Israel Oriental Society, 1971), pp. 116, 117, 120–21 (in Hebrew); N. Rose, "The Debate on the Legislative Council in the Years 1929–1936," in B. Oded, A. Rapoport, A. Shochat, Y. Schutzmiller, eds., *Studies on the History of the Jewish People and Palestine* (Haifa: Haifa University, 1974), B: 217–45 (in Hebrew); D. Ben-Gurion, *Memoirs* (Tel Aviv: Am-Oved, 1971–74), 3: 10–12 (in Hebrew).

5. A. Sela, "Conversations and Contacts between Zionist and Palestinian Arab Leaders, 1933–1939," *New East*, 22, no. 4 (1972): 406–7 (in Hebrew).

6. *Palestine Royal Commission Report*, Cmd. 5479 (July 1937), p. 117.

7. *Ibid.*, Ch. 5, p. 17.

8. The term "urban settlement" refers to a settlement in which the population exceeds 5,000. For further details see *Survey of Palestine*, 1: p. 154.

9. J. Matras, *Social Change in Israel* (Chicago, Ill.: Aldine, 1965), p. 44.

10. See A. Gertz, ed., *Statistical Handbook of Jewish Palestine, 1947*, (Jerusalem: Jewish Agency, Department of Statistics, 1947), p. 296.

11. *Ibid.*, p. 300.

12. *Palestine Royal Commission Report*, ch. 5, p. 116.

13. See Porath, *Palestine Arab Movement*, pp. 164–65; *Survey of Palestine*, 2: 900–907; *Palestine Royal Commission Report*, pp. 174–84.

14. Esco Foundation for Palestine, *Palestine: A Study of Jewish, Arab and British Policies* (New Haven, Conn.: Yale University Press, 1947), p. 475.

15. For a general discussion on the organizational developments in the Arab political center in the twenties, see Porath, *Palestinian Arab Movement*, ch. 8. On the absence of paid staff and on the financial organization of the executive see *ibid.*, pp. 230, 236–38.

16. The Zionist Commission was the Zionist political commission sent to Palestine after its occupation by the British by permission of the British government and the Entente powers. After 1921 the authority of the Zionist Commission was transferred to the Zionist Executive elected by the Zionist Congress.

17. See W. Z. Laqueur, *A History of Zionism* (London: Weidenfeld and Nicolson, 1972), pp. 462–63, 467–68. On the structure and constitution of the Jewish Agency see Ch. Merhavia, *A Homeland: A Collection of Documents* (Jerusalem: Halevi, 1949), pp. 133–41 (in Hebrew).

18. For further details see: M. Atias, *Knesset Israel in Eretz Israel: Foundation and Organization* (Jerusalem: Havaad Haleumi, Department of Information, 1944, in Hebrew); M. Atias, *The Book of Documents of the National Council of Knesset Israel; 1918–1948* (Jerusalem: R. H. Cohen, 1953), pp. 11–27 (in Hebrew); M. Ostrovski, *Organization of the Jewish Yishuv in Palestine* (Jerusalem: Rubin Mass, 1942), vol. 1 (in Hebrew); Sh. Seger, "On the Origins of the Parliamentary Regime in the State of Israel," *Molad*, 4, no. 22 (December 1971): 331–36 (in Hebrew).

19. See E. Gutmann and Y. Dror, eds., *Government of Israel: Collection of Sources* (Jerusalem: The Hebrew University, Kaplan School of Economics, 1961), pp. 459–61 (in Hebrew).

20. For the first, second and third Assemblies see Atias, *Knesset Israel in Palestine*, pp. 21, 29, 35. For the Fourth Assembly see National Council, *Report for the Period, November 1944–January 1946* (Jerusalem, 1946), (in Hebrew).

21. Y. Shimoni, *The Arabs of Palestine* (Tel Aviv: Am Oved, 1947), (in Hebrew). p. 290; also *Survey of Palestine*, 2: pp. 948–74.

22. Shimoni estimated that in the early forties the salaried workers amounted to somewhere between 23,000 and 25,000. To this figure, Shimoni suggests, should be added some 12,000 employed in domestic industry. Shimoni, *Arabs of Palestine*, p. 190. Another source cites the figure of 60,000 workers: Y. Waschitz, *Arabs in Palestine* (Tel Aviv: Sifriat Poalim, 1947), pp. 151–52 (in Hebrew).

23. *Survey of Palestine*, 2: p. 764; Waschitz, *Arabs in Palestine*, p. 152; Shimoni, *Arabs of Palestine*, p. 366.

24. *History of the Hagana*, 2, pt. 2: 658, 759, 776.

25. This theory was developed by Dov Ber Borochov (1881–1917), the theoretician of Marxist Zionism. On the essentials of his doctrine see B. Borochov, *Collected Works* (Tel Aviv: Am Oved, 1960), vol. 1 (in Hebrew). See also Y. Slutsky, *Preface to the History of the Israeli Labor Movement* (Tel Aviv: Am Oved, University Library, 1973), ch. 12 (in Hebrew).

26. M. Lissak, "Patterns of Change in Ideology and Class Structure in Israel," *Jewish Journal of Sociology*, 7, no. 1, (June 1965): 46–62.

27. Compiled from different sources, particularly Gertz, *Statistical Handbook*.

28. Porath, *Palestinian Arab Movement*, pp. 238–46.

29. M. Rinott, *Hilfsverein der deutschen Juden: Creation and Struggle* (Jerusalem: Hebrew University School of Education, Haifa University, and Leo Baeck Institute, 1971, in Hebrew).

30. Evidence for that is found in M. Friedman's article "The Struggle of the Jewish Community in Jerusalem after the British Occupation," *Ha'uma*, no. 29 (January 1970), pp. 68–81 (in Hebrew).

31. Z. Sussman, "The Policy of the Histadrut with Regard to Wage Differentials" (Ph.D. Thesis, The Hebrew University of Jerusalem April 1969), pp. 41–43.

32. The Labor movement's attitude to the issue of "Jewish labor" was expressed unequivocally by D. Ben-Gurion in his book *Hebrew Labor* (Tel Aviv: Havaad Hapoel, 1932, in Hebrew). See also B. Katznelson, *Writings* (Tel Aviv: Mapai, 1945–50), 6: 313–21 (in Hebrew).

33. D. Horowitz, *The Development of the Palestine Economy* (Tel Aviv: Dvir, 1948), pp. 34–35 (in Hebrew).

34. Repeated references to this attitude are found in the journal of the Farmers Association, *Bustanai*, e.g., 16 October 1929; also 3d year, no. 2 (1931).

35. See, e.g., Z. Even-Shoshan, *History of the Labor Movement in Palestine* (Tel Aviv: Am Oved, 1966), 2: 136–37 (in Hebrew).

36. For example, the PKP, Poalei-Zion Smol, the left wing of the Labor Brigade, and part of *Hashomer Hatzair*.

37. Sussman, *Policy of the Histadrut*, pp. 46–47.

38. See Horowitz, *Development of the Palestine Economy*, pp. 232–34.

39. R. Szereszewski, *Essays on the Structure of the Jewish Economy in Palestine and Israel* (Jerusalem: Falk Institute, 1968), (in Hebrew). table 1. See also Sussman, *Policy of the Histadrut*, pp. 51–52, and *The Yishuv's Economy: Book of 1947* (Jerusalem: Havaad Haleumi, 1947), pp. 502–6 (in Hebrew).

40. Sussman, *Policy of the Histadrut*, p. 48.

41. Porath, *Palestinian Arab Movement*, ch. 2–3.

42. H. Malamat, H. Tadmor, M. Stern, and S. Safrai, eds., *History of the Jewish People* (Tel Aviv: Dvir, 1969), vols. 2 and 3 (in Hebrew).

43. The term "Old Yishuv" refers to the Jewish Orthodox population (both Sephardic and Ashkenazic) concentrated mainly in Jerusalem, with some extensions in Safad, Tiberias, and Hebron. The majority of this population immigrated to Palestine between the end of the eighteenth century and the early ninteenth century. Various aspects of the social structure and composition of the Old Yishuv are described in Sh. Avitzur, *Daily Life in Nineteenth Century Palestine* (Tel Aviv: Am Hasefer, 1972); Y. Ben-Porath, B. Yehoshua, and A. Kedar, eds., *Chapters in the History of the Jewish Settlement in Jerusalem* (Jerusalem: Yad Ben-Zvi, 1973): B. Gat, *The Jewish Settlement in Palestine, 1881–1940* (Jerusalem, Ha'gemasia Ha'ivrit, 1963); M. Friedman, "On the Structure of Community Leadership and the Rabbinate in the 'Old Ashkenazic Yishuv' toward the End of the Ottoman Rule," in Ben-Porath *et al.*, *Chapters*, pp. 273–88; M. M. Rothschield, *The Chaluka*, (Jerusalem: Rubin Mass, 1969); M. Maoz, "Changes in the Condition of the Jewish Community in Palestine in the

Mid-Nineteenth Century," *Keshet*, no. 4 (Summer, 1970), pp. 5–16 (all in Hebrew).

44. The beginning of the "New Yishuv" lies in the first wave of immigration (*aliya*) in 1882 which founded the first settlements and the new urban quarters of Jaffa. It is noteworthy that a certain part of the Old Yishuv's people was socially integrated into the New Yishuv.

45. The "Capitulations" were the agreements signed between the Ottoman Empire and the various European states after the sixteenth century. These "Capitulations" defined the rights of the European citizens living within the area of Ottoman government and bestowed extensive rights on the European countries' citizens, who were in fact excluded from the Ottoman area of sovereignty.

46. Menahem Ussishkin was one of the Zionist leaders in Russia. With the establishment of *Knesset Israel* (the Community of the Jews in Palestine) he was for a short time a member of the Va'ad Leumi (National Council Executive). Until his death in 1941, he presided over the Keren Kayemet (Jewish National Fund) on which he focused his public activity in the years subsequent to 1919. After the establishment of the WZO, the great majority of the Lovers of Zion Association (founded in 1882 in the Kattowitz Conference) associated themselves with the WZO.

47. Atias, *Knesset Israel in Palestine*, p. 2. See also I. Kolat, "Organization of the Yishuv and Crystallizing of Its Political Consciousness up to the First World War," *Keshet*, no. 4, (Summer 1970), pp. 17–28 (in Hebrew).

48. The Palestine Office was in charge of settlement and development, e.g., the establishment of farms, providing agricultural training, and research for furthering and developing new agricultural branches. Dr. Ruppin headed the Palestine Office until the transfer of its functions to the Zionist Commission and the World Zionist Executive. He was born in Germany and was a famous scholar in the field of the sociology of the Jews. After the First World War for many years he presided over the Zionist Executive Department of Settlement.

49. In 1932 Britain conferred independence on Iraq and it was accepted as a full-fledged member of the League of Nations. Egypt obtained autonomy after the Anglo-Egyptian Treaty in 1936.

50. Porath, *Palestinian Arab Movement*, ch. 1. See also N. Mandel, "Turks, Arabs and Jewish Immigration into Palestine, 1882–1914," in A. Hourani, ed., *St. Antony's Papers,* No. 17 (Middle Eastern Affairs) (Oxford: St. Antony's College, 1965), pp. 77–108.

51. Clear evidence for this attitude may be found in M. Sharrett, *Making of Policy: The Diaries of Moshe Sharett* (Tel Aviv: Am Oved, Zionist Library, 1968, in Hebrew), and particularly the book of D. Ben-Gurion, *Talks with Arab Leaders* (Tel Aviv: Am Oved, 1967, in Hebrew).

52. M. Burntein, *Self-Government of the Jews in Palestine since 1900* (Tel Aviv: Hapoel Hatzair, 1937), pp. 19–30 (in Hebrew).

53. A concise review of this organization appears in E. Krischer, "The Jewish-Arab Labor Union in the Ordeal of Fulfillment," *M'asef: Studies in the History and Problems of the Jewish Labor Movement*, no. 3–4 (August 1972), pp. 160–70.

54. D. Ben-Gurion, *We and Our Neighbours* (Davar, 1931), p. 82 (in Hebrew); see also E. Mangalit, *The Social and Ideological Sources of Hashomer Hatzair, 1913–1929* (Tel Aviv, Tel Aviv University and Hakibbutz Hameuchad, 1971), p. 72 (in Hebrew).

55. D. Waschitz, *Arabs in Palestine*, p. 171. See also the entry "Alliance of Palestine Workers" (Brit Poalei Eretz-Israel), *Encyclopedia of Social Sciences* (Merchavia: Sifriat Poalim, 1966) (in Hebrew). J. Gorni, *Ahdut Ha'avoda, 1919–1930: The Ideological Principles and the Political System* (Tel Aviv: Hakibbutz Hameuchad and Tel Aviv University, 1973) (in Hebrew), pp. 152–57.

56. Waschitz, *Arabs in Palestine*, pp. 175–83; Y. Porath, "The Origin, Nature, and Disintegration of the National Liberation League, 1943–1948," *New East*, 14, no. 4, (1964): 358–60 (in Hebrew); G. Z. Israeli, *Mapam, PKP, Maki: History of the Israeli Community Party* (Tel Aviv: Am Oved, 1953), pp. 177–84 (in Hebrew).

57. The Palestine Communist party (known by its initials PKP) had undergone many changes. In the early twenties its founders were Jews; only later did Arab members join. In the thirties the leadership was passed to an Arab according to the Comintern's policy.

58. S. Dotan, "The Beginning of Jewish National Communism in Palestine" in *Zionism, Studies in the History of the Zionist Movement and of the Jews in Palestine*, 2 (1961): 21–211 (in Hebrew).

Chapter 3

1. On such processes of transition see S. N. Eisenstadt, *Modernization, Protest, and Change* (Englewood Cliffs, N.J.: Prentice-Hall, 1966); "Sociological Aspects of Political Development in Underdeveloped Countries," *Economic Development and Cultural Change* 5, no. 4, (July 1957): 289–307; "Post-Traditional Societies and the Continuity and Reconstruction of Tradition," 102; no. 1 *Daedalus* (Winter 1973), pp. 1–28.

2. M. Lissak, "Some Theoretical Implications of the Multidimensional Concept of Modernization," *International Journal of Comparative Sociology*, 11, no. 3 (September 1970): 196–207.

3. E. Shils, "The Concentration and Dispersion of Charisma," *World Politics*, 11, no. 1 (October 1958): 1–19.

4. E. Shils, "Society and Societies: The Macro-Sociological Approach," *Megamot*, 16, no. 2–3 (1967): 130 (in Hebrew).

5. The founding conference of the Histadrut took place in Haifa in December 1920. The Histadrut is unique among world labor organizations in that it incorporates the functions of trade union, economic entrepreneur, and provider of social services. For further information on the Histadrut see E. Biletzky, *Labor Market, Social Trends, and Organizational Patterns* (Tel Aviv: Am Oved, Culture and Education Publication, 1967, in Hebrew).

6. Ahdut Ha'avoda, Socialist Zionist Association of Hebrew Laborers in Eretz Israel, was founded in 1919. In the 1920s this was the largest Labor party. At its conception the party had a rather radical Marxist tone, though in the 1920s it adopted a constructivist orientation. In 1930 Ahdut Ha'avoda merged with Hapoel Hatzair and established Mapai. Formed in Palestine in 1905, originally the Hapoel Hatzair was a workers' party with a moderate socialistic tint and opposed any affiliation with international socialist organization. For the story of Ahdut Ha'avoda see J. Shapiro, *The Formative Years of Israeli Labor Party: The Organization of Power, 1919–1970*, Beverly Hills/London, Sage Studies in Twentieth Century History, vol. 4 (1976). On Hapoel Hatzair see J. Shapiro, *Hapoel Hatzair; The Idea and Practice* (Tel Aviv: Ayanot, 1967, in Hebrew).

7. At a lecture in January 1929 Ben-Gurion stated that "the national objective of the working class is to transform itself from only a working class into a nation of workers."

8. The three most important positions in the Jewish Agency Executive were: chairman, director of the political department, and treasurer. The head of the political department after 1931 was C. Arlozoroff. In 1933 E. Kaplan was appointed treasurer and in 1935 Ben-Gurion was elected chairman. Moshe Shertok succeeded as the head of the political department after the assassination of Arlozoroff.

9. The founding conference of the Revisionist party took place in Paris in April 1925. Immediately after this conference the Israeli branch of the party was formed and participated in the elections of the Second Elected Assembly. See J. B. Schechtman and Y. Benari, *History of the Revisionist Movement* (Tel Aviv: Hadar, 1970), chs. 3 and 7, (in Hebrew). In 1935 Vladimir Jabotinsky, the Revisionist Zionist Organization leader, seceded from the organized Zionist movement and formed a new Zionist organization, whose intention was to become an alternative to the official World Zionist Organization. The Revisionists returned to the WZO after World War II and participated in the 1946 elections to the Zionist Congress. See

J. B. Schechtman, *The Vladimir Jabotinsky Story* (New York: T. Yoseloff, 1956), and B. Lubotzky, *The Revisionist Zionist Organization and Betar* (Jerusalem: Hasifria Hazoinit Haktana, 1946, in Hebrew).

10. The activities of Knesset Israel were based on article 23 of the King's Order in Council of 1921 which states that every religious community recognized by the government will enjoy autonomy in its internal affairs and that the Religious Communities Ordinance of 1926 authorizes the religious communities to establish regulations to govern the needs of their communities and to levy taxes.

11. M. Atias, *The Book of Documents of the National Council of Knesset Israel, 1918–1948* (Jerusalem: R. H. Cohen, 1953), p. 13.

12. M. Burstein, *Self-Government of the Jews in Palestine since 1900* (Tel Aviv: Hapoel Hatzair, 1937), p. 111.

13. An analysis of the election returns shows that 412 Yemenite and Sephardic voters chose one representative while 793 Ashkenazic voters also chose one representative; *ibid.*, pp. 117–21.

14. For details of the negotiations between the parties and organizations of the Ezrahim sector concerning the boycott of the elections to the Elected Assembly of 1944, see J. Bar-Midot's oral account in the Oral Documentation Department, Institute of Contemporary Jewry, The Hebrew University, dated 5 June 1960, 11 July 1966, and 1 August 1966. See also Atias, *Book of Documents*, p. 48.

15. *Ibid.*, pp. 48–49.

16. According to article 17 of the regulations of Knesset Israel. See E. Gutmann and Y. Dror, eds., *Government of Israel: Collection of Sources* (Jerusalem: The Hebrew University, Kaplan School of Economics, 1961), p. 463 (in Hebrew).

17. See Burstein, *Self-Government*, pp. 170–71.

18. At the Zionist Congress in London in 1920, a decision was made to set up three trends in the educational system. Students of the general system comprised about 50% of the total number of students in the elementary schools while the other trends each attracted about 25% of the student body. See Ch. Merchavia, *A Homeland: A Collection of Documents* (Jerusalem: Ha-Levi, 1949), p. 246.

19. Burstein, *Self-Government*, pp. 144–48.

20. The regulations of the WZO of 1921 (article 25) state: "Every national organization of *shekel*-payers shall elect one representative for every 1500 *shekels* which is distributed and paid by it. The National Organization of *shekel*-payers in Eretz Israel has the right to choose one representative for every 750 *shekels*." See Merchavia, *A Homeland*, p. 115.

21. From the point of view of structure, the WZO was composed of "national federations" (*landsmanschaften*) and from "special organizations,"

as the political parties were called. Each individual could belong simultaneously to the national federation and to the special organization, though he
paid his *shekel* ony once. See Merchavia, *A Homeland*, p. 113.

22. *Palestine Royal Commission Report*, Cmd. 5479 (July 1937), ch. 5,
p. 35.

23. Keren Hayesod was established in 1921. The organization's primary
function was to recruit economic resources to finance immigration and
settlement in Palestine. The fund prepared land bought for settlement, set
up irrigation projects, and initiated road-building. See Merchavia, *A Homeland*, p. 197–98.

24. Keren Kayemet was established in 1907. The purpose of this fund
was to buy, rent, or acquire through exchange or any other means land to
be used for the settlement of Jews. See Merchavia, *A Homeland*, p. 180.

25. The quotas for immigration permits (certificates) determined by the
Mandate government distinguished among several types of immigrants: (1)
immigrants with capital of 1000 Palestinian pounds (LP); (2) immigrants
with capital of LP 500; (3) immigrants with capital of LP 250 (handicraftsmen); (4) immigrants with assured sources of income; (5) special
cases; (6) religious persons; (7) students; (8) immigrant laborers; (9)
relatives of residents.

26. The changes in the Hagana organization and in the political responsibility for its activities were a direct outcome of the riots of 1929. Until
then the Hagana had been subject to the authority of the Histadrut. Its
failure to protect life and property brought about the decision to reorganize
the self-defense organization and to place the Hagana under the direct
authority of the national institutions. These changes were accompanied by
bitter internal conflicts and ultimately resulted in the creation of the Irgun
Zvai Leumi (also called the Defense Organization of the Right or Hagana
B). A detailed description of these events can be found in *The History of
the Hagana* (Tel Aviv: Maarachot, 1964), vol. 2, pt. 1 ch. 25, and D. Niv,
Battle for Freedom: The Irgun Zvai Leumi (Tel Aviv: Klausner Institute,
1965), pt. 1, pp. 156–66 (in Hebrew).

27. For a detailed discussion on this subject see D. Giladi, *Jewish Palestine during the Fourth Alia Period, 1924–1929* (Tel Aviv: Am Oved, 1973),
ch. 6. See also Sh. Carmi and H. Rosenfeld, "Immigration, Urbanization and
Crisis: The Process of Jewish Settlement in Palestine in the 1920s," *International Journal of Comparative Sociology*, 12, no. 1 (1971): 41–57.

28. Harry Sacher (1881–1971) was one of the people who aided Weizmann in his political activities during World War I. Afterwards Sacher was
the legal adviser of the Zionist Executive and from 1927 until 1931 he was
a member of the Zionist Executive.

29. Fredrich Hermann Kisch served as a colonel in the British army during World War I. In 1922 he was put in charge of the political department of the Zionist Executive where he served until 1931. A brigadier-general in the British 8th army in World War II, he was killed in action in North Africa in 1943.

30. David M. Eder, an English Jew and a psychoanalyst by profession, was from 1921–23 and from 1927–29 a member of the Zionist Executive. His biography appears in J. B. Hobman, ed., *David Eder; Memoir of a Modern Pioneer* (London: V. Gollancz, 1945).

31. Henrietta Szold founded the Hadassah organization in America in 1912. She immigrated to Palestine in 1921 and served as a member of the Zionist Executive from 1927–31. In 1931 she was elected to the National Council and was put in charge of welfare activities.

32. See G. Sheffer, "Sir Arthur Wauchope and Jewish and Arab 'Notables,' " *Keshet* 13: no. 3 (Spring 1971), pp. 144–60 (in Hebrew).

33. For a critical analysis of his personality and period of office see *ibid.*

34. For a critical analysis of Chancellor's personality and period of office see G. Sheffer, "Britain's Colonial Policy towards Palestine," *Middle Eastern Studies* (forthcoming in vol. 14).

35. See *History of the Hagana*, 3, pt. 1: 35–53.

36. Before the outbreak of the disturbances the number of Hagana members did not exceed 2,000. By the end of 1937 their number reached 25,000. A large number of Hagana members served as watchmen and in paramilitary units. See *History of the Hagana*, 2, pt. 2: 737, 846–47.

37. *Ibid.*, p. 1000. On the background for the formation of the Kofer Hayishuv and its organization see Atias, *Book of Documents*, pp. 269–72.

38. *History of the Hagana*, 2, pt. 2, ch. 47.

39. *Ibid.*, 3, pt. 1: 198–201; D. Horowitz, *My Yesterday* (Tel Aviv and Jerusalem: Shocken, 1970), pp. 183–84.

40. D. Ben-Gurion expressed this idea in several ways. For example, see *In the Midst of Our Struggle* (Tel Aviv: Mapai, 1948 3: 14–15 (in Hebrew). See also Bauer, *Diplomacy and Underground*, p. 65.

41. Questions regarding the legitimacy of the authority of the Yishuv leadership arose over the status of the Jewish Agency on the one hand and the Kofer Hayishuv on the other. An important area in which these two organizations vied for control was the Hagana, especially the formation of the Hagana high command. See *History of the Hagana*, 3, pt. 1: 34, 216–25, and Bauer, *Diplomacy and Underground*, pp. 116–19.

42. The official decision to establish the Palmach was reached earlier, in May 1941; see Bauer, *Diplomacy and Underground*, pp. 119–30. See also *History of the Hagana*, vol. 3, pt. 1, ch. 21, and Z. Gilad, *The Book of the Palmach* (Tel Aviv: Hakibbutz Hameuchad, 1953), pp. 5–12 (in Hebrew).

43. The initiative in solving the problem of maintaining and supporting the Palmach through part-time employment of members on *kibbutzim* was suggested by the Hakibbutz Hameuchad. The suggestion was accepted because it helped alleviate the manpower shortage in the *kibbutzim* due to the war.

44. In 1930 the total national capital brought into the country totalled LP 4 million, as compared to LP 16 million in private capital. In 1934 the total import of national capital was still LP 4 million, while private capital increased to approximately LP 42.5. In 1940 the imported national capital reached LP 8.5 million while private capital was LP 27.5 million. See Ulitzur, *National Capital*, ch. 10.

45. This program was adopted in 1942 at the Biltmore Hotel in New York. The program called for the cancellation of the White Paper and presented, for the first time, a demand for the establishment of a Jewish state. See Bauer, *Diplomacy and Underground*, pp. 197–211.

46. The initiative in forming the Arab League belonged to Sir Anthony Eden, secretary of state for foreign affairs. The League was formed in March 1945 in Cairo. See *History of the Hagana*, 3, pt. 1: 115–19.

47. The decision to take action against IZL was taken in October 1944 and activities against IZL continued, with varying intensity, until approximately June 1945. See Bauer, *Diplomacy and Underground*, pp. 275–83. For the official version of the Hagana on this matter, see *History of the Hagana*, vol. 2, ch. 27. For IZL's version see Niv, *Battle for Freedom*, pt. 4, pp. 96–124, and M. Begin, *The Revolt: The Study of the Irgun* (Jerusalem: Stematzky, 1951) (in Hebrew).

48. This movement was established in October 1945 in order to coordinate the armed struggle against the British. Its biggest operation was the *"Night of the Bridges"* carried out by the Palmach (17 June 1946). The last operation carried out by the Hebrew Resistance Movement, in this instance, IZL, was the bombing of the King David Hotel, where the office of the Mandate secretariat was located (22 July 1946). See *History of the Hagana*, vol. 3, ch. 42, and Niv, *Battle for Freedom*, pt. 4, pp. 179–92.

49. See *History of the Hagana*, vol. 3, ch. 43.

50. On the severe economic crisis of the late 1920s see Giladi, *Jewish Palestine During the Fourth Alia Period*, pp. 231–40, and Laqueur, *History of Zionism*, p. 464.

51. A. Gertz, *Statistical Handbook of Jewish Palestine, 1947* (Jerusalem: Jewish Agency, Department of Statistics, 1947), p. 321.

52. For discussion of the concepts of "coercive-based," "utilitarian-based," and "normative-based" power, see R. W. Lehman, "Toward a Macro-Sociology of Power," *American Sociological Review*, 34, no. 4 (August 1969): 454.

Chapter 4

1. E. Shils, "Society and Societies: The Macrosociological Perspective," *Megamot*, 15, no. 2–3 (1967): 130 (in Hebrew).

2. The founding conference of the *Poalei Zion* Party took place in 1906 in Poltava, Russia. The World Union of Poalei Zion was founded at the Hague Conference in 1907. In 1920 a left-wing faction broke away and formed Poale Zion Smol.

3. The Tserei Zion Movement was formally established in 1917, although the first groups or associations of this movement arose in Russia in 1903. In 1920 the association of Hapoel Hatzair and Zerei Zion (also known as the Hitachdut) was formed. After the merger in Palestine of Ahdut Ha'avoda and Hapoel Hatzair, in 1930 a merger took place between the Hitachdut party and Poale Zion (*Zionist Socialists*). See J. Shapiro *Hapoel Hatzair: The Idea and Practice* (Tel Aviv: Ayanot, 1967), chs. 14–16 (in Hebrew).

4. On the initiative of Ahdut Ha'avoda and its control over the Hagana, see J. Shapiro, *The Organization of Power* (Tel Aviv: Am Oved, 1975), pp. 31–32 (in Hebrew); see for an English translation *The Formative Years of the Israeli Labor Party: The Organization of Power,* Sage Studies in Twentieth Century History, vol. 4 (1976). See also *History of the Hagana* (Tel Aviv: Maarachot, 1964–72), 2, pt. 1, ch. 4 (in Hebrew).

5. Non-Zionist groups such as Agudat Israel, the Communist party, and the seceding Revisionists were not considered part of the "organized Yishuv."

6. Regional organizations of agricultural workers in *moshavot* had their beginnings with the formation of the Association of *Moshavot* in Judaea. This association was preceded by economic organizations such as the economic organization Pardess (Orchards) (1900) and Organization of Grape Growers (1906). In 1914 the Association of the Galilee Moshavot (reorganized in 1923) was established. In 1923 the Farmers Association in Eretz Israel was formed. The Farmers Association, the largest and strongest of all these organizations, developed into an influential economic and political organization in the Ezrahim sector. It also participated in the elections to the first and second Elected Assembly, but boycotted the third and fourth elections. For a review of the history of the Farmers Association see D. Weintraub, M. Lissak, and Y. Azmon, *Moshava, Kibbutz and Moshav* (Ithaca, N.Y., and London: Cornell University Press, 1969), ch. 5.

7. This was founded immediately after World War I. The "Jerusalem Council of the Sephardic Community" was the backbone of the Sephardic Association. In the 1920s the Association functioned in an unsystematic manner. In 1944 the Sephardics created a new organization called the National Representative to Sephardic Jews in Eretz Israel.

8. This party was founded in 1942 by Zionist leaders from Germany who came to Palestine during the Fifth Immigration. In late 1948 the Aliya Hadasha party united with the Ha'oved Hatzioni and the General Zionists "A" which seceded from the General Zionist Federation. Together they established the Progressive party.

9. For more extensive discussion, see ch. 7.

10. For a discussion of the General Zionists Association (General Zionists "A") and the "Union of General Zionists" (General Zionists "B") see M. Kleinman, *The General Zionist* (Jerusalem: Institute for Zionist Education, 1945), pp. 13–26, 32, 60, 64, 71–81 (in Hebrew).

11. The very existence of a labor organization outside the framework of the Histadrut created dissension among the General Zionists and was one of the reasons for the split between General Zionists "A" and "B." Information on this subject can be derived from oral testimony collected by the Institute of Contemporary Jewry of the Hebrew University. For example see the testimony of C. Levanon on 28 November 1965 and J. Bar-Midot on 23 January 1966 and 6 February 1966.

12. See the oral testimony on 5 January 1965 of Joseph Sapir, and the oral testimony of Bar-Midot, Oral Documentation Department, Institute of Contemporary Jewry, The Hebrew University, 6 February 1966.

13. The tension between the commanders of IZL and the Revisionist movement was evident even in Jabotinsky's lifetime. One of the leaders of the opposition to Jabotinsky's authority was Abraham Stern, who broke away from IZL and formed the LHI. After Jabotinsky's death the conflict between the IZL commanders and the heads of the Revisionist movement in Palestine increased. See D. Niv, *Battle for Freedom: The Irgun Zvai Leumi* (Tel Aviv: Klausner Institute, 1965), pt. 3, pp. 255–56 (in Hebrew). On the echoes of the conflict between the IZL commanders and the Revisionist movement members after the Second World War, see J. Tavin, "The Military and Political Struggle of the Irgun in Europe January 1944–January 1949. (Ph.D. thesis, The Hebrew University, 1969), pp. 59–61, 89–90, 217–18 (in Hebrew).

14. The beginnings of Hamizrahi (a shortening of the term "spiritual center") were at the early part of the century. The organization was etsablished in 1902 in Vilna. In Palestine Hamizrahi was established in 1918. During the Eighth Congress Hamizrahi joined the World Zionist Organization as an autonomous federation.

15. I. Kollat, "The Organization of the Yishuv and the Consolidation of Its Political Consciousness Up to World War I," *Keshet*, 4 (Summer 1970): 17–27 (in Hebrew).

16. The authors prefer those variables which relate to the structural characteristics of the Israeli parties over other typologies, such as those suggested by Duverger and Lipset and Rokkan. This preference stems from the fact that our attention has centered on the variations among the different parties active in the Jewish community in Palestine rather than differences between these parties and parties in other countries. For a critical analysis of Duverger's approach see A. B. Wildavsky, "A Methodological Critique of Duverger's Political Parties," *Journal of Politics*, 21 (1959):303–18. For an exposition on Lipset's and Rokkan's conceptual framework see S. M. Lipset and S. Rokkan, eds., *Party Systems and Voter Alignments* (New York: Free Press, 1967), pp. 1–64. Ideological characteristics of the parties will be treated separately in ch. 6.

17. A. Bar Haim, "The Labor Relations System in the Yishuv during the Mandate Period until World War II" (M.A. thesis, Sociology Department, The Hebrew University, 1972), pp. 86–87 (in Hebrew).

18. Thus, for example, in 1934 the Histadrut Ha'ovdim Haleumit (Federation of Nationalist Workers) and Kupat Holim (Sick Fund) were established and provided medical services to federation members and to many self-employed who did not receive services from the general Histadrut. The new federation was small in comparison to its competitor, the general Histadrut, and included only a few thousand members.

19. This cooperation began only at the end of the 1920s. Before this date there were many conflicts between the Histadrut and Hapoel Hamizrahi, centering on the issue of organizing labor through a general labor exchange.

20. The first Mapai constitution was approved only in the middle of the 1950s.

21. M. Naor, "Mapai during the Years 1930–1948" (M.A. thesis, Political Science Department, The Hebrew University, n.d.), p. 38 (in Hebrew). The source for Naor's paper is Mapai's Central Committee's financial report of 30 September 1936.

22. Naor, "Mapai, 1930–1948," pp. 26–27.

23. On the organizational model developed in Ahdut Ha'avoda see Shapiro, *Organization of Power*, pp. 30–31.

24. Oral testimony of Mr. C. Levanon, Oral Documentation Department, Institute of Contemporary Jewry, The Hebrew University, 28 November 1965, pp. 6–8. On the lack of an organization for recruiting members during the election period and especially on the absence of financial resources, see J. Bar-Midot's oral testimony dated 23 January 1966, pp. 5–6. According to the testimony of the party chairman, Peretz Berenstein, in the Union of General Zionists (General Zionists "B") in 1936 there were no more than

several hundred members. See P. Berenstein, *Selected Articles and Essays* (Tel Aviv: "Published by a Committee of Friends," 1962), p. 25 (in Hebrew).

25. The Maccabbee Federation, with whom "the Young Maccabbee was affiliated, was actually under the influence of the Ha-Ihud Haezrahi circle.

26. Lipset and Rokkan, *Party Systems*, pp. 1–69.

27. This group, named after Baron Benjamin Edmund de Rothschild, was founded in 1921. One of the reasons for the establishment of the association was the demand to reform the policy of discrimination against the members of the old *moshavot* which the founders felt existed. On the background of the founding of the association and its history, see the oral testimony of one of the movement's founders and leaders, O. Ben Ami, Oral Documentation Department, Institute of Contemporary Jewry, The Hebrew University, 19 June 1964.

28. M. Lissak, "Patterns of Change in Ideology and Class Structure in Israel," *Jewish Journal of Sociology*, 7, no. 1 (June 1965): 46–62.

29. Nevertheless, one must remember that labor organizations were connected with the two branches of the General Zionists. But while the labor organization of Union of General Zionists (General Zionists "B") was weak and not influential within its party, the Ha'oved Hazioni, the organization of hired laborers and *kibbutz* members affiliated with the Association of General Zionists (General Zionists "A"), became, with time, the most important power in its party.

30. Naor, "Mapai 1930–1948," pp. 24–28.

31. Seligman made a comparable distinction when he suggested differentiating between the pluralist, populist, and sectarian Israeli political parties. L. Seligman, *Leadership in a New Nation: Political Development in Israel* (New York: Atherton, 1964), p. 89.

32. The distinction between a multirole party, a quasi-party subcenter, and a single-party subcenter can often become blurred. An example of this is Hapoel Hamizrahi Federation, which was simultaneously a multirole party, quasi-party subcenter which appeared in elections, and a single-party subcenter.

33. Chaim Weizmann himself legitimated this situation. See J. Gorni, *Ahdut Ha'avoda, 1919–1930: The Ideological Principles and the Political System* (Tel Aviv: Hakibbutz Hameuchad and Tel Aviv University, 1973), p. 287 (in Hebrew). This was expressed by the fact that the General Histadrut was the only labor federation recognized by the World Zionist Organization. For an account of the financial support given the general Histadrut by the World Zionist Organization, see Shapiro, *Organization of Power*, pp. 63–64.

Chapter 5

1. Berl Katznelson was born in 1887 in Russia and immigrated to Palestine in 1909. Katznelson was one of the great ideologists of the Labor movement in Palestine, one of the founders of the Histadrut, and the initiator of many of its economic, social, and cultural organizations. He was also one of the founders of the Ahdut Ha'avoda party and of the Mapai party. Katznelson died in 1944.

2. Shlomo Kaplansky was born in 1884 in Poland. He was one of the founders of the Brit Poale Zion Haolamit. Kaplansky immigrated to Palestine in 1912 and settled permanently in 1924 when he was appointed the Ahdut Ha'avoda representative on the Zionist Executive in Jerusalem. Upon his resignation from the Executive in 1931 he was appointed director of the Technion in Haifa, a post he held until 1948. Kaplansky was also a member of the plenary of the National Council from 1926–31. In the 1940s he resigned from Mapai and became a member of Mapam at that party's inception in 1948. Kaplansky died in 1950.

3. In relation to the term "ruling class" see: Z. Keller *Beyond the Ruling Class* (New York: Random House, 1963), pp. 54–60; W. Kornhauser, " 'Power Elite' or 'Veto Groups,' " in R. Bendix and S. M. Lipset, eds., *Class, Status and Power*, 2d ed. (New York: Free Press, 1964), pp. 210–17.

4. M. Czudnowski, "Legislative Recruitment under Proportional Representation in Israel: A Model and a Case-Study," *Midwest Journal of Political Science* 14, no. 2, (May 1970): 217–48.

5. See one of the pioneering discussions on this subject: W. Coutu, "Role Playing vs. Role Taking: An Appeal for Clarification," *American Sociological Review*, 16, no. 2 (April 1951): 180–87.

6. E. Goffman, *The Presentation of Self in Everyday Life* (Garden City, N.Y.: Doubleday Anchor Books, 1959).

7. There are few direct accounts of cooptation. However, it is possible to derive some information from various autobiographies, for example, David Hacohen's account of the suggestions he received on his return from his studies in London; See D. Hacohen, *My Way* (Tel Aviv: Am Oved, 1974), pp. 13, 95 (in Hebrew).

8. The reason the Ezrahim group is so much larger is because of extensive changes in that sector. The material on the elite is based on written biographical material, though some information has also been acquired through questionnaires.

9. The total number of people included from the Sephardic and other Oriental ethnic groups was eight.

10. See General Federation of Labor (Histadrut), *Report of the Sixth Conference* (Tel Aviv, 1945), p. 367 (in Hebrew).

11. On political elites in developing countries see, for example, E. Shils "The Concentration and Dispersion of Charisma," *World Politics*, 2, no. 1 (October 1958): 1–9; H. J. Benda, "Non-Western Intelligentsias as Political Elites," in J. H. Kautsky, ed., *Political Change in Underdeveloped Countries* (New York and London: John Wiley, 1962), pp. 235–51; L. W. Pye, "Administrators, Agitators and Brokers," *Public Opinion Quarterly*, 22, no. 3, (Fall 1958): 342–48.

12. In regard to obstacles to mobility for native-born Palestinian Jews, see D. Weinryb, *The Second Generation in Palestine and Their Occupations* (London: Arrarat, 1954), pp. 13–14.

13. On the relevance of using the concept of charisma to analyze selection of leaders in societies undergoing change and revolution see R. C. Tucker, "The Theory of Charismatic Leadership," *Daedalus* 97, no. 3 (Summer 1968), pp. 731–56; A. Willner, *Charismatic Political Leadership: A Theory*, Princeton University, Center of International Studies, Research Monograph, No. 37 (Princeton, N.J., 1968).

14. Several aspects of this subject are discussed by M. Bar-Am, "Totalitarian Elements in Jabotinsky's Approach," *Medina Ve imshal*, 1, no. 3 (Spring 1972): 49–51 (in Hebrew).

Chapter 6

1. M. Seliger, "Fundamental and Operative Ideology: The Two Principal Dimensions of Political Argumentation," *Policy Sciences*, 1 (1970): 325. For some sociological and anthropological approaches to the analysis of ideology see D. Apter, ed., *Ideology and Discontent* (New York: Free Press, 1969).

2. Seliger, "Fundamental and Operative Ideology," p. 327.

3. For a discussion of the concept "millenary movement" see Y. Talmon, "Millenarism" in *International Encyclopedia of the Social Sciences*, 1968, 10: 349–62. For a discussion of the difference between Zionism and Messianic movements in Judaism see N. Rothenstreich, "A Self-Analysis in Depth," in *Fundamentals* (Tel Aviv: Amikam, 1962), pp. 26–31 (in Hebrew).

4. In our conceptualization of ideological orientation toward fundamental attributes of social order and social action we follow to a certain extent F. R. Kluckhon in her "Dominant and Variant Orientation," in C. Kluckhon and A. A. Murray, eds., *Personality in Nature, Society and Culture* (New York: Alfred A. Knopf, 1953), pp. 349–50.

5. On Ben-Gurion's view of the Bible as a source of inspiration for national revival see *The Vision and the Way* (Tel Aviv: Ayanot, n.d.), 1: 43 (in Hebrew). Ben-Gurion often referred to Biblical figures, such as

Joshua and King David. See, for example, *Sinai Campaign* (Tel Aviv: Am Oved, 1964), p. 165 (in Hebrew). On Ben-Gurion's attitude to the Bible, see also A. Avichai, *David Ben-Gurion* (Jerusalem: Keter, 1974), pp. 32–36.

6. See, for example, E. Marmorstein, *Heaven at Bay* (London: Oxford University Press, 1969), p. 71 (in Hebrew); Y. Rozenheim, *The Voice of Jacob* (Tel Aviv: Netzach, 1954, in Hebrew); A. Gitlin, *Judaism, The Torah and the State* (Jerusalem, 1959), pp. 45–46 (in Hebrew).

7. C. Weizmann, "In the Midst of Struggle," *Speeches* (Tel Aviv: Mitzpeh, 1937), 3: 569–70, 4: 747–50 and 795–802 (in Hebrew). Also see D. Ben-Gurion, *Memoirs* (Tel Aviv: Am Oved, 1971–74), 1: 399, 406 (in Hebrew); Y. Elam, *An Introduction to Zionist History* (Tel Aviv: Levin-Epstein, n.d.), ch. 4 (in Hebrew).

8. Practical Zionism considered constructive colonization as the way to fulfill Zionism and political activity secondary. This approach is associated with A. Ruppin of the Palestine Office.

9. Vladimir Jabotinsky, "The Program for Evacuation," in *Speeches, 1927–1940* (Jerusalem: Ari Jabotinsky, 1948), pp. 195–212 (in Hebrew); *On the Front Line of the People of Israel's War* (Jerusalem: N. Kop, 1949, in Hebrew); D. Niv, *Battle for Freedom: The Irgun Zvai Leumi* (Tel Aviv: Klausner Institute, 1965), pt. 2, ch. 11, pp. 120–25 (in Hebrew); B. Azkin, "Jabotinsky's Foreign Policy," *Gesher*, no. 2–3 (August-September, 1948), pp. 36–58 (in Hebrew).

10. On the similarity between Jabotinsky's ideology and Herzl's idea of charter see Jabotinsky's speech at the Seventeenth Zionist Congress: Jabotinsky, *Speeches*, pp. 107–31, and especially pp. 122 and 131.

11. On Hapoel Hatzair's reservations and ambivalent attitude see J. Gorni, "Hapoel Hatzair and Its Attitude toward Socialism," *Baderech*, 6 (December 1970): 74–83 (in Hebrew). See also J. Shapiro, *Hapoel Hatzair: The Idea and Practice* (Tel Aviv: Ayanot, 1967), pp. 425–29 (in Hebrew).

12. J. Gorni, *Ahdut Ha'avoda, 1919–1930: The Ideological Principles and the Political System* (Tel Aviv: Tel Aviv University and Hakibbutz Hameuchad, 1973), pp. 23–28 (in Hebrew).

13. A. Margalit, *Hashomer Hatzair: From Youth Community to Revolutionary Marxism, 1905–1929* (Tel Aviv: Tel Aviv University and Hakibbutz Hameuchad, 1971), p. 138 (in Hebrew).

14. E. N. Nodlinger, "Political Development: Time Sequences and Rates of Change," in E. A. Nordlinger, ed., *Politics and Society* (Englewood Cliffs, N.J.: Prentice-Hall, 1970), pp. 329–47; M. Lissak, "Some Theoretical Implications of the Multidimensional Concept of Modernization," *International Journal of Comparative Sociology*, 11, no. 3 (September 1970): 196–207.

15. E. B. Hass, *The Unity of Europe: Political, Social and Economic Forces, 1950–1957* (London: Stevens and Sons, 1958); E. B. Hass, *Beyond Nation-State Functionalism and International Organization* (Stanford, Cal.: Stanford University Press, 1964).

16. W. Z. Laqueur, *A History of Zionism* (London: Weidenfeld and Nicolson, 1972), pp. 347–59.

17. This was expressed in the memorandum on the future of Palestine which Ben-Gurion published in 1932 and to which Chaim Weizmann agreed. See Ben-Gurion, *Memoirs*, 1: 406–7.

18. See I. Kollat, "Poale Zion between Zionism and Communism," *Asufut*, no. 2 (November 1971), pp. 47–49 (in Hebrew).

19. BILU (House of Jacob come, let us go) was an organization of Jewish youth established in Russia in 1881 some of whom immigrated to Palestine in 1882–83. The proposed aim of BILU was "the political, economic, national, and spiritual renaissance of the Hebrew people in Syria and Palestine."

20. Brit Habiryonim was established in 1930 by a group active in the Revisionist movement who criticized the relative moderation of the Revisionist movement in its struggle with the Mandatory government and with the Labor movement. The founder and spiritual leader of Brit Habiryonim was Abba Ahimeir. The organization's extreme stand was not acceptable to the established Revisionist movement including Jabotinsky himself. Ahimeir was suspected, with two other members of the Revisionist movement, of participating in the murder of Arlozoroff. On Ahimeir's trial and acquittal see A. Ahimeir, *The Trial* (Tel Aviv: Committee for Publishing Ahimeir's Letters, 1958, in Hebrew). See also A. Ahimeir, *Brit Habiryonim* (Tel Aviv: Committee for Publishing Ahimeir's Letters, 1972, in Hebrew). See especially the introduction to the book, written by J. Nedava.

21. A. Ahimeir, *Revolutionary Zionism* (Tel Aviv: Committee for Publishing Ahimeir's Letters, 1968) 1: 61 (in Hebrew).

22. D. Ben-Gurion, *The Labor Party and Revisionism* (Tel Aviv, 1933), p. 67 (in Hebrew).

23. This is what Ben-Gurion claimed in his address at the opening of the First Rehovot Conference (1953) which dealt with economic and social developing countries. See D. Horowitz, *In the Heart of Events* (Tel Aviv: Massada, 1975), p. 41 (in Hebrew).

24. Ahimeir was born in 1897 and died in 1962. He wrote *The Scrolls of Sikrikin* which is, in essence, a philosophical tract on individual terrorism. *The Scrolls* became the ideological platform of Brit Habiryonim.

25. See N. Yellin-Mor, *Lohamei Herut Israel: People, Ideas, Deeds* (Jerusalem: Shikemona, 1974), p. 146 (in Hebrew).

26. D. Horowitz, "A Pioneering Society, or Like All Other Nations," *Molad*, no. 146–147 (October 1960), pp. 413–37 (in Hebrew).

27. Arlozoroff defined heroic economics as a way of depleting and exploiting resources at the expense of rationality and future development potential, since it is based on the exhausting of the physical capacities of the settler. Chaim Arlozoroff, *A Selection of Writings and Biographical Episodes* (Tel Aviv: Am Oved Zionist Library, 1948), p. 39 (in Hebrew).

28. The comments were an oral response to Ben-Gurion's greetings at the opening of the First Rehovot Conference. See note 23.

29. See A. Shapiro, "The Dream and Its Dissolution: The Political Development of the Trumpeldor Labor Brigade, 1920–1927," *Baderech*, 3 (December 1968): 37 (in Hebrew).

30. D. Weintraub, M. Lissak, and Y. Azmon, *Moshava, Kibbutz, and Moshav* (Ithaca, N.Y., and London: Cornell University Press, 1969), ch. 6.

31. *The History of the Hagana* (Tel Aviv: Maarachot, 1964, 1972), 3, pt. 3: 1846.

32. D. Niv, *Battle for Freedom*, pt. 1, p. 204. Also see W. Jabotinsky, *The Idea of Betar* (Tel Aviv: Betar Command in Palestine, 1934), p. 19 (in Hebrew).

33. Abraham Stern (Yair) was born in Russia in 1907 and immigrated to Palestine in 1925. He joined IZL at its inception and was appointed one of its commanding officers. As a result of disagreement with Jabotinsky and the Revisionist movement, Stern left and formed LHI. He was murdered by the British in 1942.

34. From the LHI anthem, "Anonymous Soldiers."

35. J. Shapiro, "The Debate between Chaim Weizmann and Louis Brandeis, 1919–1921," *Hazionut* (Tel Aviv: Tel Aviv University and Hakibbutz Hameuchad, 1974), 3: 269 (in Hebrew).

36. One of the major groups among Eastern European Jews which favored Jewish autonomy was the Bund (General Covenant of Jewish Workers in Lithuania, Poland, and Russia). The Bund was founded in 1897. At its fourth convention in 1901, it was decided to present a demand to turn Russia into a federation of nationalities, each of which would have absolute national autonomy regardless of the territory in which it existed. See S. Ettinger, *A History of the Jewish People in Contemporary Times* (Tel Aviv: Dvir, 1969), pp. 195–96 (in Hebrew), and H. J. Tobias, *The Jewish Bund in Russia from Its Origins to 1905* (Stanford, Cal.: Stanford University Press, 1972).

37. On the secession of the "territorialists" from the Zionist Organization and the establishment of the Jewish Territorialist Organization (YTA—in Yiddish) in 1905 see Ettinger, *History of the Jewish People*, pp. 188–90.

84. "Social revolutionaries" was a term applied to the various Russian revolutionaries in the 1870s and 1880s. In its most limited sense the term applies to the Social Revolutionaries party established in 1901–2 in Russia.

85. Narodnaya Volya was a movement which fought for the destruction of tsarist rule in Russia in the years 1860–95. The movement advocated the establishment in Russia of socialism with the peasants at its center. Its members favored skipping the capitalist stage in socialist development. Their ideological successors were the social revolutionaries.

86. The ideologist of *Brit Habiryonim* A. Ahimeir, even published a series of articles entitled "From the Notebook of a 'Fascist' " in the newspaper *Doar Hayom*, September–November 1928 (in Hebrew).

87. On the Enlightenment movement see J. Katz, *Tradition and Crisis* (New York: Schocken, 1971), ch. 24.

88. On Jewish community organization in the seventeenth and eighteenth centuries see Katz, *Tradition and Crisis*, chs. 9–13. On the changes which occurred in the structure of the Jewish community and its status see Ettinger, *History of the Jewish People*, ch. 4.

89. On the negative attitude of the various branches of Orthodox Judaism toward Zionism see Laqueur, *History of Zionism*, pp. 407–13.

90. S. A. Horodetzky, *Hassidism and Hassidim*, 3d ed. (Jerusalem: Dvir, 1951, in Hebrew); B. Dinur, "The Beginnings of Hassidism and Its Social and Messianic Bases," *Zion* 8, no. 1: 107–15; no. 2: 117–34; no. 3: 177–200 (in Hebrew); and R. Mahler, *Hassidism and the Enlightenment* (Merchavia: Sifriat Poalim, 1961, in Hebrew).

91. See S. N. Eisenstadt, *Israeli Society* (London: Weidenfeld and Nicolson, 1967), pp. 52–53.

Chapter 7

1. For a discussion of the political system as a field of authority and a network of exchange see: H. Eckstein, ed., *Internal War* (New York: Free Press, 1964), pp. 57–65; K. Deutsch, *The Nerves of Government* (New York: Free Press, 1966), ch. 7; R. L. Curry, Jr., and L. L. Woode, *A Theory of Political Exchange: Economic Reasoning in Political Analysis* (Englewood Cliffs, N.J.: Prentice-Hall, 1968); P. Bachrach and M. S. Baratz, "Two Faces of Power," *American Political Science Review*, 56, no. 4 (December 1972): 947–52; A. Etzioni, *The Active Society* (New York: Free Press, 1968), pp. 313–81; and E. Lehman, "Toward a Macrosociology of Power," *American Sociological Review*, 34, no. 4 (August 1969): 453–64.

2. For a general discussion of agrarian reform and its results in developing countries see A. Hirschman, *The Strategy of Economic Development*

38. This attitude was particularly felt by Hakibbutz Hameuchad and its leader Y. Tabenkin. See Tabenkin's comments on this subject at a meeting of Mapai's Central Committee (10 April 1937) as described by D. Ben-Gurion, *Memoirs*, 4: 135–43 (in Hebrew).

39. Brit Shalom (Peace Covenant) was established in 1925. Its purpose was "to pave a way for an understanding between Jews and Arabs for living together in Palestine on a basis of equal political rights of two autonomous nations in their mutual efforts in developing the land" (from the constitution of Brit Shalom as published in a pamphlet, *Our Aspirations*, Jerusalem, Brit Shalom 1928, in Hebrew). Brit Shalom was primarily composed of a group of intellectuals concentrated in Jerusalem and especially in the Hebrew University between 1925 and 1933. It stopped functioning (though it did not dissolve formally) in 1933. The Brit Shalom leaders continued in their efforts to establish organizations with goals similar to those of Brit Shalom. The most prominent was Ichud (Unity), established in 1942. In contrast to the Brit Shalom members, the Ichud attracted members from the Palestine leftist groups. See S. L. Hattis, *The Bi-National Idea in Palestine during Mandatory Times* (Haifa: Shikmona, 1970), pp. 38–58 (in Hebrew).

40. For a discussion of the idea of "rights" and of attachment to the land in relation to the historical argument on the borders of Palestine, see Sh. Avneri, *Ma'ariv*, 5 June 1973 and 8 November 1974 (in Hebrew).

41. This idea was first formulated at the end of the 1920s and early 1930s. See Margalit, *Hashomer Hatzair*, pp. 136–58, 201–4, 227–42 (in Hebrew).

42. On the Palestine Communist party's stand on this issue see, for example, G. Z. Israeli, *Mops, PKP, Maki: History of the Israeli Communist Party* (Tel Aviv: Am Oved, 1953), pp. 88–96 (in Hebrew).

43. J. B. Schechtman, *The Vladimir Jabotinsky Story* (New York: T. Yoseloff, 1956), 1: 244.

44. Ben-Gurion, *Memoirs*, 4: 10.

45. Cited in A. Elon, *The Israelis: Founders and Sons* (London: Sphere, 1971), p. 154.

46. For testimony about attitudes toward the Arab question from the beginning of Zionist settlement see D. Harden, *Contemporary Jewish National Thinking*, Jerusalem, World Zionist Organization Publication, no. 5 (1970, in Hebrew).

47. See B. Kimmerling, "The Impact of the Land and Territorial Components of the Jewish-Arab Conflict on the Building of Jewish Society in Palestine" (Ph.D. dissertation, The Hebrew University, Jerusalem, 1975), ch. 11 (in Hebrew).

48. For Ahdut Ha'avoda's position on this matter see Gorni, *Ahdut Ha'avoda*, pp. 141–47. For an account of Hashomer Hatzair's stand on this issue see Margalit, *Hashomer Hatzair*, pp. 204–12.

49. W. Jabotinsky, "On the Road to Statehood," *Writings* (Jerusalem: Ari Jabotinsky, Amichai 1947–1958), 4: 253 (in Hebrew).

50. D. Ben-Gurion, *Talks with Arab Leaders* (Tel Aviv: Am Oved, 1967), pp. 48–49 (in Hebrew).

51. Quoted in Elon, *The Israelis*, p. 182.

52. The Jewish Agency for Palestine, *The Jewish Case* (Jerusalem, 1947), p. 23.

53. A bitter argument about the partition plan arose in Mapai itself. The differences of opinion were expressed very clearly in an argument in the Mapai Central Committee on 10 and 15 April 1937. See D. Ben-Gurion, *Memoirs*, 4: 123–64.

54. Yellin-Mor, *Lehi*, pp. 71–74.

55. The platform of the World Union of General Zionists states that "labor and capital must be subordinate first and foremost to the needs of the whole people" (*General Zionist*, 3d year [23 September 1934], p. 4, in Hebrew).

56. Jabotinsky, "On the Road to Statehood," p. 134.

57. Jabotinsky, *On Problems of Labor* (Jerusalem: Zohar and Betar 1933), p. 63 (in Hebrew).

58. Ch. Arlozoroff, "The Class Struggle in the Palestine Reality," *Writings and Biographical Episodes*, pp. 54–63.

59. Margalit, *Hashomer Hatzair*, p. 195.

60. D. Ben-Gurion wrote in *Davar* on 14 April 1930, "The country being built needs laborers as well as owners of capital. We welcome capitalist creativity if it serves the purpose of Zionism and immigration."

61. S. Lavi, *Selected Writings* (Tel Aviv: Am Oved, 1944), pp. 78–92 (in Hebrew); E. Yaffe, *Eliezer Yaffe's Writings* (Tel Aviv: Am Oved, 1947), pt. I, pp. 65–97 (in Hebrew).

62. Gorni, *Ahdut Ha'avoda*, ch. 8.

63. Shapiro, *Hapoel Hatzair*, p. 438.

64. D. Ben-Gurion, *A Political Argument with Hashomer Hatzair* (Tel Aviv: Mapai Central Committee, November 1961), p. 32 (in Hebrew).

65. Margalit, *Hashomer Hatzair*, p. 250.

66. Ben-Gurion called one of the chapters in his book "Jabotinsky in the Footsteps of Hitler." See *The Labor Movement and the Revisionists* (Tel Aviv: Labor League Publications, 1933).

67. W. Jabotinsky, *The Idea of Betar*, p. 320.

68. *Ibid.*

69. See Ahimeir, *Revolutionary Zionism*, p. 146.

70. Yellin-Mor, *Lehi*, pp. 46, 62.

71. See J. Tavin, The Military and Political Struggle of the Irgun Zvai Leumi in Europe; January 1946–January 1949 (Ph.D. dissertation, The Hebrew University, 1969), pp. 86–88 (in Hebrew).

72. M. Smilansky, *Bustanai*, 3d year (1931), no. 41.

73. See, for example, Rabbi Kook's view cited in A. Hertzberg, ed., *The Zionist Idea: A Historical Analysis and Reader* (New York: Atheneum, 1969), p. 429.

74. See B. Katznelson, "Revolution and Tradition," in Hertzberg, ed., *Zionist Idea*, pp. 390–95.

75. See, for example, Z. Jabotinsky, *Nation and Society* (Jerusalem: Ari Jabotinsky, 1950), pp. 173–80, 181–92 (in Hebrew).

76. Ben-Gurion, *Memoirs*, 1: 656; Ben-Gurion, *The Vision and the Way*, pp. 276–78; and Avichai, *Ben-Gurion*, pp. 36–38.

77. Ahimeir, *Revolutionary Zionism* 1: 146.

78. On one concept of modern nationalism and its influence on the Jewish national movement see J. Katz, "The Jewish National Movement: A Sociological Analysis," in *The Diaspora*, nos. 52, 53 (Spring-Summer 1970), pp. 9–14 (in Hebrew); B. Halpern, *The Idea of the Jewish State* (Cambridge, Mass.: Harvard University Press, 1969, pp. 55–94.

79. Jabotinsky, *Writings*, 1: 27. See also J. Talmon, *The Era of Violence* (Tel Aviv: Am Oved, 1975) p. 296 (in Hebrew).

80. See B. Borochov, "Questions on the Theory of Zionism" and "On the Question of Zion and Territory," *Writings* (Tel Aviv: Am Oved, 1944), pp. 1–16, 17–146 (in Hebrew).

81. See I. Kaufman, *Crossroads* (Haifa: Reali School, 1944, in Hebrew). Ahad Ha'am's critical essay, "Dr. Pinsker and His Notebook," in Ha'am, *At the Crossroads* (Tel Aviv: Dvir, 1947), vol. 1 (in Hebrew); M. Yoeli, ed., *Pinsker, A Precurser of the National Problem: Autoemancipation and Its Critics* (Tel Aviv: Massada, 1960, in Hebrew).

82. For more information on Ahad Ha'am see E. Simon and I. A. Heller, *Ahad Ha'am* (Jerusalem: Magnes, The Hebrew University, 1956, in Hebrew). Ahad Ha'am was born in 1856 and died in 1927. He was an opponent of political Zionism of Herzl's type, which he considered a solution to the problem of the Jews, but not to the problems of Judaism.

83. For an inclusive but condensed analysis of the influence of the various types of socialism on Jewish socialism in Palestine see I. Kollat, "Socialism in Eretz Israel and International Socialism," in Israeli Historical Society, *The Place of the History of the Jewish People in the Framework of World History* (Jerusalem, 1973), pp. 337–61 (in Hebrew).

(New Haven, Conn.: Yale University Press, 1958); B. F. Hoselitz, *Sociological Aspects of Economic Growth* (Glencoe, Ill.: Free Press, 1960); T. Shanin, ed., *Peasants and Peasant Societies* (Harmondsworth, Middlesex: Penguin Books, 1971); and G. Hunter, *Modernizing Peasant Societies: A Comparative Study in Asia and Africa* (London: Oxford University Press, 1969).

3. For a discussion of land as one of the foci of conflict between Jews and Arabs during the Mandate period, see B. Kimmerling, *The Struggle over the Land*, Studies in Sociology, Sociology Dept., The Hebrew University (Jerusalem, 1973, in Hebrew).

4. D. Ben-Gurion, *Letters to Paula* (Tel Aviv: Am Oved, 1968), pp. 123–26 (in Hebrew).

5. A testimony to this is the almost daily meetings of the heads of the Zionist Executive and the Jewish Agency which are described in the diaries and memoirs of Kisch, Arlozoroff, Ben-Gurion, and Shertok (Sharett).

6. Dr. Jacob Israel DeHaan was a Dutch-born assimilationist who joined the Zionist movement and afterwards affiliated himself with the extreme religious Orthodx circles in Jerusalem. DeHaan was suspected of instigating the formation in the mid-1920s of a united front between the Orthodox community of the Old Yishuv and the Arab Executive Committee against the Zionist effort. For this reason the Hagana central committee gave the order to have DeHaan killed. See *The History of the Hagana* (Tel Aviv: Maarachot, 1964–72), 2, pt. 1: 251–53 (in Hebrew).

7. Kimmerling, *Struggle over the Land*, p. 35.

8. Moshe Shertok (Sharett) presented the position of the Jewish Agency on this question during his conversation with the high commissioner on 28 October 1936. See Moshe Sharett, *Political Diary* (Tel Aviv: Am Oved, 1968), 1: 353–56 (in Hebrew).

9. See M. Atias, *Knesset Israel in Eretz Israel: Foundations and Organization* (Jerusalem: Havaad Haleumi, Department of Information, 1944), p. 73 (in Hebrew). Also, E. Rubinstein, "The Creation of Municipal Government in Eretz Israel," *Haderech*, no. 9–10 (February 1974), p. 40 (in Hebrew).

10. *History of the Hagana*, 3, pt. 1: 694–97.

11. Jewish Agency, *Palestine: Figures and Facts* (Economic Department, May 1947), p. 246. For a review of income by the Mandate government, see *Palestine Royal Commission Report*, Cmd. 5479 (July 1937), ch. 8; and Government of Palestine, *A Survey of Palestine, 1945–1946* (Jerusalem: Government Printer, April 1946), 2: pp. 542–50.

12. *Survey of Palestine*, pp. 574–80.

13. *Palestine: Figures and Facts*, p. 246.

14. See, for example, C. Arlozoroff, *Jerusalem Diary* (Tel Aviv: Mapai, n.d.), pp. 211–12, 228, 295, 316 (in Hebrew); D. Ben-Gurion, *Memoirs* (Tel Aviv: Am Oved, 1971–74), 4: 16. As an example of the Jewish sector's part in the government's income, see the data for the years 1944–45 which appear in A. Gertz, ed., *Statistical Handbook of Jewish Palestine, 1947* (Jerusalem: Jewish Agency, Dept. of Statistics, 1947), p. 392.

15. Sharett, *Political Diary*, 3, pp. 39–41.

16. D. Horowitz, *The Development of the Palestine Economy* (Tel Aviv: Dvir, 1948), pp. 190–92 (in Hebrew). For a discussion of tax rates, see *Survey of Palestine*, 2: p. 545.

17. *History of the Hagana*, 3, pt. 1: 730–32.

18. *Ibid.*, 3, pt. 1: 779.

19. For a discussion of the influence of the Canaanites on LHI, see N. Yellin-Mor, *Lohamei Herut Israel: People, Ideas, Deeds* (Jerusalem: Shikmona, 1974), pp. 146–47 (in Hebrew).

20. G. Rivlin, ed., *The Fire and the Shield: The History of the Jewish Constabulary Force* (Tel Aviv: Maarachot, 1962), pp. 35–37 (in Hebrew).

21. See Ben-Gurion's speech at the meeting of the Jewish Agency Executive on 2 April 1944, cited in *History of the Hagana*, 3, pt. 1: 532.

22. For the Hagana version of the events preceding the explosion see *History of the Hagana*, 3, pt. 2: 898–99. For the IZL version of these events see D. Niv, *Battle for Freedom: The Irgun Zvai Leumi* (Tel Aviv: Klausner Institute 1965–1976), vol. 4, pp. 272–81 (in Hebrew).

23. The reference is to what is called "the crises of the Fourth Immigration." For a discussion on the nature of this crises see D. Giladi, *Jewish Palestine During the Fourth Alia Period 1924–1929* (Tel Aviv: Am Oved, 1973), ch. 6 (in Hebrew).

24. See D. Giladi, "The Reciprocal Relations between the Zionist Federation and the Labor Settlement, 1908–1948," *Bashaar*, no. 3, (1971), pp. 244–50 (in Hebrew).

25. Ben-Gurion, *Letters to Paula*, pp. 98–99.

26. See D. Weintraub, M. Lissak, and Y. Azmon, *Moshava, Kibbutz, and Moshav* (Ithaca, N.Y., and London: Cornell University Press, 1969), table 4. On the General Zionists' criticism of the channeling of resources to enterprises of the Labor movement, see Bar-Midot's oral testimony dated 7 August 1966, Institute of Contemporary Jewry, The Hebrew University, tape no. 957 (in Hebrew).

27. By 1937, 5% of all of western Palestine—10% of all the area suitable for cultivation—was acquired either by the national institutions of by individuals. See Kimmerling, *Struggle over the Land*, p. 11.

28. The principle of "absorptive capacity of the country" was reaffirmed in the White Paper of 1922 and in a letter from the British prime minister dated 13 February 1931 to the president of the Jewish Agency.

29. For a discussion of the policy of selection and its causes, see Y. Elam, *An Introduction to Zionist History* (Tel Aviv: Levin Apstein Publications, n.d.), pp. 109–14 (in Hebrew). For a discussion of the selection policy proposed by Weizmann and the Zionist Executive, see Y. Gelber, "The Zionist Policy and the Transfer Agreement," *Yalkut Moreshet*, no. 17 (February 1974), pp. 47, 69 (in Hebrew).

30. The Hechalutz movement was founded in Russia in 1917 and was officially recognized at the Twelfth Zionist Congress in 1921. The majority of the immigrants of the Fourth Immigration emigrated to Palestine within the framework of this movement. The Hechalutz Center was responsible for recruiting immigrants for the labor immigration of the Fourth and Fifth Immigrations.

31. Gertz, *Statistical Handbook*, p. 98.

32. B. Habas, ed., *The Book of Aliyat Hanoar* (Jerusalem: Jewish Agency, Bureau for Child Immigration, 1941, in Hebrew).

33. The main points of the decisions were: (1) All other conditions being equal, in confirming immigration certificates, priority would be given to candidates who spoke Hebrew and were active in Zionist activities. (2) The distribution of immigration certificates to pioneers was based on the number of members of pioneer organizations in training at settlement training centers. (3) Pioneers who were listed by the pioneering organzations as receiving settlement training and who, subsequently, proved not to be in such training, lost their right to immigration on Jewish Agency permits for a period of one year. (4) Priority in the distribution of certificates was given to professionals and trained laborers and handicraftsmen who belonged to Zionist organizations.

34. See Chaim Lazar-Litai, *Nevertheless* (Tel Aviv, Jabotinsky Institute, 1957), pp. 53–68 (in Hebrew).

35. On the Revisionists' illegal immigration see Lazar-Litai, *Nevertheless*; Niv, *Battle for Freedom*, pt. 2, pp. 129–62; and *History of the Hagana*, 2, pt. 2: 1036–38.

36. See *History of the Hagana*, 2, pt. 1: 528–30.

37. *Ibid.*, 3, pt. 2: 1031, 1034. For additional testimony in this vein see pp. 1054–60.

38. See E. Biletzky, *Solel-Boneh, 1924–1974* (Tel Aviv: Am Oved, Culture and Education, 1974), vol. 1, chs. 7, 8 (in Hebrew).

Chapter 8

1. From the time of the establishment of the state (14 May 1948) until the end of 1951, 784,000 immigrants arrived in the country; by 1960 more than one million immigrants had arrived. See Government of Israel, Central Bureau of Statistics, *Statistical Yearbook for Israel, 1971* (Jerusalem, 1972),

pp. 125–28 (in Hebrew). Much has been written about the immigration
during the 1950s. Most of these articles have been collected or condensed
into several anthologies. For example, see M. Lissak, B. Mizrachi, and O.
Ben David, eds., *Immigrants in Israel* (Jerusalem: Akadamon, The Hebrew
University, 1970, in Hebrew); *Immigration and Absorption in Israel* (Jeru-
salem: Akadamon, The Hebrew University, 1972, in Hebrew). Some of the
books which concentrate on the immigration during the 1950s are: S. N.
Eisenstadt, *The Absorption of Immigrants* (London: Routledge and Kegan
Paul, 1954); J. T. Shuval, *Immigrants on the Threshold* (New York: Ather-
ton, 1963); D. Weintraub, *Immigration and Social Change* (Jerusalem and
Manchester: Israel Universities Press and Manchester University Press,
Humanities Press, 1971).

2. See S. N. Eisenstadt, *Israeli Society* (London: Weidenfeld and Nicolson,
1967), pp. 296–300 (in Hebrew); A. Perlmutter, "Anatomy of Political
Institutionalization: The Case of Israel and Some Comparative Analyses,"
Harvard University, Center for International Affairs, Occasional Papers in
International Affairs, No. 25 (Cambridge, Mass., August 1970).

3. The IZL and LHI soldiers who were drafted into the Israeli army upon
its inception served in their own battalion framework. See the details of the
agreement signed on 1 June 1948 in *The History of the Hagana* (Tel Aviv:
Maarachot, 1964–72), 3, pt. 2: 1557 (in Hebrew). In the Jerusalem area
IZL and LHI units continued their organizational and command autonomy
until the murder of Count Bernadotte, the United Nations mediator, on 17
September 1948.

4. Several versions exist regarding the *Altalena*, which sank off the shore
of Tel Aviv on 22 June 1948. For the IZL version see M. Begin, *The Revolt*
(Jerusalem: Stematzky, 1951), ch. 11, and S. Katz, *Day of Fire* (Tel Aviv:
Karni, 1966), pp. 287–419 (in Hebrew). For an account of the govern-
ment's point of view see D. Ben-Gurion, *The Restored State of Israel* (Tel
Aviv: Am Oved, 1969), 1: 179–91 (in Hebrew).

5. The suspicion that the IZL people intended to form an armed nucleus
opposed to the government was expressed by Ben-Gurion and the Mapai
ministers at a Cabinet meeting at which this subject was discussed. See Ben-
Gurion, *Restored State*, pp. 185–99.

6. J. Bauer, *Diplomacy and Underground in Zionist Policy, 1939–1945*
(Merchavia: Sifriat Poalim, 1966), pp. 260–61 (in Hebrew).

7. This name was given to the Palmach in a series of critical articles
which appeared with the publication of the book *The History of the Palmach*,
ed. Z. Gilad (Tel Aviv: Hakibbutz Hameuchad, 1953), See "Poles,"
Haaretz, 10 July 1953 and previous articles by "Poles" dated 12 June 1953,
19 June 1953, 26 June 1953, and 3 July 1953 (in Hebrew).

8. The discussion took place at the 62nd Conference of the Histadrut on 10 December 1948. See the decisions of the council in *History of the Palmach*, 2: 985–86 (in Hebrew).

9. Some of the senior officers who were also Mapam members and were fired or forced to resign from the Israeli army were Yigal Allon, Moshe Carmel, Yitzhak Sadeh, Joseph Tabenkin, and Mulah Cohen. See E. Luttwak and D. Horowitz, *The Israeli Army* (London: Allen Lane, 1975), pp. 73–74.

10. One must note that if there was no doubt as to the de facto subordination of the chief of staff and the general staff to the minister of defense, this point was rather unclear from the formal legal viewpoint. In the regulation "Israel Defense Army, 1948," article 7 states, "The Minister of Defense is appointed to carry out this order"—i.e., establishing and activating the army. See *History of the Hagana*, 3, 2: 1598. See also E. Gutmann and Y. Dror, eds., *The Government of Israel* (Jerusalem: The Hebrew University, 1961), pp. 337–38 (in Hebrew).

11. See The Law of Return, 1950, and The Law of Return (Amendment No. 2, 1970) in Gutmann and Dror, *Government of Israel*, pp. 14–15.

12. See the Defense Service Law, 1948, the Defense Service Law Amendment, 1959 and other laws relating to the army in Z. Hadar, *Military Laws* (Jerusalem: Akadamon, 1970, in Hebrew). For echoes of the argument regarding the Defense Service Law of 1948 see Ben-Gurion, *Restored State*, pp. 388–99.

13. In regard to the Druze military service see G. Ben-Dor, "The Military in the Politics of Integration and Innovation: The Case of the Druze Minority in Israel," *Asian and African Studies*, 9, no. 3 (1973): 339–70. See also J. M. Landau, *The Arabs in Israel: A Political Study* (London: Oxford University Press, 1969), pp. 13, 15, 29–30, 53, 114, 148, 166–68, 184, 271.

14. In regard to the exemption from military service given to women, see article 30 of the Defense Service Law (combined form) 1959, Government of Israel, Jerusalem, *Sefer Ha'chukin* no. 296 (24 September 1959). The exemption of *yeshiva* students from military service is based on article 28, which permits the minister of defense to exempt persons from military service on the basis of such considerations "extent of regular forces, educational needs, and settlement needs." See Hadar, *Military Laws*.

15. The main justification for national education can be found, for example, in the speeches of Ben-Gurion and B. Dinur, minister of education and culture at the time of the passing of the National Education Law. See Ben-Gurion, *Restored State*, pp. 425 and 428; B. Dinur, *Values and Ways of Achieving Them: Problems in Education and Culture in Israel* (Tel Aviv: Orim, 1958), pp. 26–40 (in Hebrew). This passage also appears in S. N.

Eisenstadt, et al., eds., *Education and Society in Israel* (Jerusalem: Magnes, Press, 1972), pp. 555–58 (in Hebrew).

16. An example of this kind of disagreement was the dispute that broke out in late 1950 between the NRP (Mafdal)—the national religious party—and the Labor party. The dispute arose on the occasion of the reorganization of the ministry of education and centered on whether the regional supervisors of the national religious schools were subordinate to the ministry of education or the ministry of religious affairs. During this dispute the NRP threatened to resign from the government coalition.

17. Pinchas Lavon was one of the leading ideologists of Mapai, twice the secretary of the Histadrut, minister of agriculture, and served as secretary of defense in Moshe Sharett's government. He was forced to resign as a result of the so-called "Security Mishap" which was a failure of Israeli intelligence in Egypt in 1954.

18. Sh. Peres, *The Next Stage* (Tel Aviv: Am Hasefer, 1965), pp. 196–200 (in Hebrew).

19. "The General Zionists," Mapam, and the Ahdut Ha'avoda movement participated in the Zionist Executive even during the periods when they were not in the government coalition. The Herut movement entered the Zionist Executive in March 1963, in spite of the opposition of all the parties of the Left, including Mapai.

20. D. Arian, "The First Five Years of the Israel Civil Service," in R. Bachi, ed., *Scripta Hierosolymitana* (Jerusalem: At the Magnes Press, The Hebrew University, 1956), 3: 340–77.

21. The two most outstanding commanders during the War of Independence, Yigael Yadin, the chief of operations, and Yigal Allon, the commander of the Palmach and the commander of the southern front, were both thirty years old at the time of the war. Most of the brigade commanders were in their middle twenties, while the battalion commanders were usually in their twenties.

22. The contrast between the formal perception of representative democracy, which stresses the role of the parties, and the perception that also sees the need for public, independent bodies possessing the right to decide specific matters was expressed in the dilemma over the establishment and functioning of other public bodies, such as the Broadcasting Authority and the Ports Authority. While the members of these authorities are appointed by the government, they are not responsible to it or to any other elected authority. However, generally, they have not taken advantage of the possibility of evolving policies independent of political party considerations. The fact that these authorities are formed on a party-key basis and that members are nonprofessionals, and therefore not bound to professional norms, makes

it possible for them to take political considerations into account in making their decisions. However, the clash between party-political considerations and professional considerations eventually did become a source of personal and political conflicts, the most prominent of which was connected with the

23. The Transition Law and The Transition Ordinance to the Constituent Assembly, which was passed in 1949, dealt with the authority of the Constituent Assembly (whose name was changed to the First Knesset). See Gutmann and Dror, eds., *Government of Israel*, pp. 9–14. The Basic Law: The Knesset was passed in 1958; *ibid.*, pp. 17–21.

24. In order to change articles 44 and 45 of the Basic Law: The Knesset, a majority of eighty Knesset members is needed. In order to change article 4, which deals with the election system, a regular majority of sixty-one Knesset members is needed (*ibid.*). The Knesset is even empowered to pass laws retroactively.

25. According to the law it is possible to arrest a Knesset member if "he has committed a crime involving the use of force, disturbing the peace, or treason." However, immunity of Knesset members is absolute in matters involving the expression of opinions or any action connected with the duties and role of a member of the Knesset. *Ibid.*, pp. 22–25.

26. These bodies were given various names such as "our members" or "our ministers," etc. For a detailed discussion of these bodies, see P. Y. Medding, *Mapai in Israel: Political Organization and Government in a New Society* (Cambridge: Cambridge University Press, 1972), ch. 6.

27. According to the Law of Jurisdiction of Rabbinical Courts, enacted in the Knesset 26 August 1953. *Divrei Haknesset* 14: 2541–63.

28. For example, the rabbinical courts give no recognition whatsoever to marriages between Jews and non-Jews and refuse to perform the service to marry Jews who, according to rabbinical law, are forbidden to marry.

29. This occurred in 1952 in connection with the dispute about drafting religious girls into national service, in 1958 in connection with the debate "who is a Jew?" which resulted from a directive of the then minister of interior to note religion in the census, and again in 1974 in connection with the question of conversion and a correction in the Law of Return.

30. D. Horowitz, *The Economy of Israel* (Tel Aviv: Massada, 1954), ch. 14 (in Hebrew); N. Halevi and R. Klinov-Malul, *The Economic Development of Israel* (Jerusalem: Akadamon, 1968), pp. 71–80 (in Hebrew).

31. Halevi and Klinov-Malul, *Economic Development*, pp. 50–56.

32. See *Statistical Yearbook for Israel, 1971*, p. 612. In the elections to the First Knesset (1949) Mapai received 35.7% of the votes, and to the Second Knesset (1951) Mapai received 37.3% of the votes. In the elections to the First Knesset Mapam received 14.7% of the votes and 12.5% of the

votes in the elections to the Second Knesset. In the elections to the First
Knesset Herut received 11.5% of the votes and 6.6% in the second elections.
The "General Zionists" received 5.2% of the votes in the First Knesset
elections and 16.2% in the elections to the Second Knesset. The religious
bloc received 12.2% of the votes in the elections to the First Knesset and
11.9% of the votes in the elections to the Second Knesset.

33. See footnote 32 above for information regarding the First and Second
Knesset elections. In the elections to the Third Knesset (1955), Herut received 12.6% of the votes, the General Zionists received 10.2%, Mapai
received 32.2%, Mapam 7.3%, and the Hatnua Ahdut Ha'avoda movement
received 8.2%. Only a few of the new immigrants who arrived in Israel in
the early 1950s voted for Herut and the "General Zionists." In the elections
to the Third Knesset Herut received only 9% of all the eligible votes of the
25 existing *maabarot*, while the "General Zionists" received only 2%. The
two splinter groups of Mapam received 15% of all the eligible votes in these
maabarot.

34. Weintraub, *Immigration and Social Change*, ch. 4.

35. See, for example, O. Shapiro, *Political Activity in an Immigrant Town*,
Eliezer Kaplan School for Economics and Social Sciences, The Hebrew
University, Research Studies in Sociology (Jerusalem, 1959, in Hebrew);
Eisenstadt, *Israeli Society*, pp. 154–55; P. Cohen, "Community and Stability
in an Immigrant Town," in Lissak, et al., *Immigrants in Israel*, pp. 228–33
(in Hebrew).

36. As a result of the establishment of *moshavim* and development towns
the rural population increased from 16.1% in 1948 to 23.3% in 1955, while
the urban population decreased from 83.9% to 76.4%. This tendency
stopped in 1957. In 1961 84.6% of the residents were concentrated in urban
areas, as compared to 15.4% who were in the rural areas. See J. Matras,
Social Change in Israel (Chicago: Aldine, 1965), table 2.5, pp. 44–45.

37. See D. Horowitz, "A Pioneering Society, or Like All Other Nations?,"
Molad, no. 146–147 (October 1960), pp. 146–47 (in Hebrew).

38. S. Weiss, *Local Government in Israel* (Tel Aviv: Am Oved University Library, 1973), chs. 5–6 (in Hebrew). One can also study local government by analyzing specific communities such as that described in M. J.
Aronoff, *The Politics of Community Building in Israel* (Manchester: Manchester University Press and Jerusalem Academic Press, 1974).

39. Thus, for example, the Kupat Holim Leumit is associated with the
Herut party and until its split in 1975 with the Merkaz Hofshi party.

40. S. Smocha and J. Peres, "The Ethnic Gap in Israel," *Magamot*, vol.
20, no. 1 (January 1974): 5–42 (in Hebrew); M. Lissak, *Social Mobility
In Israel Society* (Jerusalem: Israel Universities Press, 1967), ch. 1.

41. The traditional strongholds of the Herut movement are in the Hatikva quarter of Tel Aviv and the Nahlaot and Zichronot quarters of Jerusalem, all of which are occupied mostly by Oriental immigrants and veteran settlers of Israel.

42. For example, see H. Smith, *Everything about the Elections in Israel* (Tel Aviv: Adi, 1969), pp. 67–70 (in Hebrew).

Chapter 9

1. E. A. Nordlinger, *Conflict Regulation in Divided Societies* Harvard University, Center for International Affairs, Occasional Papers in International Affairs, no. 29 (Cambridge, Mass., January 1972), p. 3.

2. *Ibid.* Much research has been devoted to the study of political conflicts in democratic societies. For example, see S. M. Lipset, *Political Man* (New York: Doubleday, 1960), pp. 64–71, 76–79; R. Dahrendorf, *Class and Class Conflict in Industrial Society* (Stanford, Cal.: Stanford University Press, 1959); M. Weiner and J. LaPalombara, "The Impact of Parties on Political Development," in J. LaPalombara and M. Weiner, eds., *Political Parties and Political Development* (Princeton, N.J.: Princeton University Press, 1966), pp. 418–24.

3. Z. Brzezinski and S. P. Huntington, *Political Processes USA/USSR* (New York: Viking, 1963), pp. 193–202.

4. Dahrendorf, *Class and Class Conflict*, p. 211.

5. E. Gutmann, "Religion in Israeli Politics," in J. M. Landau, ed., *Man, State, and Society in the Contemporary Middle East* (New York, Praeger, 1972), pp. 122–34; A. Etzioni, "Kulturkampf or Coalition: The Case of Israel," *Sociologia Religiosa*, vol. 3, no. 4 (March 1959); A. Don Yichia and J. Leibman, "Separation of Religion and State," *Molad*, no. 25–26 (August–September, 1972), pp. 71–89 (in Hebrew).

6. On the economic cooperation between the labor sector and the private sector, see H. Dan, *On Unpaved Roads* (Tel Aviv and Jerusalem: Shocken, 1963), pp. 190 and 222 (in Hebrew); E. Biletzky, *Solel-Boneh, 1924–1974* (Tel Aviv: Am Oved, Culture and Education, 1974), pp. 267–68 (in Hebrew).

7. I. Abadi, *Between Us and the English* (Jerusalem: Kiryat Sefer, 1947, in Hebrew).

8. For a theoretical and empirical treatment of the problem of "points of contact" and "multigroup societies" as a means of softening and mitigating conflicts, see D. B. Truman, *The Governmental Process: Political Interests and Public Opinion* (New York: A. A. Knopf, 1951), pp. 508–11; A. F. Bentley, *The Process of Government: A Study of Social Pressures*

(Evanston, Ill.: Principia Press of Illinois, 1955); S. M. Lipset, *Political Man*, pp. 88–89; A. Lijphart, "Consociational Democracy," *World Politics*, 21 no. 2 (January 1969), 208–9.

9. In regard to the Communists, we refer only to the 1920s and 1940s when they were permitted to participate openly in Histadrut activities— from which they had been barred for a long period.

10. This role was filled, from time to time, by I. Rokach, mayor of Tel Aviv. See *The History of the Hagana* (Tel Aviv: Maarachot, 1964–72), 2, Pt. 2: 729 and 1063, and pt. 1: 538 (in Hebrew).

11. G. Lehmbruch, "Consociational Democracy in the International System," *European Journal of Political Research* 3, no. 4 (December 1975): 379.

Selected Bibliography

Books

Bauer, Y. *From Diplomacy to Resistance: A History of Jewish Palestine, 1939–1945*. New York: Atheneum, 1973.

Burstein, M. *Self-Government of the Jews in Palestine since 1900*. Tel Aviv: Hapoel Hatzair, 1937.

Esco Foundation for Palestine. *Palestine: A Study of Jewish, Arab, and British Policies*. New Haven: Yale University Press, 1947.

Eisenstadt, S. N. *The Absorption of Immigrants*. London: Routledge and Kegan Paul, 1954.

————. *Israeli Society*. New York: Basic Books, 1967.

Halpern, B. *The Idea of the Jewish State*. Cambridge, Mass.: Harvard University Press, 1969.

Landau, J. M. *The Arabs in Israel: A Political Study*. London: Oxford University Press, 1969.

Laqueur, W. Z. *A History of Zionism*. London: Weidenfeld and Nicolson, 1972.

Lissak, M. *Social Mobility in Israel Society*. Jerusalem: Israel Universities Press, 1969.

Lucas, N. *The Modern History of Israel*. London: Weidenfeld and Nicolson, 1974.

Luttwak, E., & Horowitz, D. *The Israeli Army*. London: Allen Lane, 1975.

Matras, J. *Social Change in Israel.* Chicago, Aldine, 1965.
Medding, P. Y. *Mapai in Israel: Political Organization and Government in a New Society.* Cambridge: Cambridge University Press, 1972.
Porath, Y. *The Emergence of the Palestinian Arab National Movement, 1918–1929.* 2 vols. London: F. Cass, 1974–77.
Seligman, L. G. *Leadership in a New Nation: Political Development in Israel.* New York: Atherton, 1964.
Schechtman, J. B., and Benari, Y. *History of the Revisionist Movement.* Tel Aviv: Hadar, 1970.
Shuval, J. T. *Immigrants on the Threshold.* New York: Atherton, 1963.
Weintraub, D. *Immigration and Social Change.* Jerusalem and Manchester: Israel Universities Press and Manchester University Press, Humanities Press, 1971.
Weintraub, D., Lissak, M., and Azmon, Y. *Moshava, Kibbutz, and Moshav.* Ithaca, N.Y., and London: Cornell University Press, 1969.

Papers

Atzkin, B. "The Role of Parties in Israeli Democracy." In *Integration and Development in Israel,* edited by S. N. Eisenstadt, R. Bar-Yosef, and Ch. Adler. Jerusalem: Israel Universities Press, 1970.
Arian, D. "The First Five Years of the Israel Civil Service." In *Scripta Hierosolymitana,* edited by R. Bachi. 3 (1956): 340–77.
Ben-David, J. "Conforming and Deviant Images of Youth in a New Society." *Transactions of the Fifth World Congress of Sociology,* Washington, D.C., 2–8 September 1962, 4: 405–14.
Ben-Dor, G. "The Military in the Politics of Integration and Innovation: The Case of the Druze Minority in Israel." *Asian and African Studies* 9, no. 3 (1973): 339–70.
Boim, L. "Financing of the 1969 Elections." In *The Elections in Israel, 1969,* edited by A. Arian, pp. 132–49. Jerusalem: Jerusalem Academic Press, 1972.
Czudnowski, M. "A Salience Dimension of Politics for the Study of Political Culture." *American Political Science Review* 62 (1968): 878–88.
———. "Legislative Recruitment under Proportional Representation in Israel: A Model and a Case-Study." *Midwest Journal of Political Science* 14, no. 2 (May 1970): 217–48.

Eisenstadt, S. N. "The Social Conditions of the Development of Voluntary Association: A Case-Study of Israel." *Scripta Hierosolymitana* 3: 104–25. Jerusalem: Magnes, The Hebrew University, 1956.

Etzioni, A. "Kulturkampf or Coalition: The Case of Israel." *Sociologica Religiosa* 3, no. 4 (March 1959).

————. "Alternative Ways to Democracy: The Example of Israel." *Political Science Quarterly* 74 (1959): 196–214.

Gutmann, E. "Some Observations on Politics and Parties in Israel." *Indian Quarterly* 17, no. 1 (January–March 1961).

————. "Religion in Israeli Politics." In *Man, State and Society in the Contemporary Middle East*, edited by J. M. Landau, pp. 122–34. New York: Praeger, 1972.

Horowitz, D., and Kimmerling, B. "Some Social Implications of Military Service and the Reserves System in Israel." *Archives Européenes de Sociologie* 15 (1974).

Katz, E., and Danet, B. "Petitions and Persuasive Appeals: A Study of Official-Client Relations." *American Sociological Review* 31, no. 6 (1966): 811–22.

Lissak, M. "Patterns of Change in Ideology and Class Structure in Israel." *Jewish Journal of Sociology* 7, no. 1 (June 1965): 46–62.

Lissak, M. "The Israel Defence Forces as an Agent of Socialization and Education: A Research in a Democratic Society." In *The Perceived Role of the Military*, edited by M. R. Van Gills, pp. 325–40. Rotterdam: Rotterdam University, 1971.

————. "Continuity and Change in the Voting Patterns of Oriental Jews." In *The Elections in Israel, 1969*, edited by A. Arian, pp. 264–77. Jerusalem: Jerusalem Academic Press, 1972.

Mandel, N. "Turks, Arabs and Jewish Immigration into Palestine, 1882–1914." In *St. Antony's Papers No. 17* (Middle Eastern Affairs), edited by A. Hourani, pp. 77–108. 1965.

Peri, Y., and Lissak, M. "Retired Officers in Israel and the Emergence of a New Elite." In *The Military and the Problem of Legitimacy*, edited by G. Harries-Jenkins and J. van Doorn, pp. 175–92. Beverly Hills and London: Sage Publications, 1976.

Perlmutter, A. "Anatomy of Political Institutionalization: The Case of Israel and Some Comparative Analyses." Harvard University, Center for International Affairs, Occasional Papers in International Affairs, no. 25. Cambridge, Mass., 1970.

Glossary

Agudat Israel (Federation of Israel)	A non-Zionist Orthodox party founded in 1912 in Eastern Europe. It was the strongest political party among the Orthodox communities in Eastern Europe until World War II. Its members in Palestine did not participate in Knesset Israel.
Ahdut Ha'avoda (Unity of Labor)	A Socialist Zionist party founded in 1919. In the 1920s it was the largest party within the Labor movement. In 1930 it merged with Hapoel Hatzair to form a new party —Mapai.
Ezrahim (Citizens)	A name given to the non-Labor sector of the Jewish community in Palestine. In its broader sense the term was similar to the French "bourgeois." In its narrower sense it was used to describe the non-Revisionist, nonreligious, antilabor groups in the Yishuv.
Hagana (Defense)	A paramilitary organization founded in 1920, supervised by the Histadrut during the 1920s and by the Jewish Agency and Va'ad Leumi since 1930. Its forces were the backbone of Jewish defense during the Arab revolt in 1936–39 and carried the main burden of the war against the Arabs in early stages of the War of Independence.
Hakibbutz Ha'artzi	A federation of Kibbutzim, founded in 1927 by Kibbutzim whose members belonged to Hashomer Hatzair youth movement. It later affiliated to the Hashomer

	Hatzair political party and the Mapam party.
Hakibbutz Hameuchad (United Kibbutz)	Federation of Kibbutzim founded 1927 by Kibbutzim affiliated with the Ahdut Ha'avoda party. Since 1930 it was associated with Mapai. Split after the establishment of the state, following an earlier split between Mapai and Hatnua Le'Ahdut Ha'avoda in 1944.
Halacha	The full body of Jewish religious laws. Also known as Rabbinical law.
Hapoel Hamizrahi (The Mizrahi Worker)	Founded in 1922. Originally the workers' branch of the Mizrahi party and its trade union movement. Later participated in elections as an independent list. In 1955 it merged with Mizrahi to form the Nationalist Religious Party—"Mafdal."
Hapoel Hatzair (The Young Worker)	Formed in Palestine in 1905. A moderate Zionist workers' party. In 1930 it merged with Ahdut Ha'avoda to form a new party —Mapai.
Hashomer Hatzair (The Young Guardsman)	Originally a youth movement which became a political party in 1946. Later, in 1948, it became part of the Mapam party. Its main political base was the Kibbutz movement—Hakibbutz Ha'artzi.
Hatnua La'Ahdut Ha'avoda (The Movement of the Unity of Labor)	A political party founded in 1944 by a group of left-wing Mapai members. It was the dominant political party in Hakibbutz Hemeuchad. Merged with Hashomer Hatzair in 1948 to form a new party— Mapam.
Herut (Freedom)	A right-wing nationalist political party in Israel. Founded by the former leaders of IZL after the establishment of the State of Israel in 1948.

Histadrut—acronym for Histadrut Klalit Shel Ha'ovdim Ha'ivrim Be'eretz Israel (The General Federation of Jewish Workers in the Land of Israel)

Founded in 1920. Combined functions of a trade union movement, a network of economic enterprises owned by its members and a provider of social services. In the 1920s about 70 percent of the hired workers were members of the Histadrut.

Irgun Zvai Leumi—IZL (National Military Organization)

A right-wing, nationalist, paramilitary organization, founded in 1931. The IZL was loosely associated with the Revisionist movement and did not abide by the authority of the Jewish Agency. During the years 1944–47 it conducted guerrilla warfare against the British rule in Palestine.

Kibbutz, Kevutza; plural—Kibbutzim

A communal settlement based on collective ownership of means of production.

Knesset (Assembly)

The official name of the Israeli parliament.

Knesset Israel (Assembly of Israel)

The official name of the organization of the Jewish community of Palestine. Officially recognized by the Mandatory government in 1926.

Lohamei Herut Israel— LHI (Fighters for the Freedom of Israel)

A paramilitary organization. Seceded from the IZL in 1940. Used terrorist tactics in the struggle against British rule in Palestine.

Mafdal—acronym for Miflaga Datit Leumit (National Religious Party)

Founded in 1954 following the merger of Mizrahi and Hapoel Hamizrahi. Mapai's main partner in Israeli governmental coalitions.

Mapai—acronym for Mifleget Poalei Eretz-Israel (The Workers Party of the Land of Israel)

Founded in 1930 following the merger of Ahdut Ha'avoda and Hapoel Hatzair. It was the majority party in the Histadrut and the strongest party in the governing coalition in the WZO and later also in the government of Israel.

Mapam—acronym for Mifleget Poalim Meuchedet (United Workers Party)	A left wing Zionist party founded in 1948 following the merger of Hatnua La'Ahdut Ha'avoda and Hashomer Hatzair, which split again in 1954. Since then the name has been used by the former Hashomer Hatzair.
Mizrahi—an abbreviation of Merkas Ruhani (Spiritual Center)	A Zionist religious party founded in Eastern Europe in 1902. One of the main partners in the leading coalition in the WZO and in Knesset Israel. Merged with the Hapoel Hamizrahi and founded Mafdal.
Moshav—plural: Moshavim	A cooperative smallholders' settlement based on self-labor.
Moshava—plural: Moshavot	An agricultural settlement based on privately owned farms which employ hired labor.
Palmach—acronym for Plugot Machatz (Striking Units)	The striking force of the Hagana.
Poalei Zion (Workers of Zion)	A federation of Zionist socialist parties in the Diaspora founded in 1906. Its members in Palestine were among the founders of the Ahdut Ha'avoda party. Since 1930 it was associated with Mapai.
Poalei Zion Smol (Left Workers of Zion)	Zionist Marxist party established in 1920 following a split in Poalei Zion party.
Va'ad Leumi (National Council)	The executive council of Knesset Israel.

Index

Abdullah, amir of Transjordan, 26
Ahimeir, Abba, 129, 150, 152, 257
Agudat Israel, 79, 136, 148–49; political contacts, 210; relation to Knesset Israel, 44; as sectarian-type party, 209
Ahad, Ha'am, 151–52
Ahdut Ha'avoda party, 40, 70–71, 74, 76; as homogeneous party, 208; leaders of, 74–75; position on socialism, 125, 151; role expansion, 207; totalistic orientation of, 145
Alliance of Palestine Workers, 35
"Alliance." *See* Israelite Universelle Alliance Association
Allon, Yigal, 267
"Aliyah B," 53
Aliya Hadasha party, 73, 79
Altalena affair, 189
American Jewry, 6, 61
Anglo Palestine Bank, 55
Arab League, 58
"Arab problem," as ideological issue, 137–38
Arabs in Palestine: agrarian economy, 29–30; attitudes toward Palestine, 33–34; Congress in Haifa, 21; economic sector, 31–32; Executive Committee, 22, 34, 162; Higher Committee, 22, 24, 34; national awakening, 32, 34; national center formation, 32–33, 49; revolt (1936–39), 5–6, 22, 30, 35, 49, 52–53, 138, 163, 181; riots (disturbances), 4, 138; secularization process, 28; trade unions, 35; traditional elites, 22–25
Arlozoroff, Chaim, 48, 77, 130, 141, 245
Artisans association, 74
Ashkenazim, 33
Assefat Hanivharim. *See* Elected Assembly
"Autoemancipation," concept of, 128, 151
Autonomism, concept of, 153
"Authority field," concept of, 167

Balfour declaration, 3–4, 34, 140
Begin, Menachem, 147, 205